Esther the Seeker

I0835192

Ally Cooper

Ark House Press
arkhousepress.com

© 2026 Ally Cooper

All rights reserved. Apart from any fair dealing for the purpose of study, research, criticism, or review, as permitted under the Copyright Act, no part may be reproduced by any process without written permission.

Cataloguing in Publication Data:
Title: Esther the Seeker
ISBN: 978-1-7643820-8-3 (pbk)
Subjects: FIC042100 FICTION / Christian / Contemporary; FIC026000 FICTION / Religious;

Design by initiateagency.com

INTRODUCTION

Happy

I muse, smiling. How quickly my emotions change after a long punishing day at school, making my way home, the long way.

Enjoying the well-ordered streets, I admire the perfect gardens running along the familiar tops of high brick walls, wishing I had my soft soled joggers instead of school issued boots.

Climbing iron fences and walls, leaping from one to the next, looking for another hand or foothold, is my private sport, challenging myself not to touch the ground for as long as possible, even though my injuries ache from an earlier beating at the hands of a relentless bully.

Approaching the home of the Golds, who are family friends, I pull myself along their high, white wrought iron fence, working every muscle in my arms and legs to support my weight. So engrossed was my quest, that I almost overlooked the drama unfolding in front of me.

Stopping to catch my breath, I reposition my hands on the intricate iron fence, glimpsing a small drone approaching above the two-storey brick house. I pause and drop lower into the front yard to fully scan the proceedings.

Suddenly, I feel cold goosebumps cover me as it continues hovering silently.

I am astonished to see Jacob forcibly removed from his house, and as he stumbles, he is kneed in the stomach by a heavily armed, faceless Law Enforcer, Several Enforcers follow with evidence bags; one is dropped on the driveway in their haste, simple clothing falls out revealing a white shawl with fringing, which is hastily pushed back into the bag. I spy a simple candelabra poking out of another bag. One Enforcer stands flicking through a book he pulls from the evidence and throws it back in disgust.

Jacob Gold's face is frozen in a grimace; his eyes focused on his wife. Rachel is silently crying, her eyes fixed on him. Their two sweet school aged children, Zach and Elizabeth, stand looking dazed in their school uniforms, holding tightly onto their mother's hands.

Quickly regaining my composure, I drop to the ground crouching behind a thick shrub, fortunately still able to observe the distressing scene from my hiding place. My heart is racing, beating so hard I am sure it will burst through my chest.

The heavily armed Law Enforcers move Jacob, a well-groomed professional man dressed in a dark suit, who is marched towards their large unmarked black transport van. The children are crying. Rachel wraps her arms protectively around them. Her eyes never leave her husband.

I hold my breath, observing this terrifying yet touching moment shared between husband and wife as they silently communicate. I slowly exhale, transfixed.

The Enforcers pause outside the transport van for a moment, discussing business amongst themselves loudly as they open the Transport doors. Jacob turns his head, and in that moment, looks in my direction. Jacob's dark pupils flicker recognition, and he quickly recovers his neutral mask again.

Having been seen, I hold my breath, feeling trickles of cool sweat running down my back, pooling at my belt observing him. Soundlessly, he mouths, "Help us, Esther, please help us," as he is pushed roughly into the dark transport.

Rachel is now sobbing hysterically as the transport speeds through their gates towards the Law Enforcement Precinct, leaving her alone in the silent front yard with her crying children clinging to her. My heart aches for them. I feel nauseated with what I witnessed.

Someone tipped them off to the law.

Why?

Observing the Enforcers have exited the property, I slip through the open gate into the expansive yard, running down the driveway approaching Rachel, who is startled by the intrusion. I have cared for these sweet children many times and wave whenever passing.

Rachel relaxes when she recognises me. I smile at the children who hug me, little Elizabeth pulls at my long ponytail. I tug her long dark braid back, and she giggles. It's our favourite game. I guide the family quickly into the house through the ornate timber front door, which has almost been ripped off its hinges. I manage to close it and lock it until it can be repaired.

Settling Rachel and the children onto the lounge, I make tea and hot chocolate in keep cups; this helps me remain calm. Their family room is sparsely furnished, like my own home - simple but cosy.

Child-minding Zach and Elizabeth is always full of fun and energy. It is one of the few avenues for me to earn points, our digital currency, which I can buy whatever I want.

After soothing Rachel with tea and giving chocolate chip cookies to the children, I whisper a promise to return with help as quickly as possible. Rachel just nods, squeezing my hands in gratitude, unable to speak and pulls her children closer.

Leaving the house through a side door, I know the only people I can tell are my parents.

Sprinting down the street towards home as fast as I can, I push my strong legs, feeling them burn. I push myself, imagining rabid zombies are chasing me, too terrified to use my slate to communicate lest I am detected by the Law and attract attention to myself and my own family.

I thunder down the long driveway, thump along the old creaky veranda, fling open the screen door, and throw myself into the kitchen, gasping and calling my parents between breaths. They are alarmed at the frantic, wild look on my face and the bruising. They are at my side, instantly pulling me onto a firm dining chair, and wait patiently until I can speak, holding my hands. My mother calmly takes our slates and puts them in the sanitiser in the laundry room and slams the door. She reappears swiftly with an ice pack placing it on my cheek.

"The Gold f- f -family up the street, y-y-you know, Jacob with the dark hair and beard, he has been taken by the Enforcers, with their stuff in bags. Rachel does not know what to do. I promised you would come. Please help them," I manage to say in-between gasping breaths.

My parents exchange terrified looks. "Did they hurt you, too?" My father asks slowly, looking at me, concerned.

"No, this is from school," I tell him, dismissing it.

"Do you know why he was taken away?" My father asks.

I shake my head as delayed tears roll down my cheeks. I manage to say they took clothes, describing the white shawl with fringes, a candelabra and a book.

"Well, let's see what can be done to help our neighbours. Ruth, please make up a dinner hamper while I contact some of our friends to meet up for tea after we pop in and see Rachel and the children," my father says calmly patting my hand.

He promptly retrieves their slates and starts messaging; after a few moments, he rises. Having completed his task, he heads for the door to help my mother with hastily laden bags, whispering in my ear as they are leaving.

"Careful, AI is always watching and listening. Do not mention a word of this to anyone, until we know what is going on."

Sitting in the silent kitchen I sob without restraint. My heart aches wondering why such a lovely family could possibly be in trouble with the law, while holding the ice pack on my cheek, then my neck and finally my shoulder. Eventually, I run out of tears, then move the icepack to my splotchy eyes to mask my distress from my younger brother Luke.

These days, any minor misdemeanour is being punished. I can barely keep up with the daily updates of new laws and somewhat mindless rules that arrive promptly on my slate every morning. Every day, the Enforcers are ready to start catching unsuspecting citizens of the latest changes in the law.

To pass the time and occupy my mind, I cook my favourite vegetable bake with lots of cream and garlic, chatting to my two best friends, Sarah, and Ruby on my slate about how crazy school was today. Thankfully they do most of the talking!

Sitting with Luke, we eat dinner together and leave enough for our parents. I make up a feasible reason for our parents' absence over dinner; he accepts it and heads outside to shoot hoops in the driveway.

I head to my room, my sanctuary, to focus on studying for my half yearly exams, as I wait for my parents to return home. It is getting very late, and it is dark outside. Feeling sleepy, I decide to go to bed, hoping all is well with my parents and the family in our street. Closing my pink floral curtains, I snuggle under my brightly coloured quilt, stitched in pink, purple and green swatches. They are recycled from clothing and sewn by my late grandmother before the pandemic took her. I feel comforted by its warmth and protective cover, reminding me of her quiet strength.

Feeling sleep overcome me, I wrap my arms tightly around my squishy pink rabbit called Bunny. Just as I am almost asleep my mother whispers in my ear, "We are home, the family is okay, but the charges are severe. Our community is doing what it can. You were incredibly brave. Goodnight, Dad and I are so proud of you, honey."

She kisses me on the cheek softly as she leaves.

CHAPTER 1

Another day breaks through the crimson sky with the promise of a fresh start. I read messages and laws on my slate; there are no new laws that concern me today - just the usual endless list.

No guns

No littering

Return takeaway cups and containers to repurpose stations

No noise after 11pm

Notify Law Enforcers of danger and illegal activity

Safety helmets compulsory…

My parents have left for work; it is silent except for the birdsong in the bush. I will speak with them tonight to learn anything new regarding the Gold family. I pack lunch boxes with fresh salad wraps, produce picked from our garden, and filtered water in drink bottles. It's been my job since I was ten, and it has helped my mother as she works long hours and several jobs.

Luke and I carefully lock the gate behind us. Crime escalates in relation to how hungry the citizens are. Our garden is a supermarket brimming with produce, so it's naturally a target.

We walk towards school through the bush reserve near our home loudly, to scare the venomous brown snakes from the path. Fortunately, none are visible as they warm themselves.

Striding ahead too quickly, and caught up in my thoughts, I stop, wait for Luke, lean against an ancient Red Gum, and breathe in its clean, familiar scent of eucalyptus.

I avoid the red sticky sap and ants, enjoying the peace, the tinkling of bell-birds calling to each other - familiar and soothing. However, the moment evaporates as Luke's grumbles erupt. I sigh loudly for him to hear.

"My legs are tired. Esther, why can't we catch the bus?"

"You know why," I snap at him throwing my satchel over my shoulder. Ouch, I still feel bruised from yesterday.

We usually walk two kilometres to school through the bush, cross the shallowest part of the river on the bend, which is a trickle - it is tough going. This unorthodox route to school adds travel time but saves us from unrelenting abuse from the town kids on the bus.

"You're fifteen, grow up!" I bite my lip; that was unkind.

I am feeling a little crazy lately. I do not understand why my family and others in our community are treated so badly, just because we grow vegetables or catch fish!

We walk together in silence. Luke is juggling his satchel slung over his shoulder and a basketball, avoiding tree trunks and branches.

Reaching the river, we remove our boots and socks swiftly, throwing them over our shoulders and deftly step across the cool, murky water on our toes to the riverbank on the other side, where our personal pathway is revealed.

Pulling on our footwear with damp feet, we quicken our pace, emerging from the bush and run down the street to the school entrance to prevent being attacked. As we enter the safety of the first school gate, Luke turns and looks at me worried.

"Is everything okay? You are so quiet. I worry when you are not hassling me." I punch him in the arm dismissing his concern.

"Just thinking that's all, little bro," I say with a fake smile, hiding my undercurrent of constant worry. My arrival at school usually starts with a round of violence.

Today, my head is slammed and ricochets off the bank of steel lockers lining the corridor. It is followed by sharp flashes of pain shooting down my already bruised cheek, neck, and shoulder.

Town Elite Jason has chosen me as his current victim!

I am in my final year at high school, year twelve, which makes this drama even more pathetic and my friends from our community are treated with the same contempt.

Because we exist!

Ritualistic abuse is bestowed on anyone who does not conform to the Town or Elite students' ideals, fuelled at home by their parents. It is exhausting and dangerous as their irrational hatred escalates and is unchecked. What determines your place in our country is education, employment, and wealth. As students, we try to see people without prejudice but even the most reasonable citizen cannot deny the yawning differences.

I was born into a minority community group, who struggle daily for survival mostly by part-time work, self-sufficiency, and bartering. My family and friends steadfastly uphold onto our values formed many, many generations ago, despite the stifling laws.

The law dictates our lives. In fact, we do not own farms or cows, just residential blocks of varying sizes, yet we have been labelled Farmers, and the label has stuck unkindly for generations.

Adjusting my satchel, I do not look at anyone directly until I glimpse a warm, familiar smile down the end of the hall through blurry eyes; it is my best friend, Sarah. She is at my side immediately.

"Esther," she says as she searches my face, seeing the signs of distress.

Sarah drags me swiftly up several flights of polished stairs to the first floor, two steps at a time by my forearm, I try not to wince at the pain. She pulls me into the unisex sanitation room, retrieves a sports t-shirt from her satchel, promptly runs it under the tap, and places it on my left cheek.

I dry my tears. Sarah hugs me then drags me to our first class. Pausing at the sliding glass door, I hover my slate over the sensor to enter technology class to the safety of my closest friends, typically sitting at the back casually chatting at their workstations. Our friends welcome our late arrival loudly with a celebratory standing ovation. However, a sharp look in their direction squashes any enthusiasm, and they slump back into their seats.

Jonah, our group comic, mimics M Spring, causing the group to erupt into laughter again. The Town and Elite class, who only operate in silence and order, stare in utter disgust.

My friends' facial expressions show how grieved they are to see the new bright red swelling developing on my face and neck.

"What happened?" they ask.

"Jason," I mouth.

"Jerk," they reply loyally.

M Spring smoothly begins the lesson, ignoring the noise. She manages this with commendable self-control.

I love technology, and I often lose myself in my current project, which is a revolutionary self-sufficient food precinct.

M Spring, a kind, middle aged, academic with an intricate Town hair style, appears at my side. She inclines her head at my progress and moves to the next student until we hear her exclaim, Jonah Murphy!

She reverts to her low modulated tone, "Move to the front slate for individual focus."

Sarah and I catch each other's eye laughing silently, knowing Jonah has found an activity to occupy his time. Gaming is banned at school, and individual focus means, you're busted!

Jonah walks reluctantly to the front, loading his work onto the huge slate that fills the wall where everyone can see his work.

The school does not permit inequality, which in turn is meant to reflect our country's standard, everyone is equal. Jonah's situation is called Individual Focus. If it was called punishment he would be humiliated, and Jonah would then be seen to be unequal and disrespected.

Any adult we address formally is M, a neutral title reflecting equality. The only inequality that exists is how my community and I are treated by the students and citizens in our Town and pretty much everywhere.

The school makes weak attempts to control the violence; it happens despite their efforts, and deliberate indifference shows their hand. They are complicit.

Indifference is a decision.

Jonah's sentence is over quickly; he sidles up to me and looks at my face as we take the stairs to our next class. We avoid the elevators. He looks concerned.

"Are you okay Essie? Your eyes and face are red."

Jonah really is caring in a goofy kind of way, which is touching.

"Yeh, Jason gave me a shove again."

"I will sort him out, where is he?" His head snaps left to right, ready to run after him, as if shadow boxing.

Laughing at his loyalty I realise he is serious. Grabbing his shirt, I pull him close.

"Don't do it, he isn't worth it," I say, hissing through gritted teeth in his face.

I drop my hands quickly to my side, stepping back, shocked by my own anger. I am concerned I could be caught touching a student.

He slumps against the grey concrete wall dejected. "You're right. Come on, math time." Jonah grabs my tiny hand in his without asking, dragging me along in his long stride, and I run to keep up.

Our math lesson is easy today; I sit with Ruby, one of my best friends, who is also a Town Elite. She strangely loves everything our group of friends is involved in.

Ruby always dresses in beautiful clothes and is always so neat in her pressed school utility pants and shirt. Her boots are polished to perfection and her hair is intricately braided.

She taps away efficiently on her slate, her eyes focused on her work. She smiles while enjoying our banter, and bounces around the tables.

M Baxter, a young nervous teacher, foolishly allows a relaxed environment, which he believes will win him favour, but always borders on a riot.

Jonah, whose self-belief astounds everyone, casually wanders over to the huge, aluminium framed windows that are the full length of the classroom. The gentle breeze floating through them cools our room.

M Baxter is entering questions on the class slate, at the front of the room. Jonah slips off his huge boots, springs cat like onto a desk located conveniently near the window, and steps onto the virtually non-existent ledge of the large open windows.

Everyone freezes in their seats. Heads snap quickly to the left, watching the next crazy act Jonah will perform. He pushes his highly skilled Parkour skills beyond the limit along the ledge.

M Baxter turns left from the front, Jonah is just disappearing out of sight, the class collectively holds its breath - M Baxter has the pallor of a dead man.

Everyone pushes for the best vantage point for the spectacle as Jonah skilfully manoeuvres his tall frame from window to window. He works in a continuous motion of moving fingertips, straining arms, and leg muscles, visibly cramping as they support him. Surprisingly, he cheats death and deprives our Town and Elite classmates of a satisfying, messy splat on the path below.

Jonah ends this bizarre show by throwing his whole body in the last window and landing breathless on his feet. "Woo Hoo." Jonah punches the air with his right fist to the silent terrified group. We are stunned. Sarah whoops with a cheer.

"That was awesome Jonah." Everyone claps.

M Baxter, I suspect, has soiled his white linen suit and is planning to resign from teaching immediately!

He regains colour and backbone, a little shaken then escorts Jonah to the security guards who have been silently alerted and now enter the classroom, a familiar routine for Jonah. Jonah waves over his shoulder, saluting his mates with boots in hand.

We leave the classroom chatting loudly to each other, laughing about Jonah's latest conquest. We find our way outside to our favourite shaded table in the yard to enjoy some respite from school.

The expanse outside is a neutral zone as the Elite and Town students detest being outside, fearing exposure to the harsh elements and premature aging.

We relax as our true selves, uninhibited, sharing food from home. We always share family style, down the centre of the table, as we generally tire of the same meals.

I enjoy swapping with my friends whose families are Fishers. They bring sushi and tuna, compared to my salads and wraps all the time.

Ruby always comes with the cafeteria meal that Town and Elite citizens love, prepackaged, orderly. She gladly swaps anytime for fresh produce, especially fruit salad.

"Ruby, why do hang out with us? Really, we are disgusting creatures with our home style food, and recycled clothes," Sarah asks giving her a friendly nudge.

"Because you guys are real," she says simply.

"That's it!" Matt exclaims. "I don't get it."

"I mean, you don't worry what everyone thinks, what you eat or what you wear or your parents' job," Ruby expands.

"Or a job at all," someone calls out.

Everyone laughs, agreeing loudly, banging the table with their fists, and rattling the lunch boxes.

Jonah finally shows up with his goofy grin, still intact. Everyone claps and the guys' fist pump him chanting, "Murphy, Murphy, Murphy."

"Anyone for a race to the top?" Andrew challenges.

"You bet," I say, tossing my lunch box into my satchel.

I sprint after Andrew to the base of a large group of robust trees with my friends behind me, forgetting about my new bruises and pain.

Behind me, I hear boots thundering to the trees in the race to the top. We love the challenge, the dangerously high branches. The trees reach the height of a three-story building, their branches spreading wide and high with a complex branch system. Great for climbing and footholds. An escape amongst the foliage.

The atmosphere is wild as we battle for the most advantageous footholds to hoist up our strong young bodies, then start swinging to higher branches.

These ancient trees have been a prized school symbol for many decades, reminiscent of our Town's history in timber. As the years have passed the trees have simply faded into the metallic landscape as the buildings have grown around them causing them to lose their splendour.

The teachers have no interest in our lunch time ventures if nobody dies.

The branches scratch my face, pulling my hair from its restrictive band. I place it between my teeth; the tree bark grates more polish off my boots. Inwardly I groan, it is not the boots I am worried about, it is the reality of never beating everyone. It's near impossible with shorter legs and less muscle, which is burning. I feel my breath becoming short and fast, and sweat tricking down my back as I climb to the top. I'm looking forward to a well-earned rest.

As usual, the boys climb to the top in minutes, unscathed by any branches. The girls follow in respectable time, looking scruffier than their male counterparts, with Ruby keeping up with us, still looking stunning. We sit amongst the foliage catching our breath.

"So, what are you going to do for your birthday Jonah? Jump off a building in Sydney City without a parachute?" one of the boys asks laughing.

"Nah, I am going to party on my Dad's trawler out on the water, you are all invited. Be there or else," he says with a mischievous grin.

"Race you to science."

Staring out the window in my last class, willing it to end, I run my fingers absently through my dark brown ponytail, trying to smooth it from the lunch time race, finally, the day ends.

I swiftly hover my slate at the security check point without slowing, a well-practised movement. I'm looking forward to breaking out of this orderly place of learning to invest some time by the peaceful river. Alone.

Moving quickly to the high protective outer fence, I exit the gate, jogging towards the end of the street, leading me to the familiar bush fire trail.

I suddenly feel myself roughly propelled forward, searing pain shoots through me, and it steals my breath. Catching a glimpse of Jason in my peripheral vision I realise that this is the beginning of yet another beating I am to endure. No longer within the school's safety.

Taking a breath, I dig my toes deep into my boots, hold my satchel against my body, and run. Running, without thinking, my heart is pounding, and racing as I push my skinny legs. My muscles are burning, lungs bursting, I leap over the low gate, and sprint down the bush trail, not daring to look back.

I keep running, leaping over low fallen tree branches, wildly pushing away small branches scraping my face and arms until I do not hear any sounds around me.

Silence!

Slowing to a jog I am now confident to look over my shoulder; I can no longer see Jason anymore. I jog down the leafy bushfire trail putting as much distance behind me and danger, forgetting the burn in my legs until deep into the bush, where only Bell birds tinkle.

Slowing to a walk I gasp for breath holding my aching sides.

Weak! Hopeless!

My self-loathing rises from my gut, I feel sweaty and nauseous. The rush of burning, bursting explosive vomit pouring out of my mouth and nose shocks me, it splatters onto the parched earth at my feet, just missing my boots and satchel. Ants scatter. urgh!

My face is hot with indignation and there's a sour taste on my tongue, even a bit of carrot too. I spit it on the ground.

"Why carrot?" I ask myself. "Why run? Why not stay and fight my battles?"

I am afraid.

Of conflict, any conflict. Wiping the vomit from my lips and nose with the back of my hand I angrily wipe it down the leg of the grey utility pants and walk towards my secret place. Where only cowards roam.

The river greets me with its gentle acceptance. Taking my satchel off, I place it near a tree and gladly lean over the riverbank on my stomach and wash my mouth and nose, enjoying the change of flavour, while splashing water on my pants to loosen the vomit.

Sitting in the shade against a paperbark tree, my sobs are like a scared child, unrestrained. I am grateful for the large pieces of soft paperbark conveniently near me to blow my nose on then toss aside.

I am spent. How will I cope with being an adult when I can barely survive school?

A snap of a dry eucalyptus branch brings me back sharply from my pity party. My heart skips several beats, then pounds in my ears again. Barely recovered from flight, I turn my head close my eyes, and accepting my fate, there is no chance of escape while sitting down.

"Wow, what happened to your face Esther? Are you okay?"

I freeze for a moment, then relax with relief; my eyes open wide, it is one of the Farmer boys, James, a childhood friend. My face is warm with embarrassment. Nobody looks good with red puffy eyes and a splotchy nose.

"Nothing," I blurt out, trying to sound aloof and cool. Big fail.

"Looks like you have been crying and taken a beating." Great, he is a genius!

James is nineteen years old, he is from one of the Farmer families in my community. He has been attending Farmer and Fisher meetings since he started working at the age of seventeen, and we ride in my Dad's truck together every Saturday to the Farmer and Fisher markets.

"Why are you here James?" After all, this is my place, I think to myself.

"I hang out here after work to get away from all that back there." He gestures towards town.

"Why aren't you at work?" I snap again, instantly sorry I was so mean, picking at my scuffed boots.

"Not enough work for a full day, you know how it is," James says. James stares at his own scruffy safety boots, missing polish on the toes, covered in mud and dirt.

"Yeh, if only we weren't Farmer kids, we would be better off!" My reply was too angry.

WOW. I am in such a foul mood I shock myself.

James looks up surprised.

"It's okay. I don't mind; it gives me time to help at home. My parents can't work in the garden and in the town as much as they need to." Great another veggie addict.

In our community, unless you have connections in high government positions, it is difficult to find work. The unemployment rate has now hit fifty percent.

Those who have jobs try to keep them, often working in less desirable conditions and can only get part time hours.

My parents say that wages have not increased for close to fifteen years, yet those who supply their needs increase the cost of goods annually.

"I'm going to win a scholarship and go to university," I declare defiantly.

James shuffles his feet in the dirt, nervously. "I better go and help with the fruit trees, heaps of apples are ripe now. See you at the markets, then your place, Sunday?"

"My place?"

"The meeting, remember it's your family's turn."

"Oh, I almost forgot," I sigh, because it is so mind numbingly boring.

"Bye," he says cheerfully, disappearing into the scrub.

I sit thinking about James. He is not rude, mean, or even ugly. He is dependable.

Opening my slate, I lose myself reading, immersing myself in the post-apocalyptic world where my favourite character Emily seems to slay zombies effortlessly in the dark inner-city streets of Sydney City like a gothic warrior. I feel completely recharged but envy Emily's ability to overcome enemies so confidently.

I dust off my uniform and walk home down a different bush trail. Time to shake off my selfishness and head home to help Mum with dinner.

CHAPTER 2

Standing in the school entrance, I stare at the sign board displaying the school laws reflecting our countries laws.

On an adjoining screen, the State Governor is announcing another venture with the Law Commander of our North Coast Precinct, vowing to track down citizens practising religion, disturbing our peace and equality.

No guns

No religious gatherings

No religious signs

No religious artefacts

No littering, return cups and trays to repurpose stations

Be aware, notify Law Enforcers of illegal activity

No pencils No Pens No Paper

No casual clothes

No coloured hair

No makeup

No sex on school grounds

No touching or personal contact with any student

Update your relationship status and agreement on Teen iRESPECT App

No gaming

Safety helmets compulsory on single and double transports…

Some of the guys from my community are reading them too.

"I'm surprised we're allowed to pee without the Governor knowing," Andrew laughs.

"Technically, touching your privates to pee is personal contact, so touching yourself means you are in a relationship. In that case, we should update our relationship status on the iRESPECT App," Thomas adds.

I move away quickly, not wanting to hear anymore crass juvenile banter.

"Esther!" Sarah calls me.

Her blonde hair is loose today, and it dances around her shoulders; she is the girl who every guy stares at. She has a quiet determination and strength I admire and why we get along so well. Born on the same day. *Weird!*

Both born into Farmer families, we played for hours at our parents' feet while they worked in their gardens. As we grew, our games became wild, much to our parents' dismay, and vegetables became victims of our games.

"Why weren't you on the bus?" She pants running to catch up.

"You know why," I say.

"You missed the big news on the bus. Jonah was arrested last night in town by the Law Enforcers for drawing some scribble they reckon was a religious symbol on the wall of the butchers, they interrogated him."

"Is he alright?" I try to make sense of it.

What could the religious sign be? Unusual for Jonah to graffiti walls; his specialty is goofing off like a ten-year-old. I cannot ask anyone, otherwise I will end up in the same situation.

"Yeah. They released him, there was not enough evidence. It was only chalk. His Dad and some Fishers came to his rescue," Sarah informs everyone around us.

This latest Jonah act affects my stomach that seems to be doing nervous flip, flops.

Feeling unsettled, it overcomes me, I cannot speak. Feeling breathless, I stand staring at Sarah, who waves her hand wildly in front of my face.

"Hey dopey where are you?" I drift back to reality and leave my thoughts.

"Sorry, I was just thinking about Jonah, he will end up in weekend detention with this stupid stuff."

"Race you to math, Esther," she yells over her shoulder.

Sarah runs, giving herself a head start, weaving amongst the other students. I love being competitive with Sarah. Laughing, pleased to have at least one good friend in this world, I sprint after her.

Today we apply for our final exams, further study, or for most students, applying for employment. Sarah, Ruby, and I find seats together in the school hall.

Year twelve sit in the hall, orderly in rows. Slates ready on our laps waiting for the applications to appear. The first, our final exam application, is easy, I complete this and hit send.

The next application is for university, colleges, and employment, and I freeze. I have not finalised my choices. The principal tells us to choose three potential career fields we would like to work in, then we will be advised after the exams if we are accepted and given our options.

Scrolling down I look for my one choice – lawyer. M O'Neill passes behind me looking over my shoulder and notes only one choice has been selected.

"Esther, you need to choose more than one. Have another look, pick two more, who knows the career of your dreams could be there, it is your time to shine," she says kindly.

Scrolling again out of the corner of my eye I see Sarah and Ruby selecting their choices and realise it is time to be focused. I am touched that a teacher cares about me.

Paralegal, yes, at least it is still in the same field, and I could work up to being a lawyer if I do not get the grades. My eyes rest on Law Enforcement, I had not really thought about it before, but it covers a few of my passions, justice, and fitness. Choices submitted.

I honestly do not know if I could be great at anything but most importantly, to my own disgust and shame, I admit I do not want to be poor. I want to be wealthy, so my family does not have to struggle, and I can buy whatever I want. That is my driving motivation.

My stomach starts flip flopping again as my thoughts conflict with everything I have ever known or been raised to aspire to.

* * *

My family sit together in the loungeroom after dinner as we always do. Tonight, the mood is sombre, Luke is sent to fulfil a task at the far end of the garden.

Once he has left, my mother immediately puts our slates in the sanitiser. In unison, my parents turn to me and proceed to update me about the general details of the Gold family I helped yesterday.

"We cannot tell you much except that our community has managed to work together with the law to have the charges of practising religion downgraded to being in possession of religious artefacts, Peter thought it was the best compromise considering the situation. The law will not be satisfied until they were punished. They will have a huge fine to pay," Dad informs me.

"Wait! Peter? Ruby's Dad?" I am slowly trying to digest this information.

"OH, that was supposed to be kept secret," my father says awkwardly,

"Too late *now*. Since when do we get advice from someone who can have us locked up, or killed? Nice guy but *really!*" My mother places her hand firmly on my arm and squeezes it.

"Settle down, Esther, this is serious. If someone can help us and the citizens in our community, we must trust. He works for the North Coast and City Precincts as a historian; he is knowledgeable on all historical and religious artefacts, so his help was appreciated."

I am struggling to understand this banned religion business. What are religious artefacts?

I calm down, resigned. "I don't understand what religion is and what the artefacts could be and why we could go to gaol for it."

My parents look at each other furtively.

"Study the laws on your slate, do not discuss this with anyone. This is the best way we can keep you safe, Luke too," my mother says.

"How will I know a religious sign or artefact if I see it?"

Dad rises and pats me on the head, suddenly a little more light-hearted. "It will be so different to anything you know that it will be hard to miss, If you do see anything, stay away from it," he warns.

I open my mouth to ask my mother for an explanation; she holds her hand up firmly. "Just don't *ask* me." She disappears and returns with our slates from the sanitiser; she places a finger on my slate, then her lips.

Left feeling ignorant about religion, I take a deep breath, trying to fight back tears. I'm so confused and feel very alone.

Calling Sarah takes my mind off tonight's discussion. It was a good choice. Sarah happily chats about birthday celebration options for us later in the year and what we are going to wear to Jonah's party, the dancing, who is coming, and career choices, most importantly.

"Esther, seriously, how are you going to get into law? I can understand Ruby, but not you. They all hate us, plus, can you pass the exams? They are so hard," Sarah groans.

Wow, even my best friend does not have confidence in me, despite how good my grades are.

Sarah talks about going into healthcare, maybe nursing. She is so patient, kind, and smart that she will be perfect at it.

I am determined to study hard and help people like the Golds. I am not sure in what capacity, but I can try.

After chatting to Sarah, I work on a history assignment. I am careful to only put in safe words to keep me from drawing attention to myself from the law through my online searchers. It must be about our town.

Looking at old photos so many generations ago, I am fascinated to see a totally different town landscape come to life. The transport vehicles were not sophisticated, they were big and there were so many, filling the sides of the streets and roads.

There were multiple food stores pictured, some called supermarkets. They were huge compared to our small convenience markets dotted throughout town, with the occasional speciality butcher or bakery. And of course, our fish co-op near the wharf.

They have pictures of citizens with a cart in these supermarkets filled with cardboard packaged food and fresh produce. The supermarkets look like warehouses.

Is that why they are called *super*markets? I wonder did everyone prepare food like us Farmers and Fishers generations ago?

I scroll to old advertisements, fascinated as I watch them, enjoying the music that accompanies them for clothing stores, supermarkets, and transports like cars with families going places outdoors, even with pets.

One advertisement draws me in; it is an organisation that provides food, shelter, and support to the poor. It is a documentary that has been accidently archived in advertisements.

The organisation has been around for over a century helping the poor. Providing food, hot meals, and a chat. They assist with housing, employment, clothing, even emotional support, through group meetings and visiting citizens.

Volunteers, workers, as well as recipients of the help, are interviewed. They are so happy, smiling about the positive change the organisation is making in the community. The narrator finishes with, "They are one of the many organisations making a difference in our town."

I log off, thinking about this world I have never experienced from the past and about organisations that have disappeared after so much time in operation. I try to digest what has changed in my world and the generations before me.

We only have one place in our town, run by the government, that supplies food trays or soup in keep cups for the hungry and homeless. I see it on my way to school; it is in the outer part of town and operates out of an office. The line almost goes around the block. The needy line up early. Supplies are only as generous as the budget allows.

When did citizens stop preparing meals like the Farmers, and Fishers? Where did all the supermarkets go? It is like they never existed. There are some sad remnants of buildings on the outskirts of town, undistinguishable to what they once were.

I am also struck by the advertisements, drawn to how citizens are smiling and looking happy and carefree, unlike our advertising that continuously pops up on our slates of serious, superior, frozen faced individuals whose only form of expression are their jerky head and body movements, like puppets, unnatural and surgically altered.

I seek out my Dad as my mother seems terrified to talk about anything. He his hunched over his beloved old truck tweaking it, the bonnet is up, a torch hanging illuminating the engine, all I see is grease and wires everywhere. He looks up and smiles.

"Everything okay?"

"Yeah, Dad, can I ask you about our town?"

Dad wipes his hands on a rag. "Come with me while I wash my hands."

We walk to the outside tap, and he scrubs his hands with soap and a small brush that seems to remove most of the grime and dries them on a towel conveniently hung above. He grins as he throws the towel over the hook.

"Your mother doesn't like cleaning grease off the bathroom sink."

We sit on his comfy wooden bench.

"Okay, ask away."

He stretches his legs out in front of him, putting his arm out indicating he is happy to chat, enjoying his daughter's company. I ask him about why there were so many forms of transport generations ago, and he tells me that the costs were lower to keep them registered. Families often had two or three vehicles. The vehicles ran on fossil fuels, not electric like now, and not hybrid fuel that is permitted for his antique truck.

I ask him about the supermarkets, and why so much food. He laughs, reminiscing about going to them as a very small child and sitting in a cart, while his parents shopped, brought the food home and cooked it.

"You could buy prepackaged meals, but not everyone did. Home cooking was normal. That is why kitchens are designed the way they are, the Town and Elite have them for show, that is all. We cook everything from our garden, it's a long family tradition, and healthier and tastier, don't you think?" he asks. I nod.

"But why don't people cook anymore? Nobody answers my questions, Dad."

"My understanding is that citizens became lazy and obsessed with free time and looking good. Citizens started ordering meals tailored to their specific health goals. Our country was sold on the idea of a dream, that you can have free time and look good. Even technology and big business got on board, personal blood testing, and prescription meals like we see today came and stayed. Like your friend Ruby's family."

"How come we don't buy meals? You and Mum work so hard." He pats my arm.

"Every luxury comes at a cost. We cannot afford it. We eat well from this garden, the weekly markets, and the seafood we can barter. Your mother and I like to know what is in our food. Also, you and Luke eat adult portions. Can you imagine the cost to fill you guys up? Anything else?"

I mention the documentary, he nods, telling me its late, it's a conversation for another day. I stand and kiss him on his forehead and thank him as I head for bed. I am a little wiser and confused.

CHAPTER 3

Hearing a rumbling engine in my dreams, my eyes snap open. Springing from my bed in the dark, I feel for discarded clothes on the floor with my feet. Dressing quickly, hopping from foot to foot on the cold concrete floor, I quickly twist my hair up in a messy bun. Pulling my old yard boots on, I hurry outside, forcing open the door of the rumbling monster with both hands, and climbing up into my father's truck affectionately named, Retro. Bang! Slamming the door shut, I rest my head on the cool vinyl seat, with eyes closed and arms folded across my lap.

"*Morning*," my father smiles wickedly, which I observe with one eye then close it before he notices. He guides Retro down our long driveway, turning into the main road, rumbling into the early morning. An electric self-driving transport glides pass us, *silently.*

It is market day. Each group of Farmer families hosts one Saturday a month near their homes around our town, then other Farmer and Fisher families join them. This allows the hosts of the market to sell larger volumes of their produce.

We pick up Sarah and James' family produce. My Dad delivers it back to a huge undeveloped lot near our home. The government and Lawmakers ignore our community markets as we keep the lot tidy, feed the poor, and earn points that are taxed. It's a win in every way.

Sarah smiles as she glimpses the truck coming around the corner, while jogging on the spot to stay warm with her younger sister, Miriam. They bound up to the truck as it shudders to a stop.

The truck is loaded quickly, and Sarah jumps in next to me, rubbing her hands together. Miriam always rides up top on a crate with her Dad. We collect them each week.

Sarah dives immediately into relaying the latest news in a continuous stream from reading her social pages. I stare through the dirty windscreen wondering where she finds the time and energy for it.

Sarah's Dad, Matt, jumps on the back of the truck, taps the roof twice and we head off to our next destination.

James stands ready at the curb with his family's produce. He moves immediately into loading the truck with wooden slatted crates bursting with red apples and produce, and he talks to my Dad and Matt in the way men do. I see him in the side mirror ruffling Miriam's hair, much to her annoyance.

James swings himself up onto a crate and we circle back to the empty lot.

I wonder where his Dad, John, is?

"James' Dad is sick, so his parents will not be here today. We will help James."

"*OKAY,*" Sarah says, millimetres from my face.

"Yeah, yeah," I say, thinking of the million other things that I could be doing today, like sleeping or studying for my ancient history exam.

We set up the market stalls. Our group is seasoned professionals; they wordlessly lay out colourful tablecloths on folding tables and arrange crates of produce. Pop up gazebos provide instant shade and festive colour. Our group has been careful to grow different fruit and vegetables to maximise sales and boost the families' incomes.

My family's crop consists mainly of cabbage, cauliflower, and ground vegetables with some fruit. Sarah's family specialises in anything you can grow on trellises or vines, as well as owning beehives. James' family has the market cornered on fruit and anything growing on trees and bushes. They have an impressive mini orchard in their yard.

The Farmer and Fisher citizens gather quickly to share a breakfast of hot coffee in their keep cups and savoury scrolls someone is kindly sharing around.

My father and older men always share words of encouragement with the group; each week they list the community friends either missing or still being held for questioning by the law. My stomach flip flops uncomfortably. Some have been missing for weeks!

The men remind us that we are well provided for despite the challenges and to be generous with our friends, supplying their needs until their loved ones return home. My Dad informs the group of John's illness, and everyone eagerly agrees to jump in and help James.

I hear laughter and light-hearted conversations of family and friends, reconnecting after a busy week, floating on the warm breeze. It's a happy rhythm of life I secretly love, despite the early hour.

Commotion down the street alerts us as buses have pulled in and hungry shoppers are heading down the street towards us.

My father quickly instructs Sarah and I to sell James' produce today, to set up across the lot. He promptly tells James to hand his slate to us; James will use mine as he will be working with my father and Luke.

I freeze momentarily. Sarah and I do not have time to discuss the decision as the first wave of customers arrives at James' stall. We immediately cross the lot; grateful James has the produce prices conveniently listed on his slate.

James' slate is like mine, so I total and take the points from the customers. Sarah's younger sister helps us, and we quickly become adept at fruit sales, bagging juicy apples and citrus into the customers recycled bags and keep containers, exchanging the usual friendly banter customers enjoy, including free samples.

Our country has not dealt in physical currency for two generations. Everything is paid for in digital currency called points via our hand-held slates - government issued and used in every communication.

The government and law makers know everything about us, except for bartering, which is rife in our communities. We are fortunate to have valuable and untraceable goods to exchange. Our community has bartered for centuries. This helps our families but does not win favour in the town. We are hated for it. We are seen as cheats and thieves.

The morning sales move quickly. I stand observing my father, James, and his best mate Simon, speaking animatedly to several men who listen to every word intently.

Their wives talk to my mother, who gives the children cherry tomatoes and homemade cookies to their delight. At the end of the conversation James passes a cabbage to them from under the table with no payment received.

My father and mother have always sold the cabbages and cauliflower, leaving the rest to my brother and me, who seem better suited to selling tomatoes, carrots, and loose items.

James catches my eye, looking across at his family stall, He caught me staring with indignation at him for giving away our family profits. I turn away, my face burning with embarrassment. I had no right to judge, we are instructed to give produce away to the needy.

James, oblivious to my daggers, waves wildly. He calls out thank you across the lot. I look towards James, his friend Simon stares at me directly as James makes a commotion. He smiles at my dark expression, his blue eyes twinkling with amusement, my daggers are lost on James. I wave back, avoiding Simon's gaze.

I take a break and wander among the stalls, chatting to my friends, who are all working alongside their families. Sarah's family has huge strawberries today, and fragrant beeswax candles her mother cleverly sells in recycled kept containers and glassware.

Feeling a tiny sticky hand slip into mine, I look down to see a little Fisher looking up at me, smiling - Phoebe who is covered in watermelon juice.

"Hi Phoebe, where are your parents?" She points a sticky finger towards their stall.

Her parents are busy with customers; she has slipped away. I lead the four-year-old to the stall and I inform her parents I will clean her up.

We walk hand in hand to a tap located near the Fishers' stalls and proceed to wash the bright pink juice off her hands, face, and cute floral dress. I then proceed to wash my own hands. As I crouch down at the tap at her eye level, Phoebe throws her arms around my neck.

"I love you Essie, you are like my *big* sister. Tell me a story."

"I love you too Phoebe, but no story today, I'm helping James."

She looks sad. "You make it fun with all the noises."

"I can't today, you know who tells better stories than me, Paul."

Phoebe looks frustrated putting her hands on her hips.

"Pauls not *here.* You are."

I inform her parents she is desperate for a story.

"Maybe ask Rachael or Skipper Andrew if Esther will take you," her mother suggests.

We pass the Fisher families, who keep their stalls in the shade to prevent the ice from melting, and see a huge array of gleaming fish. I love how the women wear colourful scarves intricately wrapped over their hair for hygiene and the guys wear caps.

Jonah is helping his family skilfully filleting fish for a customer in his apron, gloves, cap, and boots. He looks up and sees me. He grins, waving his filleting knife like a sword to make me laugh, much to the horror of his customer. His father tells him to focus. It is good to see he is consistent.

I observe Andrew from school at the next stall. He is sitting on a huge esky in the shade looking at his slate while his family is working on the stall. He waves me over. I excuse myself, embarrassed to be intruding, with Phoebe in tow.

Andrew's older brothers, Matt and Simon, pause and watch with interest and amusement, then realise we are talking about school, ancient history in fact, and they return to their activities. Our community loves match making.

"This ancient history exam prep is killing me, so many dates. I am working through a trial exam and got stuck. If it was engineering, I would be all over it," he sighs.

I am grateful to have a reprieve from the stall and look over the trial questions, realising I can help, showing Andrew where to find the answers in our digital resources. He thanks me.

"Andrew, you are so lucky to study at the markets, I'm helping James out today."

"Study trumps gutting and filleting. Mum gave me the choice, study under her nose or work on the stall... *hmmm* hard choice."

We laugh, knowing Andrew hates fishing but helps when it's needed, leaving most of it up to his older brothers, whom he resembles closely. Right down to the deep tan from surfing, bright blue eyes, and curly blonde hair.

I observe Andrew's Dad talking animatedly at the stall to some men and women, using his hands to illustrate his point. He reminds me of my father.

Skipper Andrew calls Simon and Matt over; they wash their hands, and join the animated discussion. Rachael, their mother, crouches talking to Phoebe and the children about the fish in the tubs, and I am sure a story too.

Story telling is a strong trait in our community.

Finding my way out of the labyrinth of tubs, Simon, and Matt smile, inclining their heads to me; his parents give me a friendly wave. We have grown up together, living and working side by side. I wonder what on earth Andrew is going to do if he is not going to fish. He is like me, studying like crazy to get out of this town.

Arriving back to relieve Sarah and Miriam they happily escape. I stack the empty crates, and bundle and sell the last produce to a keen customer at full price. I'm genuinely happy I helped James' family; we made a good profit. I just need to park my crappy attitude.

Sarah comes back noting the packing up is all done and produce sold.

"We sold everything," I tell her proudly

We hear the stall holders banging their fists loudly on tables. The sounds are deafening throughout the markets. Our slates freeze instantly, announcing drones approaching that block communication amongst us. The law hopes to catch us bartering.

Sarah searches the blue cloudless sky for drones. As they approach, we pull our broad brimmed hats over our faces, looking down as they pass slowly overhead. The drones pass several times very low, zig zagging and scanning us all. We are constantly under stifling surveillance. Today, they are hunting someone.

I observe my father and several of the men gather quickly to have a discussion then disperse. Something is up. They know who the law is seeking.

Kids yell, throwing rocks at the ominous black drones with their creepy red lights on their underbellies They are told off by terrified adults not wanting to draw attention to the markets or themselves.

It is a tenuous time living in our town without giving the law genuine reasons to raid the markets or place higher scrutiny on us.

It is midday, everyone packs up, sharing produce with each other, and any stragglers who know the deal. Any produce left is cheap, or free.

My father comes over to James' stall, beaming. "You have done well; James can go home happy with lots of points for his family."

He hands my slate back that is functional now the drones have passed. "Thanks Mark, it was a pleasure; it could happen to any of us," Sarah says. My father nods in agreement jogging back to help Luke, hurriedly packing up.

My face burns and I feel nauseous. How could I not trust my father's decision? I am a truly selfish creature. James comes over, smiling, thanking us. *Again.* He hands me a wrapped package. "Simon gave me this for your Dad. Fish guts or something," he mutters, unsure.

James, Sarah, and Miriam accept a lift home in Skipper Andrews' truck. Simon helps James load up, and they jump on the back, sitting on the top of the precariously high load, waving goodbye.

Simon grabs James by the back of his shirt as he almost tumbles off. They laugh despite the danger.

My father and I walk towards the house after unpacking Retro, his arm protectively around me, chatting about our regular customers and their news. He asks me if I was upset with the arrangements this morning. "I saw your famous frowny face." He smiles.

I confess, initially I was disappointed as it is one of our family rituals working together but accepted that he had his reasons, which were valid even if I did not know the plan.

"You are growing up to be very wise, Esther. I want to teach James how we run our stall in case something happened to me or your mother. He attends the community meetings, and I wanted to speak to him and Simon, they have leadership potential, like a girl I know. There is a surprise for you at the house."

He pats me on the head like I am six years old. He then disappears into his garden weaving around the garden beds whistling, signalling everything is well, even with wrapped fish guts tucked under his arm.

Dad is a strange creature, especially when he spoke about James and Simon. Who would have thought them leaders? I think of them as surfer friends, and well suited to their jobs in construction, fruit picking, and fishing. Maybe they can be both!

Running to the house, I am eager to see the surprise, and there he is, our dearest friend, Paul, sipping tea at our outdoor table.

Paul shows up when you need him the most. He is what my parents call nomadic. He travels light, up, and down the east coast with his signature worn black satchel, swag, and nothing else but the reliance on others for a hot meal and bed in return for a day's labour or two and wisdom I would challenge the government to beat.

Running to him like a favourite grandfather, he never fails to deliver a treat even to a seventeen-year-old girl. He stands and holds out a bag of brightly coloured candy with a big grin.

"You have grown; you'll be passing your Mamma soon."

Throwing my arms around his waist I rest my head on his chest feeling the steady beat of his heart. He points to my slate, which I stow away quickly in the sanitiser and return.

"Paul is the Law looking for you *again*?" He smiles nodding, his broad gleaming smile contrasting against his dark skin.

"They don't like that I travel talking to citizens. *Farmer Fisher* citizens. Too bad. I have important information to share. They are constantly keeping tabs on me, so I left my slate in the bush this time."

Five years ago, a virus caused a pandemic, resulting in our country losing most elderly citizens; it is rare to see anyone over seventy. Surprisingly, quite a few older homeless people survived, as they live and sleep rough in the bush or in parks, like our beloved Paul.

Paul is in his nineties. A friend, substitute grandfather to us all, who no longer have an elder in their family.

We learn from him and are loved by him unconditionally, like grandparents do. Paul, fortunately, sleeps outside or camps in the bush, and he remained there during the pandemic, safe.

"Paul, would you like a bowl of my secret stew tonight?" my mother calls.

"Yes, I'm happy to hang around for dinner. Why secret stew?"

"The secret ingredient is … *Love,*" her favourite joke. *Cringe.* Our family sits with Paul at our family table, enjoying a lively meal, updating him on all things new in our world.

"This is wonderful, it's time to chat to Mark. I have updates on farming from up north even some fishing tips if he is interested. Thank you for a fine meal, Ruth. Thank you for letting me lay low here."

Paul follows my father to his favourite bench, ready to relay his knowledge for several hours in the tranquil garden.

Silence is broken by screeching startled birds as drones approach over fences with spotlights scanning and searching for Paul, I am sure. Dad and Paul are nowhere to be seen. Thankfully they are hidden.

CHAPTER 4

"Good morning, the sun is up and so must you. *Esther,* can you hear *me*?" My mother sings.

"*Yes.*"

"It's meeting day, our turn, remember?" She reminds me.

Meeting day! My heart skips a beat. Getting up is not an issue anymore.

"Can you help with the food?"

"Sure, no problem, Mum."

"Thank you, see you in the kitchen."

I make my selection of sweet treats. With feats of food achieved, I move on to cleaning the kitchen quickly, then making the most important decision, what to wear, which is a joke.

I have only two choices suitable of blinding someone. Rewind, a choice of two outfits that look okay and may catch someone's eye who I have been attracted to for a long, long time.

Standing in our kitchen I wait to serve morning tea to the Farmers and Fishers who are arriving. Today is a big meeting.

My father, Paul and Luke have set up chairs cramming them in everywhere, even rows of cushions on the floor. Everyone must be coming to hear Paul's updates.

My mother has decorated a mountain of cookies in the shape of animals for the kids to eat in the garden while the meeting is in progress.

Families arrive, most come on foot or by bus as this does not attract attention, otherwise Farmer Fisher's trucks would alert the law there is a large gathering. I cannot see anyone special in the crowd as I busily greet everyone, refilling plates, and glasses.

Stepping aside for a drink, I feel someone pull at my arm, surprised at being touched I turn … it is not *him,* only Jonah, sigh!

"Hi Jonah, what do you want?" He pulls a strange awkward smile.

"I'm wondering if you have given anymore thought about going out with me?" He wiggles his eyebrows at me as he greedily crams a gooey brownie in his mouth, coating his teeth brown.

Oh, my goodness, what a mess. What an awkward offer! *Cringe*, hardly an enticing offer.

Jonah has been chasing me in a good-natured respectful way for a while, but I just cannot think of him romantically at all. Let alone take him seriously!

"Oh, Jonah, at least you make me laugh," I say smiling.

"Seriously, Essie, will I *ever* get the chance?" His voice softens.

Maybe I have been a little rude in this very candid moment.

"Sorry Jonah, we will just have to grow old together as friends." I pat him on the shoulder like a good mate.

"You can't blame a guy for trying," he whispers dejectedly, moving towards the meeting.

My confidence, which is usually non-existent, is a little boosted; I'm feeling hopeful that I might be attractive to *someone.*

Watching the last adults file into the living room, I turn towards the veranda door to join the children under eighteen outside, the older ones usually supervise.

Suddenly, I feel my feet leave the floor and my body being swung up in the air. So totally inappropriate and unexpected I get a fright.

"Did you think I was not coming today?" someone whispers in my ear.

I am going to faint, no, die of embarrassment!

"Sorry, I was busy on the trawler and had to shower before I got here." I note his sun-bleached blonde hair looking tousled and damp, a hint of soap and cologne, casual t-shirt, shorts, well-worn joggers, and those bright blue eyes.

Simon has not asked me out or shown any pointed interest beyond a good friend. He has stolen long looks at me across the room when he thinks I would not notice, he has been extra helpful lately to my parents and at other meetings, staying back and chatting to me. He must have picked up on my mutual attraction. Finally, but how humiliating.

"Um, yes, I was wondering where you were. The meeting is about to begin, and you weren't here," I murmur almost to myself.

We have known each other forever.

Simon looks briefly into my eyes, smiling before gently placing me on the ground like I am a feather.

"I'm so sorry Esther, that was wrong. I should not have touched you, without your permission. I wasn't thinking. Forgive me?" I incline my head. "Will I see you at the river today?" Simon asks shyly.

I incline my head again as though I have lost the ability to talk. My heart beats so loudly in my ears that it sounds like the ocean. What is wrong with me? I have known Simon all my life. I am very attracted to him - I am unsure when that changed.

With that, he and his very strong arms and bright blue eyes are gone, disappearing in the crowded room towards an empty seat near Jonah. He looks back at me with a smile. No longer hiding his attention to me.

I quickly run outside to help with the children, as I am not yet eighteen and not able to join the boring farm and fish talk. Plenty of time for that later, much later.

Joining the small children sitting under one of our many big shady trees, I settle myself on the grass and calm my racing heart, reading a story aloud from my slate.

"Essie, why is your face so red?" Beth, a five-year-old asks.

Sarah, sitting at the back of the group with a baby on her lap, looks me in the eye, a smile dancing on her lips.

"Yeah, why is your face *so* red?" She obviously saw Simon arrive late and swoop me in the air. Her face says it all, 'thank goodness he finally made a move.'

I read animatedly about a cute chicken, making sure not to miss any detail in the story, even adding animal noises, to the children's delight.

After story time, everyone explores the garden, eating cookies. Sarah and I lay under the tree in the shade, chatting about the river and who might be there today. I hear random words float on the warm air from open windows, *ground, planting,* and *harvest.*

I hear Paul's voice today, he seems to hold the floor talking about John, he must be a friend of his. It is interesting to observe the group, each meeting from a distance, as my friends come of age and attend their meetings. However, I have absolutely no interest in joining an hour-long discussion on farming and how to catch a fish better, not now or ever.

The meeting finishes promptly at eleven, releasing everyone, and leaving me free to do as I like until school tomorrow.

After cleaning up, Sarah and I rush to change for our afternoon at the river. We grab our bags and apples for the walk along the bushfire trail near my home leading to the river. Farmer and Fisher kids love the safety of it. Most of our friends have already left to go to the river.

The Town and Elite community do not find frolicking in the river interesting, rather they see it as something untamed creatures participate in and is dirty. We walk in comfortable silence along the bush trail, carefree chomping on juicy apples, savouring the sweetness.

"What on earth do they talk about in those meetings for so long?" Sarah blurts out.

"Boring stuff I think," I say.

"My parents don't tell me anything, only that it's all about the harvest."

"Mine too. Who cares," I say, carelessly tossing my apple core under a tree.

"Race you to the river?" Sarah challenges.

We run along the trail until we near the clearing, where we start peeling off our outer clothes, revealing our swimming costumes. As we run, we throw our bags to the side. I reach the rope, I swing first and then I'm pushed; I'm sent flying forward into the river by a very enthusiastic Sarah, who now possesses the swing.

"You win!" I declare, defeated by her wicked tactics.

I land with a belly flop then flip over to enjoy floating on my back, staring at the sapphire blue sky, alone in my world for a moment.

The gentle river is lapping at my ears. This is my private Australian sanctuary, until I spot a small drone flying low along the curve of the river. Observing us, as always.

Splash! The silence is broken by Sarah, who laughs and squeals without any care in the world, barely missing the drone.

Our friends gather, soaking up the one afternoon a week where we can be truly free. We swim, chat, and catch up with those who work. Today, we compare stories of escape, beatings, and bruises from the community bullies.

We gather as we lay on our towels in the shade. I look at Matthew from my class; I barely recognised him. His face is swollen with a split lip, and most of his body is bruised. Everyone looks at his bruises and collectively gasp.

"Esther copped abuse this week too, show them," Sarah announces.

I shyly oblige, removing my rash shirt and they all gasp at my purple and blue bruising across my back, shoulders neck and face. I quickly pull my rash shirt back on to be modest. I do not like exposing myself in a swimming costume, let alone without my rash shirt.

They all ask if I am okay, the guys are outraged, rightly so, but stop at plans of revenge, knowing it is pointless.

James, who never talks, speaks up and says we all need to watch out for each other, we are safer in groups. He makes a point of saying the girls are particularly at risk on their own, especially isolated on the buses and streets. Everyone is very quiet, digesting what he is saying, acknowledging the fact that it must be serious if James is speaking with authority about the violence.

We are not free, as these reminders come to the fore.

The group quickly changes the subject to school and work, teasing Jonah tirelessly about facing the law. He is reckless but refuses to repeat the offence for our entertainment, except he shows bruising on his wrists from restraints that were placed far too tightly and slight cuts. Maybe a sign of maturity, or a reflection on a truly terrifying ordeal.

Everyone heads back to the water. I rest my back against a huge, smooth eucalyptus tree trunk, and I am joined by Simon who politely asks if I am okay, and can he join me. I incline my head; he sits at a respectable distance and rests against the tree looking out at the river. We sit in silence on our towels for a while, until I ask him, breaking the silence.

"Don't you ever tire of being near water? Fishing all week, swimming at the end of the week."

"Not if it means being around you," he says quietly out of the hearing of his friends and not looking at me directly, suddenly feeling confident.

"Really?" I say, turning my head, surprised he is sharing his feelings.

"*Really*! I have liked you for so long and I knew that if I did not do something quickly a certain big fish," indicating Jonah with his head, "might snap you up."

I laugh to myself a little, embarrassed, being chased by two guys in the same day. Is it courting Esther season, what is going on? *Weird!*

"Oh Jonah, you are safe from him. I have broken his heart today. I love your whole fish analogy thing going on though."

"*Really!* I thought it was bit lame, but it was too late to take it back. Am I next in the firing line?" he asks half serious, half smiling raising his left eyebrow.

"Hmm, I haven't decided yet, I need to think about it." I jumped up walking quickly down the bush trail into the shaded bush away from the others to think.

Simon catches me quickly in his arms and suddenly we are face to face trying to catch our breath. He releases me immediately like a hot rock, realising again he has acted impulsively and inappropriately, it's such an awkward moment. Simon is openly revealing his feelings, and I am trying to confirm mine.

"Sorry Esther, I guess I got caught up in the moment, again. Did I bump your bruises?" He apologises profusely. Simon's eyes are shining, his red face contrasting with his blonde hair. He is clearly nervous now.

"Don't be, it was kind of fun," I whisper, standing still despite the whirlwind of emotions I am feeling.

"*Really*?" he says, surprised and relieved.

We stare at each other for a long moment, unsure of what to do or say next. "Would you go out with me and not just a one-off date?" Simon finally asks awkwardly and very old fashioned.

I think carefully about what I am about to do. Speaking slowly, knowing this is not a passing infatuation on his part, but I am relieved.

"Can we spend time together, keeping it secret, for a while until I am sure about us? This is very different from being childhood friends, Simon. I am not ready to jump onto the iRESPECT app and set up a relationship agreement with you yet." I bite my lip nervously.

"I understand, I want us to be totally honest with each other. It has taken me so long to ask you out. I was thinking about taking it real slow and if you are willing to trust me, we can leave that formal stuff to later," Simon says, looking serious.

"We should be getting back you know, not to arouse suspicion," I say.

"Yes boss," Simon cheekily replies, sneaking one longer look into my eyes and strolls back down the bush trail as if nothing has transpired between us.

I follow moments later back to where I left my towel. A new excited flutter in my stomach. I open my slate and read more of my Zombie slayer story to calm my nerves.

Sarah and Elizabeth find me lying on my towel totally engrossed in my reading and thoughts. They drag me off to the rope swing, each of us taking turns to take death-defying high swings over the river and dropping. As I swing through the air I wonder if keeping secrets is like moments on this swing, *exhilarating but dangerous.*

The afternoon is so much fun with all my friends - carefree and no responsibility. The future is looking a little brighter, unknown, and handsome.

Calling Luke in the distance, I remind him it is time to go home. We walk home down the bush trail chatting about our afternoon, and we look forward to dinner with Paul, our special guest.

My parents sit at our table on the veranda packing dried seeds into homemade envelopes. These are cleverly created from paper packaging saved from my father's recycling bin at work at the building supply store. They are talking and laughing with Paul as they pack seeds for our Farmers to share.

"So how was the river today kids, freezing?" Paul asks grinning.

"Awesome," was Luke's response, followed by a lengthy discussion of the crazy, dangerous activities that occurred, ending in the fact that nobody was killed.

All eyes turn to me expectantly.

"Just the usual, we swam, goofed around with the same people," I tell them unenthusiastically.

"Nobody of particular interest today, at all?" my Dad asks, not looking up.

I shrug, wanting this interrogation to be over, shifting awkwardly from foot to foot, looking down at the veranda, and counting the ants crawling on a timber slat.

"Surely there is a nice boy amongst them. Look how interested Jonah has been, what about James down the road?" my mother joins in the discussion.

"Yes, they seem to be growing up into respectable young guys, especially James or one of the others from your class," he adds to my mother's interrogation.

They talk about my dating prospects like they are from previous centuries. I squirm internally, looking for an escape.

"I have found the best policy is to let young citizens work it out for themselves, saving the parents from the blame of a poor match. Match making is a dangerous business, even though it has its merits," Paul says smoothly.

"Thank you, Paul." I thank him with a very grateful smile.

"How about your favourite tonight, Paul? Veggie stack," to reward my rescuer.

"Sounds great, tonight will be my last night here. It's not safe to stay too long in one place," he informs us sadly.

I scoot into the kitchen to start dinner after changing; my mother follows.

"Why does Paul sleep on the veranda?" I ask her while we prepare dinner.

"He has been on the road so long he is only comfortable outside. I think he likes sleeping under the stars," she replies without any concern.

It sounds like the best option to me too, sleeping under the stars. Paul certainly lives an interesting life on the road; I am a little envious of his adventurous life. Unpredictable, yet comfortable. Loved. Maybe not being pursued by the law though.

After dinner Luke and I excuse ourselves and clear the table and head towards our bedrooms to tackle homework.

"Every time Paul visits, I offer him my bed you know," Luke tells me.

"Really, oh well, at least you offer. He is a great guy, isn't he?"

"Sure is, I am going to miss our chats when he goes." Luke flops face down on his bed; all that can be seen is a messy mop of brown hair. He is my only sibling and we have a tight bond. He is strong for his fifteen years. He is stuck in that strange place between boyhood and manhood. His changing body is slowly winning, yet he still shows that boyish vulnerability at times, which I love.

His dark hair and hazel eyes that shift from brown to green in the light is not lost on the girls, yet he is uninterested in the attention.

Luke finds school unchallenging but necessary. He enjoys basketball, his chosen sport, and with his ever-increasing height, it has proven to be a wise decision. His strength on the court is fuelled not only by hormones but also by physical yard work at home.

He can dig and turn over our numerous garden beds with great speed and accuracy; he is able to lift large crates of produce to help our father. I often wonder if his dedication is to be helpful or determination to complete his chores to escape to basketball?

I am touched by his moments of thoughtfulness, which can be unexpected, and just as quickly disappear, like a sun shower, short - nurturing but can be gone in an instant.

He really is a younger version of our Dad. I enjoy his sense of humour, which wins every time when we fight. He is the peacemaker, even if his style is a little quirky.

I sit hugging my bunny, absently stroking its satiny ears, opening the vault in my mind, and placing the sweet moments of today safely away for another day, savouring them just for a moment.

I place bunny on my bed and work on assessments, determined to keep up with the Town classmates, ignoring all the messages from friends that pop up on my slate. I pause when one message comes in from Simon. Taking a slow breath, I open it to see a photo of a beautiful sunset, his sweet message 'this reminded me of you.'

I decide that it is a sign to stop studying. I stare at the simple words that say so much. I feel myself open my heart to the possibility of having a boyfriend for the first time and feeling confident to explore the possibilities for the future.

I am curious about dating and download the teen iRESPECT app and the Adult iRESPECT app, as I am eligible to use both at my age - over sixteen under eighteen.

Looking at the simple layout for teens I see tick boxes of what physical stuff you are comfortable with then apparently if the person you are in the relationship with reads it and agrees to the boundaries you both sign off on it.

The options start with hand holding, hugging, and kissing. I look down the detailed list, and think, oh *my,* I am not ready to think about some of this stuff and shut it off quickly.

Simon has dated a few girls, but not for long. We seem different, he has not rushed to ask me out, quite the opposite. He has taken his time, which is sweet.

CHAPTER 5

I am too late to catch Paul before he leaves. He has awakened early travelling to his next destination. I find Paul's gift on the table, a rare handwritten note in pencil on recycled paper with rainbow-coloured candy attached for our family.

The written word is forbidden. Slates are the government's law. Paul's note conveys his emotion and character through his writing. It is unlike slates, which is cold and predictable.

Carrying the heartfelt gift, I present it to my mother, placing it in the kitchen for the family to see. "We are certainly going to miss him," she sighs, busily collecting laundry.

I tell Luke we are catching the bus today, as I hurry him through breakfast, hoping to get to the front of the line. We are in luck, managing to be second and fortunately strong enough to penetrate the toxic crowd on the bus despite the verbal and physical abuse.

Sarah sits next to Josh, her best male friend. Everyone else in our group call it dating.

Josh is very protective of Sarah, a Fisher, a good match in our community. They are talking animatedly, competing against each other on a game on their slates, oblivious to the foul language being hurled at us from the back seats.

Managing to tumble out of the bus at school unscathed, we move quickly into the school entry, lining up to tap our slates. Most town students have an identity chip in their hand or wrist permitting them to go ahead of us.

We place our satchels into tubs for scanning at the security check point. A warning siren sounds. We cover our ears, wincing at the loud, nauseating, undulating sound.

"Whoops, just testing!" exclaims Jonah. "It's my Mum's fault, she packed my lunch," he babbles on exasperatedly. To security it looks like an explosive and to his humiliation we know his Mum packs his lunch. Pathetic.

"Your mother makes your lunch? You are seventeen years old," the security guard robotically says. The foyer erupts into laughter.

"You are correct, I will not let it happen again," he politely bows to security, slinking over to his locker to stash his contraband.

We join Jonah riding on the crest of his discomfort until Sarah and Josh receive another cruel jibe about their relationship from the Town boys passing by giving Josh a violent shoulder barge, sending him flying into the lockers.

"Get out of the way little kids, have you and Sarah done it yet Josh?" Jason sneers. Jonah grabs Josh's sleeve, propelling him towards their first class, talking earnestly to him with an arm around him. For all his antics, Jonah is a dependable friend.

"I am sick of it. Every time we show interest in someone, Town students expect us to act the same. All they think about is sex. We are not like that, we are good friends," Sarah sobs.

I usher her to the nearby sanitation room until she settles, then I guide her to her class, Surely Parkour will be a good diversion. I am happy to keep my new relationship a secret. We change into our PK uniforms and enter the PK training centre. We start the course from the opposite end, to chat and to hide our emerging skills and strength.

Parkour is an ancient pastime that has developed into a nationally recognised fitness programme in schools, focusing on smooth efficient movements. It is so popular that children and adults partake in it at local parks on purpose designed PK equipment.

Sarah and I throw ourselves off high simulated walls onto platforms and rails, chatting in between, and catching our breath. Our teacher asks us to remain behind after class. She surprises us by applauding our increased proficiency.

We thank her, then quickly change back into our uniforms. I see on my slate a picture from Simon featuring a huge shiny fish on the trawler with the ocean as a backdrop and a cute note saying, sorry you are not here. I am glad I was not there to smell it. I message that sentiment back to him.

"I am feeling better, Esther, thanks for being there," Sarah whispers. I nod hurrying, late for our next class.

We take the shorter route to communications, which passes the chaotic administration desk to make up lost time in PK. I stop and stare; there is a figure at the counter who looks like my mother in scrubs. Why is she here and not at work?

"Mum, Mum is everything alright?" I ask, running to her in a panic.

"Yes Esther, I was just sending for you," she replies casually.

"Why?"

"Today is your last day of school, a really good job came up. I put your name forward to my supervisor, Rose, and HR at the Medical Precinct, and you have been approved. Naturally, I accepted on your behalf. It is an incredible opportunity. The shift starts at midday, so we must hurry, she simply informs me.

Standing in shock - school is over for me in an instant. I have seen students leave in their last years when employment opportunities arise, but I did not picture myself as one of them, especially with my excellent grades and class rankings. I had great plans. University. Law. This swirls around my head.

It is a rare opportunity in our community to gain employment, which I am not fully appreciating at this moment. I am moving in slow motion; the world is rushing past me in a blur. I am queasy and lightheaded.

Sarah just hugs me firmly, her eyes say, "Call me later, everything will be okay." My mother puts her arm around me, happily shepherding me to the door.

"The position came up unexpectedly. I decided this would be perfect for you."

"Mum, what have you signed me up *for?*" Jerking back into reality and thinking the worst.

"Helping out in the Medical Precinct wards, of course." It appears from what she is saying someone had to be fired for stealing.

Numbly, I sit in the sleek white medical transport car she has borrowed. She clips my seat belt around my school utility uniform and expertly programmes the self- drive transport, and we glide away from the school grounds.

Arriving at my new life in minutes, the huge Medical Precinct looms in front of me. Multiple stories of glass reflect the expansive blue sky, and Mum parks the vehicle in the designated parking station.

We enter the fancy entrance through glass sliding doors. The floors gleam, with polished granite, the ceilings are high and the air is filled with a scent of cleanliness.

After passing the security check point my mother gives me a reassuring squeeze with promises of meeting me at the same place at six pm and assuring me that I can do this job.

She directs me to the nurses' station that I need to report to and hurries back to work. I have barely digested the whole scenario. The Medical Precinct is buzzing with activity and smells of disinfectant mixed with illness. Working for the rest of my life! A distant thought suddenly came to the forefront.

Presenting myself at the nurses' station I am met by a falsely cheerful young Town girl, Candy. She energetically drags me to a disused corner of the back entrance of the Medical Precinct that doubles as a locker room, where relics of previous staff uniforms have been left for new initiates to fight over until they are formally on staff. She hands me the clothes and stands staring expectantly at me.

"Try them on," she demands impatiently, jiggling from foot to foot.

"What, here?"

"Yes, yes, strip, hurry up or the CEO will not be happy. Time is everything in this misery factory."

I move at lightning speed. The top is huge and the pants are manageable, so I roll the waist band to tighten it; she grins watching me struggle. I am feeling more confident, on the outside, my school boots peeking out underneath.

"You'll do, let's go. Candy stands hands on her hips. She directs me to a locker nearby. "You choose a new one each time and a new code. I will give you a tour of the outpatient clinics, just once, then work it out yourself."

For the few moments that she grants me, I am directed to the zone where I am to perform my role. My head spins from the rapid tour.

"In this clinic, you will report to Rose over there. Bye."

"Will I see you again?" I ask, unsure of this crazy place.

"Don't you get it, schools over, *Farmer girl*, suck it up, if you can't hack it, go back to the farm. Plenty of others will take you place. Her tone was cruel.

She flies off, leaving me feeling the sickening weight of my responsibility. She bluntly stated my situation with no sweetness sprinkled over it. Just the ugly truth. Dreams crushed.

Without thinking, I keep moving towards the outpatient nurses' station, trying not to worry, fearful that an unending torrent of tears will erupt.

Rose approaches me, a middle-aged woman who exudes efficiency and Town prejudice. I introduce myself and her demeanour shifts, greeting me warmly; maybe my white, bloodless face softened her.

She shows me my supplies cart that I will work from and hands me a Medical Precinct slate with a list of tasks and time assigned for each. She takes my slate and puts it on charge. Thanking her I look around; the air is alive with the sights and sounds of citizens and medical staff, swirling together.

My slate beeps already! Wow I am already two minutes behind schedule. Fortunately, I am given the task of restocking all the treatment rooms with intriguing supplies, which is generous on the Precinct's part to help me find my way. I suspect this will be one of the easier days.

My heart pounds with nervous energy as I try to beat the timer; success is easily achieved when it is almost predetermined. I push my cart quickly, trying not to knock over any patients and staff.

Proudly, I seek out Rose who barely acknowledges my heroic efforts. She just nods and keys in another set of minor tasks that the staff will not touch, without looking at me.

Cleaning the treatment rooms, emptying bins… I scroll to the end. The slate shows six pm is the end of the day. This conclusion only comes after all the tasks are dutifully completed, of course.

"You did well, I had my doubts. Hit the end button now."

Rose acknowledged my meagre existence, and to my delight the slate shows the points I have earned. She places it in the recharging rack, ready for tomorrow and hands mine back.

"Do not get excited, these can be deducted, you know. Ruth was right, you are very trustworthy and a hard worker, we will message your shifts." She picks up her bag and leaves.

Seeking out my locker, I grab my satchel and school uniform, grey and shapeless. I change back into my school uniform in the change room this time, stowing my scrubs into my satchel.

Messaging Sarah, Ruby, and Simon my big news, I wind my way back through the labyrinth of corridors and gladly find my mother waiting for me, staring thoughtfully at the stunning water feature. She is comforting and unchanging.

She has managed to secure herself two permanent part time jobs, but the hours are long. Her least favoured place is the fancy skin Precinct where the wealthy attempt to remain youthful. The pay is fair and the clients are always happy when they achieve their goals, youth, or a poor representation of it.

The job, where her passion for citizens is ignited, is the Medical Precinct. Farmers and Fishers are generally not given these positions but she is able to soothe the difficult patients. The precinct recognises this as an asset and has designated her a role as a nursing assistant and unofficial crowd control. I silently hug her for a long time, grateful she has helped me bridge the gap between childhood to present and to be here at the end of a hard first day.

We walk home chatting about our day, revelling in the opportunity to share our day, the thirty-minute walk home seems like minutes.

I shower quickly and prepare a simple meal of brightly coloured salad and finely sliced chicken as if it were a celebration meal. Employment is worth celebrating in my family and community.

My father and Luke arrive at our family table as soon as the clatter of plates is heard. Luke asks what the occasion is?

"Mum got me a job, and I have already started at the Medical Precinct with her."

Luke takes a moment to absorb this news. "Awesome Esther, hope you have to wipe a million butts." I knew it was impossible to escape a cheeky comment.

After savouring the chicken meal, our family gravitates to the lounge to relax and chat, enjoying the evening together. Ruby and Simon message back a million questions and congratulate me. I will reply later.

Sarah arrives at the door. She is incapable of waiting for an invitation, so she joins our family where my parents have been excitedly grilling me on my first day of employment. She sits wide eyed, listening intently, hugging a pillow while I tell them about my day and the race to beat the interminable clock. My parents radiate pride, happy to share their good news.

"How does it feel not to be at school?" Sarah finally asks. I can only deliver a shrug with my tired shoulders. I produce my scrubs for inspection, which finally releases all my pent-up emotions into waves of laughter, which everyone joins in. They are truly bland and shapeless.

"Those handsome medics will be fighting to be near you," Sarah giggles.

"I can arrange your own set. Josh will not be able to take his eyes off you!"

"Yuck," she throws cushions at me.

A perfect ending to a crazy day. Family and friends are the pressure valves of life, and laughter of course.

CHAPTER 6

I have been assigned ad hoc shifts. They provide me with enough hours to earn points to help my family while continuing to study, hoping to keep up with my class and be permitted to sit the HSC exams. My school has continued supplying lessons.

My days are repetitive, consumed by preparing meals, cleaning, studying, and tending our vegetable garden, allowing my father to rest. Grudgingly, I see James's point; the balance between paid employment and helping at home is very important. My only reprieve is messaging Sarah, Ruby, and Simon.

Simon and I have fallen into a pattern of messaging or chatting daily. This has helped break the ice in getting to know each other as adults. Our schedules have not aligned to meet up in person, but regular contact is building our bond. Simon is a guy of few words but takes great pictures to illustrate his days when words are few.

Today, I help prepare the produce for market; we will be travelling to another group's market site across town tomorrow. My mother and father insist on packing all the cabbages and cauliflower and force me to go to bed to rest.

I take extra care choosing an outfit for tomorrow, Simon and I will be able to finally talk to each other face to face. Happy with my choice, I sleep. Kookaburras joyfully call at dawn, so happy, warning of rain and waking me.

My mind turns pleasantly towards market day and helping my parents. We will take less produce, which frees me for more social time.

I surprise the family by hurrying them for a change. Our truck picks up Sarah and James' family produce. Sarah and James jump on the back with Luke and me, and their families will follow.

We sit astride the crates yelling at each other over the truck's noisy engine, laughing when we cannot make any sense of each other.

We arrive at the park that is furnished with brightly coloured children's play equipment, and well-established ancient trees - they provide much needed shade. Our family quickly completes the task setting up and seeking out breakfast, *mmm* warm savoury scrolls again.

My father speaks briefly to the group then we disperse. I feel warm breath on my neck giving me goosebumps as Simon whispers covertly over my shoulder. "Good morning beautiful, can I see you today, when there is a break?"

"Sure," I whisper back separating quickly.

Citizens arrive in droves today; my parents are relieved of their cabbages quickly. They are talking in earnest to the same people I saw last week over cabbages and many new customers too.

Bored with the market today, I drift from stall to stall chatting to friends and tasting produce until I find myself at Simon's stall, overflowing with vibrant seafood, the fish so appealing with their bright eyes and shimmery scales resting on crushed ice.

"Hi Esther," Simon greets me, casually, his eyes lingering.

"Hi Simon, I would like to buy two Bream."

"Sure, would you like me to fillet it for you as a treat for your good news about the job?" he asks, keeping the conversation neutral with his mother nearby.

Simon wears a large, white plastic apron, gloves, boots, and a cap to keep his curly, blonde hair out of the seafood. He impressively fillets and cleans the fish and finalises the transaction by packing it into my keep container, handing it over with a flourish.

"For you!" Then mouths, "Because you're beautiful." Aww so sweet.

I giggle at this shameless flirting. Nobody thinks anything of our interaction especially, as I transfer points.

"Can you help me with my slate, Esther?" he asks.

"Yeah, bring it over to me later," I say within earshot of his parents. This is ridiculous, I feel like I am performing in a school play.

I sit with school friends under a nearby willow tree, who seem more enthusiastic about my job than I am.

A familiar face appears in the crowd, it is Paul. I run to him, wanting to share my news. Glad he has not left town yet.

"Hey, what's the rush?" Paul asks.

"Have lunch with me." I invite him to sit.

Paul agrees, listening intently as I share my lunch of rolls, salads, and details of my opportunity to work at the Medical Precinct.

"This is wonderful, Esther, I am happy for you. Can I ask you something? Why does that boy Simon Allen keep looking at you? Have you caught a big fish?" Paul leans towards me his eyes dance with amusement.

"Shhh, it is a secret, it's very new. Yes, I have hook, and line I suspect." I laugh, holding my finger to my lips.

"Well, it won't be for long if he keeps that staring up. I'm happy for you, think carefully when you are at work. Ask yourself, are you working for yourself or for others?" He stands, picking up his signature satchel, and looking at me.

As I contemplate his words for a moment I look up and he is gone. For an elderly man, he moves quickly.

Simon appears at my side crunching an apple, his apron, gloves, boots, and cap are gone. He's just wearing his blue company t -shirt and cargo pants, with his slate in hand, keeping up the charade.

"Paul knows about us," I say to Simon resignedly.

"He is a very wise man, Esther; you would be surprised how much he knows. Am I *that* obvious?" He is miffed at his appalling acting.

"Apparently so. I have to go to the city tomorrow to register for work, I'm nervous about getting lost." Leaning closer to him, our shoulders touching.

"I can come with you, like a guide, if you want and skip the meeting. What time?" Simon offers gallantly.

"Six am, but you cannot be seen by anyone we know on the train. Okay?" I insist.

"Okay, that is early, just as well you are pretty. Otherwise, no chance!" he exclaims good humouredly.

He sure is persistent with flirting and knows how to win my heart. I am surprised he called me pretty and beautiful today.

"Bye. I had better help my poor Dad, he seems a bit overwhelmed," I tell him, while observing a huge crowd at the table.

On my way back to the stall, I see Ruby. She stands out in the crowd, with her Elite hair style and clothes; she hugs me, congratulating me on the new job.

"Come for dinner tonight so we can catch up, I miss our long talks. Sarah's strawberries are amazing as always." She gushes biting into one.

"I would love to, is seven, okay?" I'm pleased with the invite.

"Of course, Esther," Ruby replies.

Jonah wanders past with his lunch - I grab him.

"Jonah, please keep an eye on Ruby." He nods obediently, knowing she is vulnerable and naïve, wandering around the park.

Bouncing up to my father, I work beside him, and he instructs me how to carefully place the cabbage into the person's carry bag. This is belittling but I bite my tongue. I am nearing eighteen, surely, I could be trusted.

A man approaches our stall, and points at my father with a grubby finger, I stop, unsure. Graciously, my father steps in quickly, speaking to the man who has many questions on how and where to plant seeds.

My father directs me to other tasks while he spends time discussing the finer points of ground and soil types, the man is totally engrossed in the discussion.

Finally, my father indicates to me to carefully get a cabbage from a box under the table. For a fleeting moment I see some odd marks on the cabbage amongst the leaves and then it is gone, the cabbage is handed over, no payment is taken. It's a gift my father insists.

We sell most of our produce, giving the remaining vegetables away to the homeless living in the park. My father and I load the truck together silently side by side, then he stops for a moment and observes me.

"I think you are getting stronger; this new job and lifestyle is good for you."

"Thanks, Dad."

Maybe PK and gardening are the reasons I can load the truck with as much speed as the Farmer boys now.

I insist that my father go inside to rest when we arrive home. I can easily pack the empty crates away with Luke, except he has disappeared again, like a magician's assistant.

Working my way steadily through the stacking and sorting in the shed, I step backwards onto a box as I try to squeeze in one more crate, noticing it is full of rice paper. Sitting on a crate to rest, curiosity takes hold. I have never spent much time in here. It is dirty and spiders have made it their sanctuary. Red backs are plentiful.

I am shocked at how many rice paper sheets there are - more than our family could eat in a year. I quickly cover up the box.

I prepare a basket of fresh produce to share with Ruby's family, I rest and then study all afternoon.

I dress into the best outfit I own, a blue tailored dress. I carefully style my hair suited to Elite standards. It is easier to hide camouflaged.

As I am farewelling my parents, Ruby arrives unexpectedly on our veranda. "Hi Esther, I thought I could pick you up as you have been working so hard this week, is that okay?" she asks apologetically.

"Oh, course Ruby, you are sweet!"

Walking to her transport I realise it is brand new.

I look at Ruby expectantly.

"My parents could not wait until I graduate so they gave it to me today. I wanted you to be the first to ride with me."

"Ruby, it's perfect." I am happy for her.

It is a sleek two-person self-drive transport in deep metallic red like a beautiful ruby. The dome is tinted, adding to its elegant sporty persona.

We hug jumping up and down like children with a new toy. "Let's go, Ruby."

The doors swing up and we slip into the soft white leather seats. She speaks to the transport AI, directing it to drive home. We sit back as it chauffeurs us zig-zagging through the community to her home; it feels like I am riding on air.

Ruby is truly lucky; her parents are very wealthy as her father is a City, Town and Precinct historian with the Lawmakers, her mother is a paralegal for a prominent lawyer. Ruby prefers hanging out with the Farmers and Fishers at school, even joining us at the river on occasions.

We have always dined at each other's homes, wanting what the other takes for granted in a good-natured way but always happy to share what we have.

Sadly, my entertainment is over quickly arriving without a sound into the spacious driveway. Entering Ruby's immaculate home I am greeted by her mother Krystal, looking flawless with long dark hair, as if from a slate advertisement. The Elite are all the same, they have the appearance of being manufactured. Krystal politely inclines her head. She inquires after my family and excuses herself.

We happily find a cosy corner in the opulent house and talk about everything, and finally, my work.

"Tell me honestly, are you truly happy at the Medical Precinct? If you hate it my parents will find something else, I promise," Ruby asks earnestly, grabbing my hands.

"Ruby, I love the challenge, the patients, and the silly little jobs they give me. The work is not very regular. I would love more than two shifts a week," I confess.

"Why don't you ask?" She encourages me.

"I could, I guess," slowly thinking through the logistics. It is a fine balance between asking and appearing ungrateful.

"Are you hungry, Esther?"

"Always at your place, especially if you are cooking." It is our inside joke, Elite do not cook. They heat pre-packaged meals.

We enter the spacious kitchen, which has never cooked a meal. The pantry houses cooling units with glass doors displaying their contents. Clearly labelled for each household member like a retail store.

"What do you feel like Esther, chicken, beef, vegetables, spicy, creamy? What is your wish? Just pick from my side." Ruby spreads out her arms, twirling.

I have eaten at Ruby's home many times and remain speechless at the choice before me. For a moment, I feel shame being so excited about dinner, remembering the needy who visited the park today. This quickly passes as I select my favourite, creamy chicken.

"Good choice, my favourite too," Ruby enthuses. Ruby places the meals into the heating unit. In minutes we have our aromatic meals in front of us at the kitchen counter.

"Hello, you two, how were the markets today?" Peter, Ruby's father asks.

"Oh, the fruit is wonderful, I bought you some of James' fruit, the peaches and apricots are delicious." Ruby informs him, clutching her stomach. Peter and I look at her alarmed.

"Are you okay? Is it the usual pain after eating? Make a note for your doctor and we will track its ingredients. Do a blood test straight away," Peter instructs Ruby, and she nods, reaching for medication.

"It was the usual chaos today, Peter," I continue, while Ruby pricks her finger placing a single drop in a scanner, sending it off to who knows where.

"How are you, Peter?"

"I am well, Esther; I hear wonderful reports of your work from friends. How are enjoying being one of us workers?" Peter is always friendly and relaxed when chatting to me, unlike his indifferent wife.

"Very much," I answer, acutely aware nothing is private in this town.

"Can you get your father to register his truck ASAP? It would be in all your interests," he says as he leaves the kitchen more as a directive than a suggestion.

"I will, thank you for the kind tip." Ruby raises her perfect eyebrows. "Something's going on again Ruby, I am worried that the Law makers have found another way to make our lives difficult."

"Don't worry, there is always dessert, a double fudge sundae," Ruby says mischievously as she takes my empty dish throwing it in the kitchen sanitiser.

"Absolutely! If your tummy is okay." She dismisses it with a wave.

We grab tubs of gooey chocolate delight, wandering barefoot around her cultivated garden, and enjoying the mild autumn evening. The grass feels like velvet. I lick fudgy delight off my spoon savouring it.

"What do you think of Jonah? He is so funny and adorable." Ruby sighs staring at the stars. All I can do is not choke and spray chocolate fudge all over the garden.

"Ruby, has he asked you out?" I ask.

"No, but we had a great time eating lunch together at the markets today, just us chatting. It was nice. We have always got along. I don't know, I have felt attracted to him for a while now. He looked at me *a lot* when I was talking and just listened."

Recovering quickly, I look at Ruby. She is serious.

I realise she is in the same situation as me. There is a small pool of guys in our town we can date; the shift can be subtle from mates to dates.

"Ruby, do you realise if you date Jonah you are stepping into my world? It is not really dating; we call it courtship. Like a slow dance…lots of boundaries to navigate together."

"You really care about me. Yes, it is what I really want. I *know* I do not want to date an Elite. It is literally all about sex." Ruby tilts her head looking at me.

"Ask him out. It will surprise him and speed up the dance just a little or it could be ages. Wait, what about your parents?" "*Oh crap*!" she says, realising the dilemma.

"My Dad would be cool; my Mum will freak out. She thinks I should be aiming for Uni then the ultimate Elite partner." Ruby grins.

Ruby kindly drops me off home and thanks me for the chat, promising to keep me posted on the Jonah situation.

CHAPTER 7

I shiver in my black hoodie and cotton cargo pants, pleased autumn is here. It's a relief from the insufferable Australian summer. The sun is just beginning to rise.

Staring at the train rails I am contemplating my trip today; I acknowledge it is daunting travelling to Sydney City. It is comforting that Simon will be by my side. I want to know him better without prying eyes.

The sleek carriages of the bullet train glide into my station, I am the only person about to board. Suddenly, out of the shadows, a figure appears at my side.

"Good morning," Simon murmurs, looking around.

"Oh Simon, you're here. Let's find the best place to sit; we have exactly twenty minutes until we reach the city." I pull my hoodie back smoothing my hair escaping from my long braid.

Simon pulls back his hoodie too, revealing unruly blonde hair, which I cannot deny is very cute. My Dad describes it as 'classic surfer dude hair,' meaning messy.

We settle into a corner seat, away from passengers who do not hide their distaste for us as Farmer and Fisher – typical! We dismiss their stares and focus on us.

Simon tells me he needs to look up today's laws. He offers to share his slate with me. We quickly scroll the endless list of current updates for today.

Simon starts the conversation about his week, battling high seas and low yield. A worrying time for any fisherman he informs me. The most harrowing is when they almost lost a valuable member overboard on Friday, even with safety harnesses.

The Fishers choose to keep these moments from their families, protecting them from the harsh realities of the job. I feel closer to Simon now, compared to the casual small talk in groups with friends and chats via our slates.

I am shocked at how brutal his work is and the cruelty of the sea. Farming and working in our town pales in comparison.

Turning our conversation to my work, I share my disappointment at the few shifts assigned to me. I am desperately hoping for more, I am needing the points. I am so organised at home; I even have more time to practise my parkour around the community and find myself challenging my times daily to improve.

Simon looks at me intently, listening to my woes, and offers to rub my cold hands between his, while asking my permission.

I nod, giving permission; he shows such patience listening defiantly a skill a Fisher would need to possess. I look down at his Fisher hands, tanned, slightly calloused. Very short, clean fingernails.

"Sometimes we have to be patient," Simon says, smiling at my impatience.

"Maybe, but I'm getting very impatient, I'm so bored." The announcement for Sydney City Terminal rouses us from our private conversation.

We make our way off the train from the country platforms and head to the exit of the terminal, ready for the next step in our adventure.

We are intercepted by Law Enforcers at the turnstiles asking for our identities, which we produce quickly opening our slates.

They separate us and ask what our purpose for visiting the city is. I inform them, looking down at the ground staring at the Enforcers huge black boots, that I am registering for work and Simon is my friend. They nod and give me my slate back and indicate with their head that I am released.

Simon is searched from head to toe. He patiently submits, standing with his arms out, letting this humiliating process be carried out. He is excused and his slate is thrust back at him. He walks over to me frowning.

I ask him if he is okay. Simon nods, putting his finger on his lips as if to say not to talk, AI is listening. "I wonder why they didn't search me?" Simon shoots me a surprised look.

"You are underage, that is the *only* reason. I don't want them touching you. *Ever,*" he says, with an edge.

I am moved by his protectiveness. Swallowing hard, I acknowledge the fact that my age was the only reason I was not searched. Not for much longer.

We tap our slates passing through the turnstiles and head quickly to the Pitt Street exit of the terminal.

"Esther, why are we here so early? The office does not open for another hour."

"To spend more time with you Simon."

I bounce out of the Terminal exit onto the cold street, blasted by incredibly powerful wind tunnels, while catching my breath, it is so cold. Simon grins acknowledging my cheeky plan.

We find a cosy cafe open with the welcoming aroma of brewed coffee and baking, almost like home, and order freshly baked cheesy rolls and coffee to warm us. Simon kindly pays.

We gaze out the huge window into the city of glass and steel. It's a landscape completely foreign to us, yet strangely enticing in its orderly artistic architecture. It reflects the breathtaking pink and gold hues adorning the skies as a beautiful day begins again in Sydney City.

We chat lightly about the future for each of us, which is very similar, as our upbringing is almost identical. Yet we both secretly crave more than our predictable existence.

"Simon!" I reach across the table grabbing his hand with such ferocity I almost knock his hot coffee over. He quickly steadies it. I apologise immediately for touching him and withdraw my hand.

"It's *Okay* Esther, relax."

"Simon, is it wrong to want more? Trying to find real meaning in life, away from our families our community or town. I am terrified I will never discover what is out there." Simon leans back in his chair, his hands clasped behind his head, laughing at me.

"There is plenty of time for that, why so serious? I thought we were having fun today."

"You're right, the office will be open soon. Let's go!" I say, ready for fun.

Stepping into the freezing street, I brace myself again against the icy gusts, pulling my hoodie over my head. I consult my slate for directions.

"You don't need that when you have me," Simon informs me confidently. Simon pulls up his hoodie and drags me along by my free hand, not asking permission. Very bold. I am impressed how well he knows his way around.

We arrive at the Services office, entering its warm interior. I see a variety of citizens gathered in one place treated equally. A rare moment to observe. I love the glimpse of a possible future. The Services office is open seven days a week to cope with the workers' schedules, to and keep them compliant paying points.

I wait with other keen workers who want this process over as well. My number flashes, reaching the assigned counter, I have my details processed and place my hands on the scanner to have my identity confirmed by fingerprints and my cheek swabbed for DNA to match with my birth records. Nothing is private.

I inquire about the registration fee for a truck like my father has and am informed of a registration fee that is unattainable. How can my father afford it? I thank the attendant and seek out Simon who is relaxing on a seat observing everyone around him. I smile to myself; he is the only one not looking down at a slate.

Now officially a worker for the rest of my life I gaze down at my new identity number. I am no longer a person, just a number to the government now.

"What's up?" Simon asks, approaching me, seeing my frown.

"I thought being an adult would be more fun, and exciting. Well, I am almost an adult," trying to hide my worries.

"It is! You must wait," he says mysteriously.

"Really? You're just trying to sugar coat it."

"How about a quick tour of the city before we head back?" Simon suggests.

"Why not! how do you know so much about the city?" I am intrigued considering he fishes most days. I am grateful for Simon's offer to tag along.

"I have got some friends who study and live in the city; they let me crash there when I feel like a change from home. You remember them, Lizzy, Isaiah, and Mark."

I recall Lizzy being lots of fun and smart, Isaiah super smart and wild, and Mark smart, serious, and into music.

We spend the next hour touring the retail Precinct, business Precinct, and recreational Precincts, which are resplendent in the sunlight with the emerging blue skies reflected in the vast expanses of glass. It is so quiet.

Sleek, single, and multi-person transports are parked in the immaculate street, there are many different models and colours, unseen back home. I love seeing the single transports slip silently through the streets on their two wheels, gliding and weaving. If I could own a single transport, it would be shiny and black.

Simon and I admire the transports that are parked, discussing what we like about each one. Simon is drawn to a custom decorated transport in red and black with flames emblazoned down the sides – it's far too busy and showy. He seems to be incredibly knowledgeable about them.

We walk and talk about transports and the merits of each model, not aware of our surroundings. Simon suddenly grabs me by the hand pulling me, running in the opposite direction.

Drones appear overhead; they are so low, it is terrifying, and they are tracking all the citizens on the street. We stop as one stops at our eye level, scanning us, then moves on.

"Don't look back just keep moving, and don't say a word," Simon whispers with surprising authority.

I do not question his request until we stop at a busy shopping precinct to catch our breath. Thankfully, the drones are heading in the opposite direction on a mission to search for someone. I stop and look up at him expectantly for an answer.

"There are bad people in the city too, Esther; they can even be the law, so be careful," he whispers in my ear.

Simon has barely finished his warning when the Police and Medical Transport sirens are heard through the streets towards the direction of where we were minutes ago. I am oblivious to the ways of this world.

We walk on further until we approach the recreational precinct, a large open area where the sun filters through the imposing buildings. It feels so good to be warmed by the sun.

"Are you okay?" Simon pauses, pulling me into his arms, holding me tight.

I nod into his shoulder then step back and look around. I cannot believe they have Parkour parks this good. The early rising citizens are already climbing and hanging off girders at dizzying heights by one arm or jumping excitedly off angled structures, acknowledged by friends who sit around the perimeter sipping warm drinks and cheering each other on.

"Pretty awesome isn't it." Simon enthuses, looking around him.

I cannot speak, I'm too engrossed in the scene before me. Dropping my bag on a seat I yell to Simon.

"Catch me, I dare you." Did I really say that?

This city has an alluring carefree pull that I love, despite its dark side. Running to the nearest concrete ramp, I sprint up the ramp, propelling my weight forward to land on a low, narrow wall. I climb up, seeking another hold to grasp, Simon is not far behind me.

I leap without stopping, my momentum grasping the wide steel girder above me. My legs dangle free, and I walk my hands down the cold girder until I reach the end and drop three metres onto my feet, dusting off my hands to see Simon land seconds behind me. We stop breathless with exertion, grinning at each other, loving the challenge.

"Race you to the Terminal," I challenge, grabbing my satchel throwing its strap across my body and running effortlessly like I was born to do it.

"You have good memory to find your way back. How did you get so good at climbing?" Simon asks as we reach the Terminal entrance.

"I practise all the time, remember, I use Pk to get to work quickly, and besides, it's so much fun."

"Well remind me to be very careful challenging you. You have too many secret talents. I take it you enjoyed this morning?" he asks quietly looking at me.

"I cannot believe how different it is here; I have loved being here. Thank you for coming." I look around to break his intense gaze.

"I loved it too, more than usual today, with you." Simon's willingness to share his feelings surprises me a little. He is being very clear in his attraction to me. We enter the terminal, passing Law Enforcers patrolling the perimeter.

Simon moves quickly through the turnstiles while they are occupied. We wave our slates over the sensor and head to the country train platforms, fortunately stepping onto an awaiting train, heading home to a more predictable afternoon at the river.

I must have drifted off for a moment. As I awaken, I find myself resting on Simon's broad shoulder. "Oh, I'm so, so sorry." I sit up immediately, moving respectfully apart and checking my face that I have not drooled on him.

"No problem, so do we call today our first date?" he asks smiling.

"Remember, I have not decided about us yet," I say gently.

"Oh, I was hoping you might have decided about us because that would mean when we meet at the river it will be our second date…," he says hopefully.

"Hey, no rush." I give him a friendly punch, secretly enjoying his pursuit.

"No pressure." He smiles at me, looking a little too long and deep into my eyes. His gaze travels to my lips and back up to my eyes again. My face gives me away, turning pink.

"You like me. James was right." he says triumphantly.

This puzzles me. What do these guys talk about? Maybe I am too naive for my own good. Was I that obvious to my friends? Surely not. We sit in quiet companionship, each retreating to our own thoughts about this potential relationship.

A small monitor fixed in the corner of the carriage animates, moving side to side, scanning the occupants in the carriage, and within seconds, our slates flash with requests for our status with each other. I immediately open the request and type in *friend* and show Simon who does likewise.

Keeping our relationship secret will be harder than I thought. The slates have already picked up we are together now more than in the past. How long will it be until our friends or community realise?

Our station is announced. We rise feeling the deceleration of the bullet train as it approaches our station. Stepping out, we squint into the bright sunshine, a relief from the constant government surveillance.

We walk through the exit tapping our slates. We are in no rush to leave, standing outside the station and agree to meet at the river later. Simon stretches out his arms asking if it's, okay. I incline my head as he pulls me close.

I am impressed that he follows society's personal interaction laws. I feel safe. He is looking down at me with intensity in his big blue eyes, his curly blonde hair falling across one eye.

"I don't know how long I can keep my feelings a secret from everyone," he whispers with great emotion.

"Just a little longer, see you soon," I whisper. I avert my eyes from his gaze which, is making my heart race again.

I slowly move backwards away from him, releasing our intertwined fingers, reluctant to be on my way. I start to jog the five kilometres home, looking quickly over my shoulder. I see Simon still standing watching my retreating figure, smiling.

I will never understand guys, especially Simon. I keep wondering why he likes *me*. He could chase far prettier girls than me. Besides, I have not let him kiss me, but I really want him to. Kissing is kind of weird really. If you think about it…

CHAPTER 8

I visit the river early to rest, read, and reflect. Grabbing my backpack I sneak out of the house wanting to be alone.

Walking along the familiar track, I see Paul in the distance resting against a tree, his belongings next to him. He appears to be sleeping. As I approach, he stirs, making a shallow, gasping sound. I realise immediately he is not sleeping, he is struggling to breathe, is pale, sweaty, and dying. Calling his name desperately, terrified, I grab his face, yelling at him, "Look at me, Paul, open your eyes."

I yell repeatedly, pulling him quickly onto his back, ready to start CPR, his breathing is now quiet and slow. As I am leaning over listening to his breath, my hands are positioned to start breathing life back into him and start compressions. He opens his eyes, his face shines in that moment with sheer joy, and he smiles broadly looking into my eyes as he utters words that almost stop my own heart.

"See you in heaven, Esther." With that, he fades away. I hear his last breath float away into the bush.

Shocked, I sit back on my heels patting his warm hand, silent tears rolling down my cheeks, Paul was supposed to be around to help me, be my friend forever, not leave.

Where is this heaven? How do I get there if he is dead? I was taught at school, you live, you die, that is it. This world is all there is.

Picking up his swag, I place it over him respectfully, pausing. A thud of a heavy black book falling from his bedding snaps me out of my shock momentarily. I have rarely ever held a book, only for special history lessons. They are usually displayed behind glass.

Why would Paul have a book in his possession? We only read slates. We're only allowed a slate, this is illegal! Sitting next to Paul, still in shock, I flick through the front pages of this book feeling the texture of the thin paper pages between my finger and thumb. My heart races at the realisation that this could be a religious book. I am not sure; it has a t symbol on the front and a word I cannot pronounce *Bible*?

Turning the pages, I am shocked that my own name is listed in the contents and some of my friends too. Bewildered, I madly fly through the first pages trying to decipher what this book is about until I find the first chapter *Genesis* …… talking about '*In the beginning God created the heavens and the earth…*' I panic dropping the book, like a boiling pot burning my hands.

This book cannot be found, or I will be imprisoned. Digging through Paul's meagre belongings I search for a waterproof covering; I wrap the book quickly in a towel, throwing it into a hollow of a tree, terrified. I hear birds screeching and flying away as several drones approach slowly then hovers over Paul and me. They have finally found Paul and me in his presence.

My mouth is dry. I feel sweaty, with nausea rising and falling. Stumbling to my slate, I hold it high to get a signal, despite the drones watching me, and send an urgent message about Paul and my location to my parents, hoping a signal will get out.

I put my slate in my bag throwing it across my body and blindly start running. I leave everything behind, including Paul, crying, not seeing, because the tears are blurring my vision. I violently throw myself through the low scrubby bush, thrashing at the low branches with my arms, not following the bushfire trail, the branches grab my braid pulling it free from its tight weave scratching and tear at my clothes and face. I do not feel them or care. The drones are down low tracking me. I am terrified.

Paul's gone. *Forever.*

My mind swirls with words and moments from the past, creating an abstract picture that was right in front of me, yet the full picture remains unfocused. I am unsure of what it all means.

Am I am living in two worlds? One known and one unknown?

What is the truth?

What is so dangerous that they hunt Paul?

Somehow, I manage to blindly stumble onto the familiar bush trail, colliding with Simon and James. "Paul's dead by the tree near the river, Paul's book is in the tree," I gasp, collapsing to the ground.

I cannot speak coherently. Pointing behind me, my eyes are wild, I struggle to blink away the tears, and I thrash my scratched bleeding arms about, hysterically crying, and babbling. I place my hands over my face to shield myself against this world that I do not understand and the devastating loss of Paul, the predatory drones depart when I meet Simon and James on the trail.

Simon crouches beside me, gently pulling my hands away from my tear-soaked face. He carefully wipes the tears away with the corner of his t-shirt. Lifting my chin, my face meets his; he looks firmly into my eyes unwavering, calm and speaks in a low voice almost a whisper. A practised tone for all of us with our slates always listening.

"Is it Paul? Did Paul die? Do you know something? Did you open the book? Or both? Are you okay? Those drones were locked and tracking you. Trouble is coming." I nod, sobbing and rocking uncontrollably. "I don't understand, I'm scared, Simon."

Simon and James look at each other stricken. Then Simon whispers in my ear, "You would have found out soon, but not this way. I know you are confused and upset but you cannot tell anyone. Not even your parents.

"When everyone turns eighteen in our community they learn the truth, earlier if you are like James and me who are working.

"We are part of a religious group. We believe in our Creator, called God, and his ancient writings, written in books like what you found, it is a huge, amazing secret."

James nods agreeing shuffling his feet nervously in the dirt, unsure what to do.

"We will say that we discovered you upset about Paul, the rest we will discuss later when it is safe.

"We are at risk; the law will look for an explanation of what happened today. Stick to this story, it is true. I am sure they will be sending Enforcers and paramedics here soon."

Slowly, I regain my regular breathing back with Simon speaking softly and calmly. Nodding numbly, I understand the gravity of the situation. I literally have stumbled onto a huge dangerous secret.

Unable to move, I feel myself fall into Simon's arms. He scoops me up, and I immediately feel safe with darkness and heaviness overtaking me.

* * *

Awakening with panic, my heart races again remembering Paul dead by the tree, I then realise I am safe at home in bed covered by my beautiful quilt. I am supported by my community friends sitting quietly on my bed, and on the cold concrete floor, waiting for me to recover from the afternoon's events, mourning Paul's passing. My eyes open and they ask if I am okay. How did I handle being with Paul all alone? Telling me tearfully how much they loved him too. I cry again, this time for the deep ache in my heart of losing a precious friend. I am not alone this time in my grief.

Sarah wipes my tears. Ruby rubs soothing aloe vera on my scratches - our other friends just sit quietly. They are such a comfort even in their own grief. I see Luke looking in the door. I put my arms out, and he comes and sits on the bed, allowing me to hold him.

My friends eventually leave the house. Our parents sit with Luke and me in the lounge room, telling us that it was very upsetting to lose Paul, our friend, and it's okay to be sad. He lived a full life. They express their gratitude that I was there as he passed, which I thought terrifying, but they assure me no, it was good, important to comfort Paul in his last moments, and they are proud of my strength.

They are thankful for Simon and James, who found me and coordinated getting me home and the collection of Paul's body as well as explaining to the law what happened. That would have taken great courage.

"Esther, Simon carried you from the bush to our house, and James stayed with Paul until the men came, honouring him. They are exceptional young men. It was fortunate that all your friends had planned to meet up today," my mother says gratefully.

We retreat to our rooms to reflect on our loss. I lie on my bed holding a few handwritten notes from Paul retrieved from my keepsake box. They help me feel a little better and I fall asleep.

* * *

Several days later Paul's memorial is held in the memorial room at the Town hall. It is expected that every citizen who passes has their life honoured by a series of short predictable talks from loved ones, they are the words provided by the government. You just insert the name, and the body is removed for cremation.

These memorials are sad and unremarkable for a wonderful life lived only to end as another governmental procedure.

Paul's passing is the same, yet the Farmers and Fishers gather for a simple meal at our home to soften the blow and somehow make the passing more meaningful, by sharing wonderful stories and memories. We also sing songs and dance, knowing he would have enjoyed every moment well into the night.

I observe my parents consoling each other in the garden with Luke, who is all cried out. Turning towards the house I am comforted by Simon's strong embrace, resting my head on his chest, no communication needed. He loved Paul too.

Paul's life was remarkable and he was loved as much as he loved. He left us richer and wiser for knowing him, that is his legacy.

* * *

Paul was a storyteller, using his dark weathered hands to transport us into his world, illustrating them perfectly with words that painted pictures in colour about fish, storms, and fishermen, of course.

When we were at school, Paul took us to explore caves, showing us hidden artefacts of his ancient ancestors. Ash, and fish bones were evidence of sustainable living from the ocean.

There were remnants of hand-woven fishing traps. Paul reminded the Fisher kids that they are part of an ancient tradition, an important one, as they fish and protect the sea life like his ancestors, keeping it for future generations.

When Paul took us to these special places, we followed his instructions, to 'stay here, go there, boys go, girls stay.' We never questioned him. We sensed on these teaching trips the significance and reverence he had for these places that held his ancestors' stories.

My favourite place was the rock paintings in caves hard to access, protected from the weather and tides below controlling who could reach them. We would sit perfectly still, waiting on the cool, smooth rock floor. Paul would tell us the stories so beautifully illustrated on these walls, hoping we could carry on the tradition almost lost, as he had no children or family left. His legacy was to keep the rich culture alive by teaching us.

Paul also cared for us during the school holidays. He would take us to the outer skirts of town where there were many disused buildings - a stark contrast to the sleek flashy structures in the town centre. He would tell us what was previously there, such a rich history. His memory was astounding. He often stopped in front of some broken buildings, head bowed, eyes closed, reanimating moments later, informing us this was a special place once, but the law stopped citizens using it.

Sarah and I would find small pieces of coloured glass at Paul's special places. Paul told us that they were from broken windows. I would add the shards to my collection at home. When the sun shone through the jar, it would create a beautiful rainbow.

Paul always shared words that soothed, sprinkled with wisdom, occasionally correction, and kindly putting our problems into perspective.

He was a safe person to share and test our worries, to see if they were well-founded or blown out of proportion, generally the latter. As we grew into adulthood, Paul could easily transition his chats to fishing and farming. The boys often asked him cheekily if he had ever been out on a trawler.

He replied many times, much to their amusement, retelling stories of deep-sea fishing with Simon and Jonah's families chucking up over the side when the sea got rough. How he was only trusted to manage the bait, the job assigned for the most inexperienced fishermen. Paul told us he was happy to stay on dry land these days.

Ruby and Paul had a unique relationship. She adored him like a grandparent, and he loved her happy, kind disposition and the fact that living as a Town Elite she remained unchanged. On occasions, Ruby's Dad, Peter, would invite Paul for a meal in their home, which intrigued me, as I wondered what they would talk about. I realised Paul was very knowledgeable about local history, which would fascinate Ruby's Dad, who is a town and city historian.

There were so many memories, but I know one thing for sure: I am ready for a remarkable life wherever that takes me, like Paul.

CHAPTER 9

The days following Paul's passing are difficult to recall but today I rise in the cool darkness, feeling a greater sense of direction and peace. I choose to take control of my ordinary life and turn it into something unique, unpredictable, and most importantly, exciting.

The challenge is to earn enough points to achieve it.

Dressing in old yard clothes, I emerge into our silent garden with its shrinking shadows, startling some wallabies who are cheeky enough to venture into the garden at dawn, through a small gap in the fence. They hop away quickly, leaving bushes stripped of their leaves. Who could be upset at such beautiful creatures? I will mend the fence later.

After several hours, I complete my daily tasks, weeding and maintaining the gardens, and return to the house, showering and dressing for a day's work.

I have not been allocated any shifts for several weeks, which is difficult to survive on. My plan is to ask if there are any extra shifts available every day. It is daunting, but I really have nothing to lose except my remaining single thread of self-respect. I figure there must be someone away unexpectedly every day.

Walking with my mother to work, I explain my plan. She is unsure about it, seeing a potentially good long-term job disappear that she has secured, yet she admires my determination.

We farewell each other at security. I observe the patients calling out to my mother by name, vying for her attention. She patiently greets each of them by name with a smile. They must be regulars. She is beloved by the patients, not a characteristic I see in the Town employees. I wonder if I could ever possess even half her patience and kindness.

Finding myself at the front desk, I take a deep, wobbly breath and inquire if there are any shifts available today. The staff member is surprised, then frowns, asking me to take a seat in the waiting area, promising to check with HR and let me know.

Making myself comfortable, I browse my slate's messages and study. In the background, I hear soft, calming music interjected with the daily law updates stated in neutral modulated tones. I feel like I am waiting in an airport transit lounge as I see in the movies. Not that I have ever been to one or will ever experience flying, the privilege is only bestowed on law officials and high-ranking business executives who are permitted to leave Australia and only travel to New Zealand, the rest of the world is off limits.

An elderly lady next to me asks where the sanitation room is. I happily assist her with directions.

I return to my slate, reading my friends' updates, seeing more pictures of Simon's day that make me smile, and within minutes, another patient needs a specialist's office, so I direct them. My morning flies by.

I am struck that there are few Farmer or Fisher citizen patients, almost none. We are entitled to basic care like everyone else. It is just the Town citizens dominating the hospital for care.

It is not difficult to come to this conclusion as they dress so distinctively, especially the Elite Town citizens, who must enter through the front doors of the hospital before being ushered to private physicians. The perception is one hospital for everyone; everyone is equal.

Accepting there are no extra shifts, I jog home via the river to think about my next crazy scheme for tomorrow.

The river is now a bittersweet place, soothing me as I sit quietly on the riverbank, eating my packed lunch and splashing my feet in the cool water. My mind drifts like the gum leaves floating on the gentle breeze, landing on the water, floating and swirling. I am them.

I remember the book that was hastily buried. Drying my feet on paperbark, I pull on my socks and joggers, walking across the clearing to the hollow in the old Redgum, instinctively checking for snakes with a stick. Relieved, I discover it is still there. Pulling the book free, I settle my back against the Redgum's broad base in case I am caught unawares.

The first chapter reads 'In the beginning...' After that, I was hooked; I had never read anything like it, speaking with authority. I read for hours, feeling a little sleepy. My head jerks when I hear footsteps approaching. I fling the book into the hiding place; Simon appears through the scrub, surprised to see me. Zeb, his beloved rusty coloured kelpie, peeks around Simon's legs then bounds over, giving me a lick, snuggling into my side, ready for attention.

"He wanted to come with me but did not realise how far it was." Promptly Zeb lays down panting. Simon pulls from his satchel a portable water bowl for the grateful Zeb, which is sweet.

"I hang out here sometimes, you know," he mumbles shyly.

"Yeh, I know, I miss him too," I whisper.

"How are you handling everything?" Simon sits down in front of me cross legged looking concerned, reaching for my hands and entwining his fingers with mine.

"Up until today, I felt numb, but now I feel good. Happy again. Can you help me understand the book and why is my name in it?"

"Ah, so many questions. We need to start at the beginning, and a few other places, then look at Esther, much, much later. Can we meet up with James soon to explain everything better?"

"Sounds good," I say, feeling glad.

"How about a swim?" Simon asks, standing, pulling me to my feet.

"Sure, but I haven't got anything to wear, Simon?"

"Well… Adam and Eve felt no shame," he says slowly with a mischievous smile.

"Stop it! I just read about them, I will swim in my clothes." I feel my cheeks burn, declaring my choice to be modest, removing only my socks and shoes. Simon is better prepared, arriving in board shorts and a t-shirt. Zeb jumps in after us to cool off and then retreats to the bank to sleep.

We spend a relaxing afternoon racing each other across the river, floating on our backs, talking about everything that happened in our week, remembering Paul, and reminiscing about our time with him.

Talking to Simon becomes easier as the afternoon progresses. I still feel shy talking to him alone, even though we have known each other forever. When I talk, he looks intently at me, listening so sweetly and respectfully. He seems more at ease with this situation than I do, maybe having dated a few girls before helps.

We eventually climb up the steep riverbank to dry off in the sun; fortunately, our clothes are almost water repellent. Most clothing thread is made from one hundred percent recycled products and are designed to need very little water to clean them, just steam sanitation reducing resource consumption. The wealthy wear cotton, linen, and wool clothing that requires dry cleaning.

Remembering the book, I carefully wrap it up again, placing it in its hiding place, vowing to read Esther next, even though Simon said to wait.

Sadly, it is time to go and prepare dinner for my family. We walk slowly down the familiar bushfire trail, Simon confidently reaches for my hand not asking for permission and holds it as if we have been together forever, I welcome it. Zeb happily trotting between us.

Simon pauses on the track and pulls me close, holding both my hands, gently looking in my eyes with great intensity. I look back, my gaze unwavering up into those calm blue eyes. Simon's gaze lasts for seconds but feels much longer. We look at each other and smile.

I am smiling with happiness, Simon is smiling with relief that I did not reject him, but as if he really wanted to kiss me, however unsure if it was okay. I am grateful that he is taking his time to get to know me first.

I am so glad I waited to see if Simon was the right guy for me, and most importantly, to see if he is authentic and genuinely cares about me.

"Well, I guess you will have to come home with me, it is almost dinner time," I say as we emerge from the bush fire trail close to home. I lead him down our driveway by the hand. Simon stops walking, looking puzzled.

"Does this mean you have decided to put up with me, go out with me and you don't care who knows about it?" he asks hopefully.

"I don't care who knows, I'm willing to give us a chance if you are," I declare.

"I don't mind at all," Simon shouts, punching the air. "Yes!"

He picks me up briefly, spins me around in his arms and gently places me back on the ground. His arms linger around my waist for a moment. He releases me as if suddenly remembering his manners, stepping back a little.

As we enter the house, we leave Zeb to explore the yard. My mother and father are chatting over tea at the table. They stop talking mid-sentence, regain composure quickly, and greet Simon and me.

"Simon's joining us for dinner tonight, and Zeb too," is all I offer.

"Hello, Mark and Ruth, nice to see you again, can I help with dinner, Esther?" Simon says, trying to sound casual as he and I hang our satchels over the dining room chairs.

My parents exchange a secret glance of amusement.

"Sure, I'll just change Simon. I return quickly.

"I am a total wreck, I'm suddenly terrified of your parents! Look what I'm wearing, I'm a mess!" Simon exhales loudly, whispering in my ear, after we escape to the kitchen.

I laugh, looking at him in his faded board shorts, t-shirt and scruffy joggers, thinking this is going to be an interesting night. I'm touched that he wants to impress them.

We work well together. In thirty minutes we have produced a great meal of veggie lasagne and a big salad. I show Simon the finer points on preparing vegetables as he mainly lives on fish and his mother does most of the food prep.

I call Luke for dinner. He emerges from his room, to be greeted by Simon helping to set the table. Luke looks at Simon then me, with a smirk on his face.

"Are you two going out?" he asks point blank.

"Yep!" I shoot back, as it is all I can manage in front of my family.

"Awesome," he responds, diving into the salad for a carrot stick and flicks one high in the air for Zeb to catch.

"Well, that is one way to tell your parents, Esther." Simon thankfully saves this embarrassing scene, smiling at my parents seated at the table.

"Sorry, this was not how we planned to tell you. Esther just agreed to go out with me about forty-five minutes ago," Simon says very seriously.

"It's fine. We could not be happier for you both. We certainly did not see this coming," my father responds.

"I did," Luke announces proudly, taking a loud, crunchy bite of his carrot stick.

Everyone stares at him; Luke is so casual about it. He leans back in his chair smugly.

"I've seen how Esther and Simon stare at each other all the time, and how Simon stares at Esther when she is not looking, poor guy. Oh, sorry dude," he says to Simon.

"It's fine Luke," Simon replies embarrassed.

We all laugh, the tension in the air finally evaporates. Zeb sits next to Luke knowing a steady stream of food is coming his way.

They have a great relationship. Luke's not allowed to have a dog, and Zeb is happy to step in and be a substitute pet with all the treats and pampering.

We chat over dinner with my family, sharing our city trip highlights with them. I see my father is grateful Simon was with me.

I collect everyone's slates and put them in the sanitiser and close the heavy steel door. I return to tell my father about the kind warning about the truck registration from Ruby's Dad.

My father looks grave; we all know how valuable the truck is to our community. I offer to help him as I am now working. He nods and is appreciative of the offer.

"We will manage Esther; Peter is a good guy for an Elite. If he is warning me; trouble is not far away." He looks briefly at Simon who nods.

"It will be okay Mark, I know our community will help. I will talk to my father and the men tomorrow at work."

After dinner, Simon is invited by my father to discuss business in the garden while the rest of us clean up after dinner. Zeb hangs around the kitchen cleaning the floor for us and is rewarded with a bowl of left over veggies.

Trying to overhear the conversation, I hang around the veranda door hoping Dad is being kind to Simon, not grilling him like a Tuna steak. I have heard rumours from other Farmer girls about interviews by fathers in the Farmer and Fisher community.

My mother calls me from the kitchen. I slowly walk to the kitchen.

"Esther, hurry up, will you? You can trust your father; Simon is good for you. Does he make you happy Esther?" Mum looks earnestly into my eyes.

"He does, we have been spending lots of time together, talking and messaging to see if it will work. We seem to have the same interests and have a good friendship. I would not allow it to be known about us until, I was sure," I assure her.

"A very wise decision," Mum says proudly, giving me a side hug.

I rush out of the house once the cleaning up is complete. Simon walks towards me.

"I must go, off to work tomorrow, remember. Early."

"When will I see you again? I try not to sound needy.

"I will send you a message of course. Walk me to the gate?" We walk very slowly to the gate, lingering and staring at each other silently, we say goodbye, Simon pauses. "Okay?" I nod, he leans over and kisses me on the cheek, very gently. I am loving his courtship.

I watch him jog towards home, with Zeb by his side, it's easily seven kilometres. Having no transport keeps us all very healthy.

Bounding down the driveway, I release my hair from its restraint, letting it fly wildly in the breeze, singing loudly, not caring who hears me, after all, I am the luckiest girl in the community.

My father looks up from his vegetables, smiling. He calls me to him discussing the truck, and he reassures me that our friends will help. He is more concerned about the reason behind it, maybe some new law, which may be enforced soon.

"I'm pleased you and Simon found each other, my wish was always that you would meet someone who respects you and adores you as much as I do." He returns to his task looking happy despite the difficulties.

Walking to my room I message Sarah and Ruby the news about Simon and I then I unlock my mind's vault and carefully place my happy memories in there.

CHAPTER 10

My daily routine now consists of politely asking at the reception desk for available shifts, taking my usual seat at the medical precinct. I have made a home in a corner seat. Farmer and Fisher staff greet me by name, sharing in my disappointment.

An attractive young executive citizen approaches me dressed in a vintage white shirt with buttons, and a tight-fitting grey suit. His dark hair is very short and Elite styled, and on his left wrist is an enormous antique stainless-steel watch. He stops in front of me, looking just past me.

"Williams, Esther, I'm CEO Ward, please follow me," he says quietly. The Town and Elite do not look citizens in the eye; it is seen as disrespectful.

Damm it, I thought he was just another citizen needing directions. Not the *CEO.*

Crap! He even knows my name!

I mournfully follow, feeling nauseous. My eyes are fixed on the smooth, flawless, grey carpeting of his sophisticated office, all glass with massive slates covering two walls, filled with images and documents. Two chairs, no desk.

"Williams, *Esther*," he greets me warmly, shutting off the wall slates. He continues to look subtly near my eyes, not to appear dismissive, and inclines his head, which is respectful.

"Have a seat." He points to a designer chair, and I pretend to concentrate on an imaginary piece of lint on the carpet. If only there was.

CEO Ward smoothly continues his conversation, oblivious to my appalling childlike manners. He sits upright on the opposite chair observing me silently, with slate in hand.

"Esther, you have been with us a short time, with excellent progress and productivity. You have not been scheduled any regular shifts for weeks, yet you continue to arrive and annoy senior staffer Nichols daily in reception. *That is brave*. Why?" His tone neutral.

"I need the points," I whisper humiliated.

"Sorry, what was that?" He leans towards me.

"I need the points," I reply.

He sits back, looking at me with his dark, serious eyes for a long excruciating amount of time, with no expression.

"Thank you for your honesty. I have personally observed your work. You are honest and never steal. I need citizens like you in this precinct, Esther," he says quietly. I look up, shocked. He is surprised by my look and unexpectantly smiles; he has shown a human side to his very reserved demeanour.

"You thought I was going to fire you? Sorry Esther, I should have been direct, you Farm.... think everyone is against you. I have an unusual request. I need to recruit someone very trustworthy and undetectable, like yourself." His eyes briefly meet mine then he looks away.

My attention shifts quickly from self-preservation to curiosity.

"What is it?" I ask like an adult.

"It is a covert job, minimal danger, not difficult but you must agree to the terms before full disclosure." He looks grave passing me his slate with terms, conditions, and salary. The job description is missing.

It is the most disastrous job offer ever; my father would leave. Full disclosure before signing and seek counsel is his mantra. I am curious, knowing desperation is not a valid reason to skip his advice, but the salary is incredibly generous, it steals my breath and any remaining common sense away.

"Is that figure real?" I whisper. It is as much or more than my father earns.

CEO Ward inclines his head.

"Do I have to clean sanitation pipes, donate a kidney?"

"Nothing like that," he says smoothly, dismissing my rudeness. "So what do you think?"

"I would be an idiot not to sign." I sign immediately.

He inclines his head taking my slate, placing it with his on the chair and indicates to follow him. He waves his right hand over a sensor which slides open a glass door revealing an internal office.

"So, the job is … delivering packages between here and the City Medical Precinct and any other medical precincts I direct you to. You will be on call all the time and keep working in your regular role as well," the CEO informs me.

"That's it! How soon can I start?" I ask incredulously. I laugh, then cry tears of happiness. I am excited.

"Right away, if you want, I have a delivery for the City…" He pauses, looking at me. "You will need to change your look, dressing as a university student would be helpful. I am responsible for your induction. No one else. Your regular work will be here and, in the city, to keep up the validity of your presence."

The CEO deftly places his right hand on a security panel, revealing packages wrapped with encoded labels. "We share resources with the city and other medical precincts; due to the value we must hire our own couriers rather than outsourcing the work," he informs me.

He scans then places several packages in one of the unremarkable satchels stored in the room, informing me I will be contacted and have all my transport costs covered by the Medical Precinct. He gives me verbal instructions of the procedure.

"You will use the train, metro and bus systems until you are eighteen then you will ride on our single transports after your eighteenth birthday."

"I can't ride!"

"Well, we will have to arrange lessons for you. Would you prefer the city to be discrete?" he asks.

I nod, and he understands my situation.

"Okay, do you know where the City Medical Precinct is?" I nod.

"Enter the back entrance using your work ID on your slate as if you are on a shift. Do this for your ordinary shifts too, use the application I will upload to your slate to open the security boxes, which looks like an ordinary locker. It is marked with this number. The application is set up securely to all the secret lockers in the precincts; you hover your slate over it to unlock. It is very secure. Do not be detected. Place the satchel in there as if you are going to work. You will learn quickly how to remain undetected.

"Communicate with me only. I will contact you when deliveries or pickups are required on your personal or assigned work slates, otherwise continue to work your regular shifts that I will guarantee. Never come to my office unless instructed to. If I need a delivery during a shift, you will get a notification to clean the locker room. Please leave looking like you have been told off by me and deliver your first packages. I am relying on you Williams, and so are the Medical Precincts and their patients, stay safe."

I slink out looking miserable with the satchel across my body, to the satisfaction of the staff who despise me. I will not have the pleasure of telling them about my fabulous new job. I run to the station across the road, hover my slate, and leap onto the first available bullet train heading to the city, happy.

I decide to pay a modest percentage of my regular wage towards my father's truck registration. For a moment, I am saddened by the prospect that I cannot share my success with anyone.

Watching the blur of the city appear out the window, I step off at Sydney City Terminal. I easily blend in with the morning crowds in my work scrubs and braided hair, holding my satchel close to my body on the busy streets. Glancing up at the tall buildings, I walk with confidence to the huge City Medical Precinct.

The back entrance is clearly marked and there is no sign of any staff. My slate easily activates the automatic door as I stride in. My eyes adjust to the light, and I see the locker door I seek marked as described.

Hovering my slate over the panel, the door opens easily, I place the satchel inside, shut the door, and hear it automatically lock again. I head out the exit just as a group of staff enter on shift change talking loudly. They nod as I pass; I look like them in my scrubs.

I tap *delivery complete* on the app, notifying the CEO. He responds that he has confirmation from CEO Copeland that the package has arrived. That was fast!

Clear of the building, I breathe easily. I savour my surrounds, stopping to buy an indulgent cup of hot chocolate on my way to the retail precinct because I can now afford it. I shop for a few casual university student styled outfits for work as the CEO requested.

Sitting on the country platform at the Sydney City Terminal, I stare at the tracks, realising for the first time in my life I never have to be hungry again and hot chocolates are going to be a regular part of my life. I feel myself sigh with satisfaction; life is good. Even better when I learn to ride a single transport. I quickly message Simon to come to my house for dinner, giving no indication of why except that it is good news.

Whoosh, cool air awakens me from my daydreams; the train has arrived and I scoop up my shopping bag. The train swiftly delivers me home.

I was not instructed to return to work today, so I take the opportunity to grab my satchel from the work locker and enjoy the walk home.

Passing through the busy retail precinct, I stop at the florist's shop purchasing a simple arrangement for my mother. I exchange my points with the florist and notice Ruby's mother, Krystal, who looks surprised to see me. I incline my head to acknowledge her as I leave, knowing she does not like me.

Ruby and Sarah are invited for dinner to share my good news, well, some of it anyway. I buy chicken at the butcher shop, a rare experience, then head home.

Preparing a feast with the best produce and skills I can muster for family and friends is fun.

I shower, changing into a pale green dress.

My family arrives home from a long day, immediately suspicious of the aroma of baking and the overdressed family member.

Mum, very practised at hiding her thoughts, kisses me on the cheek on her way through to change. She reappears quickly waiting for an explanation. "What is going on? I was not told we were having company. Is there something that I need to be informed about?" Dad is not subtle.

All I can do to allay his fears, is smile, assuring him that there is nothing to be concerned about. He must wait until dinner time.

Luke sits patiently at the table, waiting for a feast to be served to him. I admire his cool exterior. Simon arrives barely off the trawler and showered. I suspect he hosed himself at the wharf and got changed. Sarah and Ruby arrive in a flutter. "Is everything okay Esther?" they ask.

Everyone is invited to take a seat as I place dishes of steaming vegetables, grilled chicken, and homemade rolls on the table. I present my mother with the floral arrangement and take a seat beside Simon who has not taken his eyes off me. I calmly butter a roll addressing my family.

"I have good news, I have been offered permanent shifts at our Medical Precinct and the City Precinct too, and any additional shifts as I will be on call."

Everyone erupts into cheers of relief. My mother thanks me for the gift of flowers. My father appears to be breathing evenly again; I often forget about the difficulties of our life and all its rules.

Simon just smiles, continuing to stare at me with admiration, a little weird but nice. "Esther, this is amazing news. How is this even possible? Permanent regular shifts!" Simon asks.

I thank Mum that she managed to get me started at the Medical Precinct and acknowledge I was not grateful at the time.

"I was told that I had a good work record and they could offer me permanent shifts. Of course, I said yes. Maybe it is because I have been hanging around the reception area asking for work and being a major pain to HR."

I encourage everyone to fill their plates with my cooking.

Sarah, through a large mouthful, declares this is the best meal I have made yet. What a loyal friend.

"Mark, fish guts for your fertiliser from Dad," Simon says, throwing a wrapped package to my father.

"I wondered what the smell was, it's you!" Luke says. Simon immediately chases him into the lounge room, wrestling him to the ground. The wrestle continues as Luke fights for supremacy - foolish when Simon comes from a family of boys.

Ruby is shocked then quickly regains her composure as wrestling on the ground is not the usual behaviour of the Elite.

"Kill him," Sarah encourages Luke, grinning.

My father excuses himself asking Simon to bring his strength with him to help pack for market. They each take a cookie on their way out. Simon gives me a long look before he disappears.

"Oh, Esther, Simon is under your spell, don't you agree, Ruby?" Sarah nudges my shoulder, Ruby nods in agreement.

Ruby for an Elite born has shown a great understanding of the job offer and is very happy to be part of the celebration.

"Will you help me find a hair stylist?"

"Absolutely!" Ruby replies, shocked.

"Can I come too?" Sarah begs.

"Of course, I am relying on you both to tell me what looks okay and we can share clothes too!"

"Don't let this go to your head, Esther." My mother frowns.

"I won't Mum; I just want to have some fun."

Ruby and Sarah leave, promising to set up a day to go to the stylist and shop.

Simon has finished helping my father. He asks if I am free tomorrow afternoon, then I check my work schedule.

"I'm free so far, what's the plan?" I ask Simon.

"I thought we could have a picnic maybe swim at the inlet near the wharves?"

"I'm in, how about we both bring something to share from home?" I farewell Simon, looking forward to a day of leisure.

CHAPTER 11

Rushing through my chores I check my slate for messages - no shifts, or deliveries today. I am free and pack a selection of food from the cooler.

Carrying my vintage picnic basket and backpack to the bus stop I think about the afternoon ahead, it's a wonderful change from the river.

The bus transports me quickly to the wharf on the other side of town. I step off at the co-op and pull on my wide-brimmed hat, holding it firmly as it flutters in the breeze.

Simon is waiting with James, what is he doing here? They both approach and offer to carry my bags, which is sweet.

"Remember how I said that James and I would meet up with you at some stage. Today's the day," Simon quickly says seeing my frowny face. James nods.

I adjust my mindset and embrace the opportunity to finally get some answers about the book. We walk to the inlet, and I see the guys have set up a blanket in the shade and other picnic items, including Zeb, who has been guarding the food. He bounds up smiling waiting for his usual greeting with me. I scratch his rusty, velvety ears looking into those warm doggy eyes.

"What do you recon? Swim first then eat and chat?"

I shed my outer clothing, revealing a modest swimsuit with a rash shirt over the top. The guys remove their T-shirts and quickly replace them with rash shirts too. Simon and James run into the water with Zeb who is having a great time swimming out deep to Simon in the calm water of the inlet. I take my time looking around for sharks and easing into the cold water.

We cool off in the protected inlet; nobody is around as it's a weekday. I eventually drag my tired self out and sit on a towel removing my rash shirt and pulling my dry clothes over my swim wear and I lay out the food. James has contributed a huge fruit salad to graze on. I wait until we are all together.

The guys dress quickly and Simon puts his hands out for our slates. We know this means there will be forbidden chatter.

"Put your slates over here to keep them safe from the water and sand." He puts his finger to his lips. We dutifully put them in a heavy esky lined with metal. He closes it up.

"We do not know who is listening. This blocks any signal," Simon reminds us. "Let's say grace first." Simon looks at James who nods. This is new to me.

"Heavenly Father, thank you for the food you have so generously provided and for the hands that have prepared it. May it bless our bodies. Help us to be faithful teaches of your ancient word today." James echoes Simon's words.

Simon explains that we can speak to God anytime and what they just did was called prayer, talking to God, and giving thanks and asking for help.

"This God person, can he hear you at the beach?" I ask looking around, embarrassed.

"Yes," Simon replies, "we can pray quietly in our heads or aloud. God is the Holy Spirit known but unseen, like the wind. As we show you what we have learnt hopefully it starts to make sense. It will be a lot to understand. Tell James and me if you are confused or lost." It feels like I have discovered a new world.

After lunch and feeding Zeb our scraps, we pack our bags and I wait for direction from Simon and James. We instinctively pause as a small Law Enforcers drone cruises along the coastline above our heads.

"We should be safe for a while now they have passed. Esther, please go and collect as many shells, small pieces of wood and sea glass as you can. Simon and I will get things set up." James says, as he sees my grumpy face.

"Are you five? Stop acting like a spoilt brat! Trust us, it will all make sense."

Simon looks hard at James, as if to imply that is harsh and not to talk to my girl that way. James apologises immediately.

I am surprised, James is usually so quiet and sweet. I acknowledge I deserved that scolding and get up and obediently collect as many as I can. I see them with a stick drawing a very long line, along the wet sand parallel to the water.

This is weird, I sit on my towel waiting for my next instruction.

They proceed to take turns telling me about the book I found, they call it the Bible, God's revelation of Himself to us through the ancient words.

I am directed to look at the end of the timeline they call it, which has an arrow pointing left. Simon says it represents the time before God created the world, but He already existed.

"Esther, pick up a handful of items and we will take you along this timeline. We cannot write anything down on paper or a slate, or we will be locked up, so sand is perfect," Simon instructs.

They proceed to instruct me to place shells and glass on the extra lines they have made incrementally marked down the timeline. They explain our Creator's words, books of the Bible and significant events, starting at the beginning, which I have read already so it's sort of familiar.

I am instructed place a shell here on this part of the line, on the sideline. James tells me about Genesis, which I'm told is the first book of the Bible. Along the long line they tell me about each part of God's timeline of events and James tells me the names of the books of the Bible at the appropriate places on the timeline. I can start to understand the books of the whole Bible I saw listed in the front, coming to life. I find the significant moments marked with items better than words, which helps me.

"What's this?" I am intrigued.

We reach the centre where a huge line intersects the original horizonal line.

"This is where the Old Testament ends," Simon points on the left of it, "and the New Testament starts."

"Oh," is all I can say.

We work through the New Testament times. They send me back to my marked areas in the Old Testament side and say to pick up the shell there and bring it and place it here, in the New Testament side.

"Why?" I am so confused.

"Because," Simon says, holding my hand, smiling, "these are some of the many places in the Bible written where God's promises back there," he points to the left in the Old Testament section, "are fulfilled here in this side." Simon indicates to the right side.

They briefly explain about this man Jesus who was God's Son who came to be with us, live amongst us as a human and was born as a baby, which I find amazing. Especially when it was known back in the Old Testament times he was coming.

James and Simon race through his life's timeline and then we continue to the end of the line with an arrow pointing to the right.

"What does that mean?" James tells me this is the time we wait for Jesus' return.

"Oh, it's not very specific, no date? You said Jesus died well over 2000 years ago."

"That is the challenge we have. The lessons Jesus taught and with God's word helps us to prepare for his return and so we can be confident we will be ready to be with him for eternity when we die." Simon says very seriously.

"Like Paul said to me about seeing him in heaven, he was meaning I could be with him when I die forever. What do I have to do to be ready?" I look at Simon.

Simon holds my hand and looks into my eyes smiling.

"It's quite simple really, we'll help you learn and then you can make your own decision."

We scatter the shells and encourage the rising tide to wash away our marks in the sand, hiding the knowledge of these ancient words. We sit in the shade quietly thinking about what we have been discussing, enjoying the soothing sound of the tide coming in.

"So, everything they told us in science at school is so different to this; they told us about how some big explosion started life, like it was a huge accident," I say to them both.

"Yes," they say.

"I'm confused. I do not get it. What is so scary about a group of people believing all of this?" I stretch out my arms indicating the fading marks we had on the sand.

James says his understanding is because we choose to live by these ancient writings that are very powerful, influencing how people live and treat each other. When people understand them, it is life changing and that our world is very ignorant about what they do not understand. If they do, they quite often chose not to follow.

Apparently, many generations ago, our laws were based on the ancient writings. People who followed these words thousands of years ago were known as Christians in the community and for their noticeable kindness, mercy and caring for the poor and sick, as well as many citizens of our own community generations ago.

"So, who decides what's right and wrong in our country if people don't follow the ancient writings?" I am trying to digest this information.

"The government, and it seems to be whatever they want it to be or change it to suit what they want to do and make it the law," Simon says grimly.

"That's scary! Nothing is going very well in our Town and at the markets with the hungry, homeless, and sick."

I realise all these laws that keep changing so quickly are made by people who serve themselves. Well, it seems that way.

"How come you know so much?" I ask, looking at them both.

"Our families teach us; we learn at meetings, and I learn on the boat when it's only a Fisher crew, they share their knowledge and God's writings," Simon replies slowly. He looks at James with a small smile who grins too.

"What! you're kidding, how? All I hear is farming and fishing stuff in the background while the kids play." I cannot believe it!

"If we say directly what we are talking about our whole communities would be locked up, so we kind of use farming and fishing terms like the guy Jesus did, well the older members of our group do. Also, we do not have anything on slates and only a few booklets of the ancient writings we call God's word to share around, so it's hard to learn on your own, that's why we remember so much, we must," James says very quietly.

"So, do you both believe all of this? How do you really know this is real, that God and Jesus are real?"

Simon says, his face lighting up, "Yes, I do, there have been many times where God has spoken to me or shown himself to me, I want to learn more about what Jesus taught on how to live as a Christian.

"The minute I heard that he spoke to fishermen and hung out with them, like my Dad and me I was interested. They dropped everything to follow him when he asked them to, which was amazing.

"I was determined to find out about how a thirty-year-old guy who could change the hearts of fishermen. They are tough and have strong opinions on everything and fishing is their life. Like all the blokes I know and work with.

"I have been learning what it means to really follow Jesus, and it is not easy sometimes. I have been shown what the steps to be saved are, living with God forever. I have accepted Jesus as my Saviour. I just need to commit and follow through by changing how I live.

"We usually have a special day when someone commits their life to following Jesus in front of a small group. It keeps us more accountable if the group witnesses your commitment and they encourage you.

"We used to wait for Paul to come to town, who would be a part of the commitment, as it was so important, but he won't be here for us." Simon looks sad realising Paul will not be here for his special day.

"What about you?" I turn to James.

"I have learnt a lot, but I need to learn what it means to me personally and how I need to change my life. I'm not ready to commit in front of the group yet. I know I believe Jesus came to save me though, and he speaks to me. I just don't think I am good enough for Jesus."

James is uncertain in his answer. He says this with his head down looking miserable. "Mate, you forget Jesus dying for us makes us right with God," Simon says patting him on the shoulder speaking so confidently.

"I know, but it all seems too simple to me." James' struggle is real.

I observe this conversation, marvelling at these new revelations about our world and our existence, and most importantly, we have a Creator. I realise I have so much to understand but I am at peace finally understanding we were created by God on purpose not a cosmic accident and even a mistake.

I have never heard people talk on such a deep personal level before. Especially people my own age.

Simon speaks with such happiness, passion, and authority on the subject, with no hesitation. He truly believes. This has made me curious to learn more. So, if this guy Jesus can convince surfer guys like Simon and James to follow him, then whatever he is offering must be pretty good.

"How about we do an overnighter soon into the city and catch up with others?" Simon suggests to James.

"Yeah, it would be good and go to a meeting with them," James says happier.

Simon asks me, "Esther, would you like to stay at our friend's place too? Its cosy when we all stay but it's so much fun and good to be with old friends."

"Sure, why not," I say excited, thinking of the conversation with my parents. Simon senses my reservations.

"You remember Isaiah, Lizzy, and Mark? They are all at Uni sharing a small unit in the city."

I nod, remembering them, and glad another female will be there, otherwise it would be totally inappropriate.

"Sure, tell me when and I will tell the roster manager so I can go to work in the city if needed."

James excuses himself to go and help at home, leaving us to chat and hang out.

"You did well, Esther. We threw so much info at you, but you managed to make some sense of it. James and I have been learning this stuff for years. We taught you the basics in a few hours." Simon moves closer to me on the towel and puts his arm around me drawing me in close, kissing my cheek.

"Simon, how do you *really* know the Holy Spirit you talk about, is it a feeling? Or do you see something? I cannot see anything even though you tell me about it." I feel comfortable asking Simon alone on the beach.

"When I sit quietly, away from distractions and just listen, I hear a quiet voice speaking to me, it can be at the beach, or on the back of the boat. I talk to God when I am alone, aloud or in my head around people, especially before going out to sea or in a scary storm when the trawler feels like it's going to flip. It is called prayer. I ask God to help me, and I give him thanks for all the good things, like keeping me safe and I say sorry when I make mistakes, asking God to forgive me even though I don't deserve it. Most importantly," he says, looking out at the water and leaning into me.

"I ask God to help me be a good guy and to show me how to get it right with you. A lot!" He laughs to himself colouring a little.

"I'm going to make my commitment very soon; I really want you there to witness my decision," Simon tells me.

"I would love to be there for you," I whisper to him, totally moved by his words.

He holds me close. We look out at the water, our bond now deepened beyond friendship and romantic feelings. We both know the gravity of what our knowledge means keeping it a secret, and the challenge to be the difference in this messed up world.

The Fishers and Farmers have managed to safeguard this knowledge for generations and it is the foundation of how they live, which is extraordinary and selfless. It is all finally making sense.

CHAPTER 12

I rise early for work and shiver as my feet touch the cold floor. I am in the clinics today.

I scroll the laws while eating breakfast, most are repetitive and petty. I almost scroll past a simple notification…then pause 'all possessions carried or worn by citizens can be seized if not easily identifiable by the law.'

Arriving through the back entrance of the Medical Precinct, using my slate. Most of the Town citizens have an implant in their hand for smooth transactions for everyday tasks.

Farmers, Fishers, and some citizens choose *not* to have the chip implanted maintaining some privacy. This is one of the few things the law has not enforced. Maybe spying on us through our slates and street surveillance is enough.

Placing my satchel in a locker I head to my first clinic in the maternity wards, my favourite, seeing those cute little squirming bundles.

The Town and Elite mothers fascinate me. They have painless planned births, then sit in bed immediately working on their slates like they went on a lunch break at the office.

Farmer, and Fisher citizens happily recover from delivery napping, cuddling their babies and chatting to visitors popping in for a visit. Their husbands stay by their side; I often make up a bed for them on the lounge in their room to stay overnight, which is so sweet.

Today I admire more cute babies as I mop and restock supplies in the numerous rooms and delivery suites. My slate beeps reminding me to move to my next destination, the women's health hub. I have never been assigned there before. The hub is beautiful with leather lounges, soft lighting and ambient music creating luxury.

I report to the hub manager who uploads my slate with tasks with zero acknowledgement. No mangers do. I race against the clock again observing young teen girls with their parents, they go in and come out of the consulting rooms rubbing their arms.

I realise they are having the birth control implant placed under the skin. This is a revelation to me; at that age I was too busy doing homework and managing bad skin. I keep my head down and keep working, emptying the bins.

There is a commotion in the corridor. Workers are being called by name, including me, and told to line up against the corridor wall facing it. To my horror the Law Enforcers burst into the women's hub in full combat gear, eyes only visible, armed, demanding that anyone called go immediately into the corridor. I am trembling and my heart is racing. We have been singled out by the law.

Staff and patients pour out into the corridor standing, watching, unsure what is happening. Some are scared, many show delight that those of us who are different are being interrogated.

These citizens happily support the Law Enforcers' actions, nodding, clapping, even heckling us; this sickens me to the core. In this moment the work environment has become volatile pitting staff against each other. The current enforced respect for each other, now gone. Good luck, HR, dealing with the fall out.

Now the Enforcers have located all the staff on their check list. We are informed the law has been tipped off that some of us are involved in highly illegal activities and have banned religious items in our possession.

We are ordered to remain facing the wall, arms behind our heads and legs spread apart. The Enforcers start patting down staff members, yelling at them repeatedly. "Hand over your religious items now. It will help the rest of these citizens if you come clean and confess." More cheering and clapping from the crowd.

The elevator doors barely open as the CEO sprints down the corridor and he is angry, his usual reserved demeanour gone. He looks like a tall charcoal lightning bolt with a red face.

He orders them to stop immediately, in a loud firm voice, and the Enforcers pause momentarily staring at him. He speaks now with authority back to a low modulated voice that he is the CEO having jurisdiction over this Medical Precinct.

The captain puts his hand up, signalling to stop the searches, then saunters over thrusting the CEO a slate with an order on it waiting expectantly for the immediate go ahead to continue. Peeking over my shoulder I observe what is happening, noting the silence that has descended over the whole corridor, which is excruciating.

I observe CEO Ward; he appears to be reading every word of the order to the captain's annoyance, *leisurely*, leaning on the wall casually. He asks a staff member politely to get him a long black coffee. This is amusing to me and the girl next to me, and we smile despite the drama unfolding.

The CEO takes so long; the captain's clear goggles fog up as he gets angrier and almost explodes when the coffee arrives for CEO Ward. He extracts himself from the wall smoothly, pausing to sip it, and eventually looks the captain in the eye.

"Very well, but *do not touch* these citizens, that is a direct violation of their privacy and equality in this facility; some are minors. They may turn, stand, and take everything out of their pockets instead, for you to examine. Do not yell at anyone. This is a Medical Precinct not a training ground for your lot. Agreed?" The captain grunts, inclining his head.

The CEO has a hard closed look on his face, containing his true feelings. He stands watching the proceedings, following the captain closely. As he passes me, he pauses.

"*Okay*?" Ceo Ward whispers.

I incline my head. He keeps moving watching closely and pausing every so often checking in with the younger and distraught staff.

We obediently turn and pull everything out of our pockets, holding them out for inspection, which to the captain's utter frustration (which he barely contains) consists of sweet packets, rolls of dressings, scissors, hair ties, and jewellery on our person. That's all!

Some of the women of Indian descent near me start to cry, panicking as they hold ornate gold necklaces, and inform me they are very important to them. It is what they receive on their union day from their husbands but are worried they will be taken from them. It is an ancient long-held tradition.

Peter arrives; Ruby's father walks quickly to the CEO; he is immaculately Elite dressed. They acknowledge each other like colleagues. I overhear Peter say, "What is going on mate? I was down the hall and heard about this crap going on."

The CEO replies, his voice very low and calm but his body indicates he is containing his rage.

The Enforcers approach me and the weeping women. Enforcers look me over asking me to open my mouth, stick out my tongue. They look at my few non-descript items and move to my left.

They start yelling at the woman next to me, "What's this?" They are looking at her necklace and looking at their slate to check if it's religious. Peter starts to walk towards the Law Enforcers; the CEO tries to stop him, but he angrily shakes him off.

Peter strides straight to the Enforcer interrogating the woman and opens his slate quickly, showing his credentials. The Enforcer stops to read the slate briefly, then shows Peter the item.

Peter makes a deliberate show of carefully examining the item, declaring it is a family heirloom passed down through the generations, with both families represented on it when a union takes place.

He dismisses it with a wave of his hand like it is nothing to allay the Enforcers' concerns. He warns them to do their homework before upsetting hard working citizens or he will report them to the Commander.

The Enforcers move quickly finishing their search, and leave, not bothering to check lockers, which was their original plan. An announcement of return to work is heard throughout our floor.

Peter runs to me and gives me a fatherly hug. "Are you okay?" he whispers with concern.

I nod, shaking a little. He informs me Ruby is having more tests as her stomach pains are worsening and tells me he is sick of the increasing harassment of local citizens. The authorities are getting desperate to find law breakers.

"We are so fortunate in this Medical Precinct, despite his young age, to have a CEO who knows the law, and can easily interpret it. He is a lawyer as well as having several degrees in business, which helps," Peter informs me.

CEO Ward gives us a ten-minute break and then instructs us to return to work. He adds that our task list will be adjusted by our managers accordingly.

I observe the other staff still hanging around talking. Many look the CEO up and down in a way that makes me feel uncomfortable as they are so blatant about it. Several staff gossip to each other. "I wonder if he is available? *Never* seen him with *anyone* or on any of the dating apps..."

Peter invites me to come with him and visit Ruby. "I think you will be good for each other."

Looking at him gratefully, I cannot listen to the chatter, which is getting worse as we walk toward the allergy clinic. I see Peter's jaw set in a firm hard line.

"Are you okay, Peter?" He relaxes and smiles, looking down at me.

"Yeah, I was terrified facing those guys, they are scary military robots, just eyes."

I ask him about the staff and that they stare at the CEO making me feel uncomfortable. He nods agreeing grimly.

"People are so focused on themselves; they forget about how that makes others feel. He's their boss for goodness's sake!"

We enter the clinic, and Ruby sits in the waiting area with dressings on her arms from more tests. We embrace and Peter informs her what happened. She looks shocked.

"You are so brave Esther." I shrug.

"I am so glad the CEO and your Dad were there to help," I inform Ruby.

Peter sends us off to the café while he does business.

We enjoy a quick hot chocolate and share a decadent slice of cake as we stare out the huge windows. I freeze for a moment and gulp. There is a long convoy of Enforcer Transport vans pulling out of the precinct driveway. They really meant business today. My mother appears at my elbow observing the convoy too, frowning. She immediately calls Rachael.

"Hi Rach, I just heard there's a huge swell coming in anytime now; might be worth securing everything on the wharfs and trawlers." I hear her say thanks and is gone.

My mother wraps her arms around me. "You, okay? The Enforcers never came to my floor; I was so worried." I smile.

"I'm fine, the CEO got to our floor fast and got rid of them; he deliberately drove them mad too. It was hilarious."

"Did he *really*? Good for him." My mother kisses Ruby and me on the cheek and is gone.

"Ruby, should you be eating cake?"

"Who cares, nobody knows what's wrong with me, so it doesn't matter." She shrugs.

Peter arrives back and I excuse myself as I have several hours of my shift to complete. Ruby and Peter say goodbye, and they make their way through the crowd leaving me to complete more cleaning and restocking. It's a happier place to be than in front of the Enforcers.

Finishing my tasks in good time, I am about to head home when my slate alerts me of a delivery. I head to my locker and change into civilian clothes. Throwing my scrubs into my satchel, leaving it there and move to the secret locker, I retrieve the satchel, throw it over my shoulder and head towards the station for another city trip.

Looking out the window of the train, all I see is a blur of towns, and think about today's events. The law seems to be increasing its pressure on the community, to what ends I am unsure, although it seems to be an endless pursuit.

I enjoy just sitting - glad that moment is over. I unravel my braid and restyle my hair into a fashionable Town messy bun, sadly a new ritual I have adopted.

Finishing my delivery at the city Medical Precinct, I message the CEO and take my time browsing the huge display windows in the city, as it's only early afternoon.

Drawn to a Transport store with shiny new single and double transports all lined up, I browse while sipping my coffee and place the empty keep cup in the repurpose collection station located in the street. Everything is sanitised and re-used. I enter the store and look around; there are different sizes of transports and most importantly it seems any colour or design your heart desires.

An enthusiastic sales assistant gives me their sales pitch and asks me what license I am currently riding on. I inform them I will apply for my license in about six months. They show me the smaller versions of the transports as I will only be permitted to ride these as a learner. My eye lingers on a solid, black shiny one and I am determined to own it, eventually. I thank the sales assistant.

I head home with indulgent plans of being finally independent and able to ride. I will still use the train and metro for the city trips, as it is so efficient.

Browsing second hand transports on my slate helps my dream feel attainable. I will need to buy the right clothing too, picturing myself wearing the full-face helmet and leathers.

Where would I hide it? Nobody will believe I earnt the money working part time mopping floors at the Medical Precinct in my community without suspicion.

Taking the metro back to the Sydney City Terminal I enjoy the short trip taking in the sights and smells of cafes and restaurants swirling around me as I stand in the open doorway. Then I head into the terminal, grateful the Law Enforcers are too busy hassling other citizens.

Sitting on the country platform, I wait, happily scrolling my social pages. I see Simon, James and a few other guys have posted pictures of them all surfing today and raving about the waves in their surfer lingo. It looks like a great day. They must have had a rare day off today.

Simon rarely posts anything, but he has today. A few artistic shots of the surf and candid fun pictures of his mates goofing around on the beach, burying each other and a beach BBQ. Zeb is featured in the pictures smiling! He really lives a charmed life for a dog.

Simon sent me pictures of his day and a super cute close-up of Zeb and him chilling on the beach, and Zeb riding on his surf board in the shallow water. The pictures make me smile.

I message saying I wish I could have been there.

CHAPTER 13

Jonah's birthday invitation arrives; it will be a celebration for leaving school too. Plans are in place for shopping with friends. I shower, ready for a fun day of fashion and fun. Jonah's celebration is several days away. Ruby has told me where to buy a new dress, so naturally I will follow her guidance with Sarah in tow.

Sitting at our family table, I stare at its worn surface, tracing it with my finger, every chip and dent. Sarah and Ruby arrive talking loudly, snapping me out of my reverie. I grab my bag, grinning, putting my arms around them.

"New beginnings today and becoming an adult. I have accepted its happening so I might as well enjoy the adventure," I inform them.

"Me too." Sarah nods approvingly.

My mother appears from the lounge room with tea, wishing us well. "Make sure the dress is suitable."

Sarah and I assure her it will be fine, knowing the standard expected is modest. I am determined it will be on trend. If I am to embrace adult status I must dress the part, after all, I am paying for it.

Ruby parks at the retail precinct, leading the way with a clickety clack on the polished granite floors in impossibly high heels, just like in the movies.

She is dressed in full Elite couture, including hairstyle and attitude. Truly terrifying. I had never really thought of Ruby as an Elite until today; it is a revelation. I look at Sarah's stunned face; she feels the same.

Our friend is a super-rich Elite.

"Hey! it's still *me!* I'm putting on a show, coffee? My treat." Ruby hands us cups of aromatic coffee from a barista cart.

We sip slowly, following Ruby to her stylist, having never entered one of these salons. My family has a Farmer friend who provides haircuts. Naturally, we exchange goods with them in return.

Sarah and I stare at the lavish décor in the salon; Ruby is already chatting animatedly to the stylists. Passing the front counter, I glimpse the prices on the wall and forget to breathe for a long minute. The prices are insane, some are a week's wages, so many points. It feels wrong being here.

Propelled into a chair, I turn to Ruby. "Sarah too!" Several stylists look at Ruby.

I could pay for Sarah's hair to be styled and a new dress saying it is a best friend's gift, otherwise there would be no reasonable explanation of how I could afford it. I am already realising the difficulty of earning so much.

"No Esther, you can't afford it, this is crazy." I grab Sarah's hand looking into those eyes swimming in tears.

"Happy best friend day," I whisper.

Ruby barely nods to the stylist and Sarah is swiftly seated next to me and we are transported to the new world of the Elite. The stylists stare at our hair for so long that I fidget uncomfortably asking Ruby what is wrong.

"They don't usually style… *Farmers* and are unsure what will be okay."

"We will be turning eighteen later this year, I want to be treated like everybody else. Sarah needs something conservative," I politely announce, Sarah nods.

The stylists reanimate appearing with a slate preloaded with styles to choose from. Once chosen they load our images into it. Sarah and Ruby nod quickly.

"Esther, that's you." I stare at my virtual image.

"Please leave it long enough to tie up for work."

My hair is cut to a long shoulder length, with sharp angles, highlighting my jaw line. My hazel eyes seem huge. I stare back at the grown-up version of myself, smiling.

Sarah has a conservative style, and it is stunning as her hair bounces on her shoulders. Ruby chats to the stylists about Jonah's party on the trawler; they are curious as it is not at a private club.

"Won't it be a bit fishy?" Pearl asks Ruby.

"*No*, there won't be any fish except the ones we are eating; it's a floating venue," Ruby informs them.

"Oh," both stylists say.

Sarah and I look at each other smiling. Our world is a mystery to the Town citizens, as they never take the time to get to know us. I am guilty of my ignorance of Town citizens too.

The stylists show us tips on how to style our hair for the party that are easy, which is sweet. I transfer points for the styling and Ruby produces small gifts from our stylists who packed sample bottles of products for us to try, knowing we could not afford them.

"Now dresses," Ruby announces.

Ruby moves swiftly to a store that represents a luxury mansion. Sarah and I drift along behind her admiring the staircases, glittering lights.

Arriving in what appears to be a loungeroom, a well-dressed middle-aged woman sits in an armchair busily typing on her slate. She looks at us like most, because we are Farmers and wondering what we are doing.

Amusing rather than insulting!

Ruby informs her of an appointment. The woman nods, revealing a secret panel holding an enormous rack of evening wear, which looks to be our size, preselected. Unbelievable how these people live.

After many outfits and disagreements on style I emerge like a mermaid on land in a shimmering sapphire blue dress that hugs my body, revealing a little flesh on my shoulders. Mostly covered, very modest. I feel like a beautiful mermaid without the tail. Ruby and Sarah jump up and down cheering. I immediately turn to Sarah. "Your turn." She shakes her head.

"No, Esther you can't."

"Yes, I can," I say, reminding her it's best friend day.

"Go for it, you can wear it for lots of parties."

We all agree on a beautiful white flowing dress with gold embroidery, which highlights her hair. Stunning!

Looking at Ruby expectantly the sales assistant reveals a simple silver dress with a delicate swirling pattern embroidered all over it, which looks beautiful and understated. We stare in awe. Ruby did well to choose something stunning but will blend with her friends.

We carefully carry our purchases to the transport, thanking Ruby for the day, sadly resuming our normal lives.

* * *

Simon and I stay in touch chatting daily. It is more comfortable sharing on a deeper level about ourselves. Our schedules are so challenging that it's hard to meet up in person.

In the early mornings we chat as he heads out on the trawler until the signal disappears. I enjoy starting my day seeing his smiling face with the water and trawler as a backdrop, occasionally seeing the sunrise.

Some days the crew yell out laughing, "Stop talking and do some work." They will tease him all day for sure. Simon does not care.

We discuss Jonah's party, which we are looking forward to. We can finally catch up in person. Simon has been working at sea for many days at a time for weeks. He assures me that he dances, and he shyly reveals he loves the latest music and going to the occasional night club in the city with his friends and wants to slow dance with me.

Jonah's party finally arrives. I slip into my shimmering dress with my low-heeled sandals peeking out. I leave my hair down, letting it naturally settle with just a touch of product to keep it in place.

My parents proudly escort me to the wharf and wave me off as they chat to the other excited parents. Everyone is talking with Ruby's Dad like they are old friends; there is no sign of her mother, not surprising.

Simon smoothly slips his arm around me escorting me to the trawler. He bows like a fool and helps me carefully gather the hem of my dress while stepping onto the enormous fishing trawler from the wharf to the deck, resplendent in lights.

Simon's younger brother Andrew nods awkwardly as we arrive. I see him exchange a quick look with Simon, which I am sure was a secret brotherly acknowledgement he is happy for him. I see fairy lights wrapped around every fixture - a beautiful and unusual scene for Fishers. I feel free to be me tonight.

Ruby smiles broadly, the fairy lights reflect off her dress highlighting its detail. "Isn't this incredible, Jonah let me decorate and plan the details with his parents."

Jonah bounds up grinning and explaining in detail everything Ruby was responsible for. He is so proud of the girl by his side. His shirt is in an elegant grey with a hint of shimmer matching Ruby's dress.

Simon and I exchange amused looks as if to say, are they dating? "Are you guys going out or what?" Simon blurts out, to their embarrassment.

Looking caught, they say nothing and disappear quickly as the trawler slowly pulls away from the wharf on this beautiful, clear night. Everyone cheers signalling it is time to party, without the parents' scrutiny.

"Ahh, that's better," Simon whispers in my ear.

"You look so beautiful tonight. I have you all to myself, finally on my turf." He leads me by the hand, giving me a tour of the trawler saying it is very much like his family's one.

Simon pauses at a symbol of an anchor discreetly carved into the door frame near the cabin. He holds my hand and traces my finger over the cross part of it. I look at him.

"This is an ancient Christian symbol; we have one on our trawler too, you see them from time to time. People think it is a common anchor, but what it contains is much more; it is a sign post declaring God is with us and in some cases his people meet here," he says quietly.

"Thank you for showing me, Simon." I trace the carving, feeling its detail.

He draws me close as we sway to the music on the deck, a temporary dance floor. He admires my dress and the way light reflects off it and whispering that I remind him of a gorgeous mermaid from old sea legends.

"I'm in trouble, you could lure me into danger, danger of falling deeply, deeply in love with you, I'm already under your spell," he says, smiling mischievously.

I am stunned and flattered by his very romantic and candid declaration.

"You are too handsome to be an old crusty sailor." Moving closer to him.

I snap a picture of us with my slate; his blonde hair looks even lighter against his black, long sleeve shirt and pants. We stand holding hands watching the spectacular colours fade away as the sun slips into the ocean. The trawler is now anchored in a quiet bay.

We share hours laughing, dancing, and singing badly to our favourite music. We take fun pictures, eat too much sushi and a giant three-dimensional blue whale cake Ruby organised.

We laugh at Jonah's emotions of delight and surprise. Especially when he pretends to be eaten by it.

"It will spew you out Jonah," one of the guys yells out, everyone laughs.

We gather on the deck sharing fun and touching stories about Jonah as his oldest friends. His parents and younger siblings bring us all to tears with their heartfelt speeches. Such a special moment to share.

We find quiet places to sit, looking out on the water, reflecting on the great night as the trawler slowly chugs its way home again. The music plays softly in the background. Our friends sit in small groups chatting on the deck.

Ruby and Jonah talk very close in the shadows. Ruby wrapped in Jonah's arms, and Sarah and Josh talk animatedly, holding hands at the side, staring out into the water.

Simon leads me by the hand to the back of the trawler, helping me sit on a pile of giant cushions and placing his arm around my shoulders. I curl up next to him, snuggling in close, loving his familiar, subtle scent of soap and cologne.

I tuck my feet up under my dress grateful for Simon's body heat on this chilly night. We stare up into the sky, looking for constellations which Fishers know so well. Simon names all the ones I do not know; my favourite is the southern cross, always guiding us safely home. Simon agrees.

We fall into silence. Simon turns, leaning over me, looking into my eyes searching, then draws me closer, and places his fingers under my chin. His gentleness surprising me as he leans towards me. I feel in that single moment every possible emotion, nervous, excited, and panicky, not knowing what to do, but wanting it to happen.

"Okay?" Simon pauses, whispering, inclining his head and asking for permission.

I nod, ready for the unknown; he kisses me gently and confidently without hesitation. I respond.

When we separate, I think of his gentleness; we are so close I can feel his breath on my lips and see every detail in those bright blue eyes that are focused on me. He pulls back a little looking at me worried.

"Are you *okay* Esther?" He reaches for my hand.

"Did I push you away Simon?"

"*No,*" he says, slowly smiling.

"I was thinking that was a perfect first kiss." Simon is surprised at my revelation.

I rest my hand on his cheek and lean up to him, returning his kiss, not as confidently, but confirming my attraction to him. Simon kisses me with less restraint, showing me how he feels, and we enjoy the intimate moment. I remain wrapped in his strong arms resting my head on his shoulder, comfortable in this next step of our relationship, while looking at the town lights in the distance. Simon sighs, I look at him.

"You, okay?" I ask him.

"I don't want this moment to end." He kisses me on the cheek.

I am touched by his romantic revelation.

The engines slow signalling we are nearing the wharf. We separate sadly; Simon helps me to my feet, kissing me slowly.

"I have wanted to kiss you for so long," he whispers in my ear.

"I'm so glad you did," I whisper back promising to message soon.

The parents cheer when they see us approaching, with the engines slowing. The lights from the trawler illuminate the wharf bringing it to life.

I am disappointed that we are arriving so soon. The Dads, including Ruby's, deftly catch the ropes securing them to the moorings. Ruby's Dad acts like he has done it a million times.

Simon pulls me close; in the reflection of the trawler lights, his eyes are bright.

"See you soon beautiful. I am glad we are together," he whispers, helping me with my jacket and escorting me off the trawler.

Simon kisses me on the cheek quickly as my father stands watching us with his arms folded, leaning against his old truck in the distance. He just gives a short nod to Simon.

"I'm *terrified* of your father, Esther," Simon murmurs.

"Really? He's a teddy bear," I say surprised. Simon shakes his head.

"Dating his daughter is a game changer. His look alone keeps me accountable. I would never upset you Esther, you are his precious jewel."

Approaching the truck my father helps me up. He asks how the night was as I wave to Simon who waves back staring into my eyes. Jonah approaches, whispering in his ear; he grins, putting his arm around his shoulders, as we pull away, and I see them talking animatedly about something...

Driving home, my father asks me about the party, who was there, if we all behaved, and whether Simon was a gentleman ... Once satisfied with my answers we rumble along in a contented silence.

Arriving home, my mother appears in her pyjamas, peppermint tea in hand and waiting. She puts the steaming cup down, smiling.

"Why don't you tell me all about tonight while I help you out of your beautiful dress."

She helps me undress, propelling me to the shower. Refreshed, I return to my room in baby pink pyjamas feeling very tired. Mum sits on my bed, holding Bunny on her lap stroking its ears. I sit next to her, putting my head on her shoulder.

"How was the party, Esther?"

"It was *perfect.*"

"Simon kissed you, didn't he?" She smiles.

"How do you know?"

"A mother knows, I was a girl your age and in love with a boy."

"Dad?" She nods, lost in thought.

"Esther, take your time getting to know each other; guard yourself like we have talked about," Mum says gently.

I reassure her Simon is very respectful and I feel safe. Satisfied, she tucks me into bed with Bunny.

"Good, because your father and I cannot watch our precious girl be disrespected. It will be hard to let you go one day but worse if you were disrespected."

Mum turns out the light. I cannot sleep! My first kiss! It was amazing.

CHAPTER 14

The weeks following Jonah's party are tiring as I travel between Medical Precincts doing deliveries, averting suspicion and questions of my whereabouts from family and Simon.

There have been dangerous moments at the Sydney City Terminal, which I have managed to navigate and slip away from. I walk with confidence, not like a victim, and most importantly blend with the crowd. I have mastered the Town look on a tight budget.

Simon has been away at sea a lot, on longer trips. My schedule has prevented us being together too, but we message every day and share photos, knowing Simon will only see them when they are in range.

We have changed our slate settings to 'in a relationship' as the prompts from the government to clarify our relationship status are persistent. He writes the most beautiful messages to me every day; I guess you could call them love letters.

I rise again, early this morning, pulling on warm socks, checking my slate for deliveries, messages from Simon and law updates.

I pause over several *interpersonal relationship* laws. No touching permitted unless permission given.

All adult relationships status must be updated and agreements on iRESPECT to be completed by all parties involved.

Teen relationship status and teen iRESPECT agreements are voluntary but recommended.

I think of Simon's discreet vigilance seeking permission to physically interact with me. He obviously has navigated this before. He has not mentioned the iRESPECT app since our first interaction in the bush. I guess we are communicating well enough without it.

Today is my day off. After completing chores, I take the bus to the lookout. The bus slowly ascends the hill to the lookout, which is almost a circle with one road around it, homes in the centre, ocean views on three sides, and a pine forest reserve on the remaining. The views are spectacular.

Tapping the sensor to get off, the driver lets me out near the children's playground, and I am greeted with the refreshing ocean breeze carrying the smell of pine and the sea.

I am transported back to my childhood as I walk through the children's playground, dropping my bag on the weathered outdoor table, and running my hands over the swing with its robust chains and recycled tyre seat.

Sitting on the familiar swing, I let my mind drift. My feet dangle, recalling my beautiful Pa taking me here as a very small child and teaching me how to swing using my whole body and legs to reach great heights.

I swing high, and carefree, trying to touch the sky, feeling the tension and sorrow of the last few weeks dissipate. Jumping off the swing while it is still high, I smugly land on my feet.

Scooping up my bag I stroll down the street to the pine forest reserve. As I enter, beautiful Zeb comes bounding up to me, smiling; he is such a cute kelpie.

"Hi Zeb."

I scratch him behind his velvety ears. Zeb has jumped the fence again, to say hello. He always finds his way home, especially at dinner time. He has been known to be on the wharf too. Waiting. He stands next to me waiting with anticipation for directions.

"Come on, Zeb, I am going for a walk. Want to come?" He happily trots by my side as a furry escort until he sees a rabbit and runs off.

Walking silently through a reserve, I follow the worn path on the thick carpet of pine needles. I have missed this place, its cool dark interior, the sounds of the wind through the pines so easily mistaken for the ocean.

I walk towards the bright sunlit grass clearing near the cliff that looks out onto one of the many bays we have. This view stretches out to the ocean. Inhaling deeply, I stretch out my arms feeling the gentle breeze blowing my hair and long dress around me. Looking out to the horizon, I think of my wonderful Simon fishing. Hopefully home soon safe.

Pulling on my wide brimmed hat I sit, settle my back against a small clump of rocks well back from the steep cliff edge and stare at the expansive ocean. I feel the gentle rays of sun on my skin feeling overcome with a sense of peace.

For a moment I hear a faint voice calling me.

"*Esther, Esther, Esther.*" I look around, no one is there.

Weird! I sit still, closing my eyes and focusing. I hear a quiet voice again a whisper on the wind that is in my heart and head at the same time.

"*Esther, Esther, Esther.*"

I hold my breath, terrified and happy all at the same time, the voice swirling around me again calling my name and then it is gone. I open my eyes to feel tears running down my face and feeling completely at peace.

Zeb reappears, panting from his pursuit and snuggles next to me. He looks up at me with unconditional love like he understands something just happened. We sit in companionable silence lost in our own thoughts, for a long time trying to make sense of what just happened. I share my sandwich with him.

I read my slate, feeling better and not so overwhelmed yet still puzzled about what just happened. It is late afternoon as I walk back to the entrance of the reserve ready to head home. As we emerge onto the street, Zeb shoots across the road to my dismay in front of a Law Enforcer's transport van, fortunately unscathed.

I realise he has spotted Simon's mother, Rachael, walking home. She looks at the van and Zeb's narrow escape, worried, and then at me and smiles.

"Esther, come over and have a cuppa with me," she calls out.

I wave and nod, looking up and down the road then towards their home. "He hasn't been annoying you, has he?" she asks concerned.

"No, he's been quite the cute companion." Zeb looks a little offended.

"In a male household, he doesn't get called cute, it's mate. Lovely to have female company, especially when the men are away," Rachael says. She makes tea and places a plate of large chocolate chip cookies on the table to share.

I observe a huge pile of woollen clothing taking up half the table. Wet weather gear is stacked near a sewing machine. Farmers do not wear wool as it is too costly, but Fishers need warm clothes on the water under their waterproof clothing.

When Rachael sits at the table with me, she automatically picks up a piece of clothing and proceeds to repair a hole in it. I realise there is not idle time in a Fisher's life either; she looks after the family and home and keeps it running while they are out at sea or processing their catch. Zeb must be great company.

Rachael pauses, looking me in the eye.

"Did something happen in the reserve? You can trust me Esther, even if you do not know how to talk about it," she says kindly.

Rachael is very perceptive, maybe a mother's instinct. I look into those warm eyes, that remind me of my mother's that have just a few lines around them when she smiles.

I feel tears spilling out everywhere. She immediately drops her sewing and crouches beside me, wrapping her arms around me like a child.

"What is it?" she says, deeply concerned. Managing to stop crying, I smile, which shocks her even more.

"I think I just heard God speak to me and I feel totally overwhelmed. I don't know what to do," I inform her.

Rachael is shocked. She has never seen me at a meeting only with children. "How do you know?" she asks slowly, hiding our slates.

The tale of Paul's passing, Simon and James discovering me in the bush and teaching me on the beach tumbles out, giving her greater understanding of the situation. She squeezes me very tightly.

"You are truly blessed, Esther. God has spoken and revealed himself to you. How do you feel?" I tell her I felt so many emotions at once.

"I know it's amazing isn't it. I could see something had happened. Don't talk to anyone except maybe Simon and your parents; spend time waiting and listening for God to speak to you again, you can speak to him too, it's called prayer." I just nod, not knowing what I believe or know.

She squeezes my hand, asking about Jonah's party, I get the sense she got few details from Simon and Andrew about the night. I retrieve my slate and fill her in on the details, decorations and what everyone wore. She smiles, nodding as she sews yet another item of clothing, knowing all the characters at the party.

She is overwhelmed when she sees pictures of Simon and me. She stops for a moment, sewing in her lap and looking at me, smiling.

"Simon doesn't say much, but when he talks, it's always about you; he lights up. Seeing the pictures of the two of you I understand why," Rachael says.

"Really?"

"Why are you so surprised, Esther? He doesn't look at anyone else. He only desires your company, even under your Dad's watchful eye, that is commitment." She laughs.

I sit wondering what kind of conversations he has with his parents.

I excuse myself to head home. As I'm about to leave, I hear Zeb barking excitedly, realising the family truck has just pulled up, and a load of very tired, dirty fishermen climb out, glad to be home. Zeb naturally is welcomed with wrestles from the men.

Simon strides towards the house, boots in hand, and placing them neatly at the front door, he opens the screen door and is shocked to see me.

"Esther!" His face lights up then gestures his dirty clothes.

I run to him anyway and put my head on his chest, wrapping my arms around him tightly and feeling his heart beating strong and steady. I receive a slightly awkward but warm hug as his whole family stand watching. He smells like sweat, fish, and grease. Curly blond hair sticking up everywhere.

Rachael saves the moment.

"Everyone in the shower now, I will prep dinner. Want to join me?" she asks me like a friend.

"Sure, I will message Mum."

I observe Simon's parents discreetly withdraw into the kitchen, kiss, and embrace. I see relief in Rachael's eyes; her men are home safe.

We look in the fridge and quickly assemble a huge meal suitable for hungry fishermen while clearing the pile of mending.

Simon appears quickly, looking much better, still smiling. Delighted that I am here, he puts his arms around me and his Mum.

"Maybe we need Esther here more often to prepare feasts."

"I need Esther to come over more often for girl talk." She smiles at me.

We laugh and sit down at the table, waiting for the family to join us. Younger Andrew wanders in the front door, acknowledges his mother with a kiss on her cheek, notes my presence, inclines his head, and then turns to climb the stairs to his room.

Andrew's mother calls his name, and he reappears knowing the tone, "We eat as a family, and we have company."

Simon reaches for my hand under the table and squeezes it as his Dad gives thanks for the hands that prepared the food, and the bounty the earth and ocean provide. I know this is a thinly veiled prayer, as Andrew and I do not attend meetings yet.

The family proceeds to devour everything on the table, joking, laughing, and making fun of each other, especially funny anecdotes of the recent trip. Skipper Andrew teases Matt and Simon tirelessly about how they moped about missing their girls while at sea.

Rachael just smiles and listens as Skipper Andrew looks at her steadily across the table smiling and subtly inclines his head in a secret romantic communication. I sit and observe the banter and his mother's happiness that her table is full again, and her undeniable love for her husband and he for her.

After the early dinner Rachael offers to drive me home as the fishermen are heading to bed after many long days at sea. Simon pulls me into an alcove and kisses me slowly, his kiss lingering, seemingly not wanting it to end. I welcome this moment having missed him and worried about him for days.

Simon is almost asleep standing up and insists we catch up soon.

Rachael drives me home in the truck, and she tells me to visit if I need to chat about anything. The evening has given me great insight into Simon's family. I am grateful I do not have to struggle with everything alone, deciding to find my parents and tell them everything, from Paul's passing to this moment.

Arriving home, I gather all the slates, putting them into the sanitiser. I ask my parents to sit as I must tell them something important. They sit and do not speak until I finish. They looked at me the whole time, nodding to reassure me they are following my retelling of events, which I am grateful.

At the conclusion I sit with my hands in my lap. My mother and father just hold me tight and tell me they are so relieved I have been cared for by Simon, James, and Rachael with so much being revealed and that I have not been caught.

"Esther, we have to retrieve that book called the Bible. We have so few copies it needs to be protected and hidden." My father looks grave. My father smiles and proposes we go 'fishing' tonight.

We pack our fishing buckets and pull-on head lamps and warm jackets, leaving our slates behind. We walk quickly down the bush trail, and as we approach the tree, I check for snakes with a stick pulling the Bible free of its hiding place. Relieved it is still there.

My father stands for a moment, quite emotional. He swiftly lifts the bag of bait and places the Bible at the bottom of the bucket in its towel and places the wrapped bait and hand reels on top. He mutters, "Sorry Paul; I am sure you would approve."

As we walk toward home through the bush chatting, I inform my Dad I don't know what I believe and am not ready for meetings yet. Dad suggests maybe he and Mum can lead me through some of the ancient writings like at the meetings. I am happy with this plan as I navigate my way through this forbidden world of religion and faith.

As we reach the fire trail entry, I hear my father swear under his breath as we bump into a group of Law Enforcers gathered with several dogs. They incline their heads, asking if there were any fish biting, we reply, there were none. Looking sad, we move on knowing they do not care.

It is terrifying as we pass without a stop and search. There are so many drones circling above our heads. They must have their sights set on trouble elsewhere.

As we walk away, I feel the tension in the air. We were so close to being arrested that it takes my breath away. I could have lost my father in that moment. Arriving home, my father places his bucket down and embraces me for a long time, looking down at me.

"Esther, this is what the Enforcers are looking for and things like it. Living out our faith in secret is dangerous, but right, until the day we can freely express our faith openly."

My father lifts a concrete slab on the floor of the shed to expose a solid metal box and asks me to leave.

I lay in bed exhausted; it has been an eventful day and I try to talk to God. "Hey God, it's Esther, thank you for keeping me safe tonight, I guess you are there. Amen." I add that remembering that is what Simon did after his prayer at the beach. I feel a sense of peace wash over me as I fall asleep.

* * *

I work in the City Medical Precinct for the remaining days that week, Simon has some time off after his long days at sea and tries to meet up with me whenever possible, always holding my hand. His courtship is very intentional and beautiful.

Simon joins my family for dinner tonight; he mentions that his brother Andrew is preparing for the HSC exams soon and it is a challenge to keep him focused. His family want him to at least complete his final exams before working on the trawlers. Even Jonah is sitting the exams despite being a fisherman now. Everyone turns to me.

"Esther, will you sit the exams? I have seen you secretly studying late into the night," my father asks me.

"I'm not sure I am prepared, I could ask, I guess. I already have completed the application and all the assignments," I say unsure.

Everyone agrees that it is a great plan but stressing if that is what I want. I sit and think through the logistics and decide to go for it. I will talk to the roster manager and see if I can have some time off if that is permitted.

After dinner Simon and I walk around the garden talking about the future; we have been together for many wonderful months now. So much is happening, possible exams, working, us as one. So many things to consider, exciting but scary. We arrive at my Dad's bench and sit, enjoying the peace and privacy.

Simon draws my face to him with both hands; he looks into my eyes and kisses me with such emotion and intensity. He slides his hands down my neck and shoulders, resting them there, gently kissing me down my neck and back to my lips.

I feel the heated intimate connection between us and respond, for far too long, and I'm breathless when we separate. This is the first time it has been this intense. We both look at each other steadily knowing that our attraction is growing deeper, our bodies giving away our feelings.

We sit quietly looking out into the garden, our own thoughts swirling around us. I curl up on the bench, tucking up my feet and rest my head on Simon's shoulder, and he gently places his arm around me.

Our unspoken dilemma hangs in the air; our growing attraction is moving along at a pace I am unsure is the same. Or is it?

I thought we would arrive at this place a long time into the future but being inexperienced in love and relationships I had no idea how this plays out.

I have only observed what goes on at school, in dark corridors, hurried encounters and students hastily tidying their uniforms walking to class like nothing happened.

Very different to what I observe in the Farmer Fisher community, day to day where relationships start with friendship and we see how it goes. It is always discreet and private. If we cannot be great friends, enjoy similar interests, and communicate, the relationship ends.

I look up at Simon who looks out into the garden, his face hard to read. "Simon," I whisper, looking up at him. He looks down at me.

"I know," he says softly.

"My parents always said to us growing up to guard our hearts, minds and bodies but I didn't think it would be this difficult. I have never felt like this about anyone before."

I look into those gentle eyes.

"What are we going to do? I love you." It comes out of my mouth so naturally before I can stop it.

Simon looks at me relieved, and smiles, which surprises me.

"I'm seriously in love with you, Esther. I have been for a long time, but didn't want to say anything, as it's still so early in our relationship, even though we've known each other forever." We sit quietly in this new revelation.

"I'm not ready to be with you in *that* way yet. I always planned to be in a union with someone," I say nervously, even though my body seems to want to be the boss, I muse.

Simon nods in agreement, then says quietly looking out into the garden again, "I hear guys and girls at the wharf talk about sex all the time, they are so casual about all the different citizens they have hooked up with, and they don't seem to care about them, *at all.* It seems different from what we have; our relationship is not casual."

"Agreed, maybe we need to give ourselves some time to think about what we want and talk about boundaries we can agree on, without an app."

"And cool down, not a long break, because I'll miss you, especially surrounded by fish," Simon says, agreeing.

"Okay, let's take time to think for a week then meet up again for a dinner date, my treat," I say, smiling while forming a plan in my head.

"I will message you the details."

"Deal." Simon seems relieved that the tension has lifted.

"Off you go, I have study to do."

"I'm glad. You are incredibly smart."

He stands looking into my eyes, lingering for a long moment, then breaks his gaze, smiling as if satisfied with what he was looking for, reminiscent of our first kiss at the party.

"Bye beautiful," Simon says casually heading for home.

"Bye," I whisper as I stretch and shake off the last few heated moments.

How can I concentrate when I just found out this incredible guy with intense blue eyes loves me? I laugh to myself at how mushy it all sounds.

Oh well, it's true and I love him too.

CHAPTER 15

"Simon, Simon, lunch time," my older brother Matt calls me in from the back of the trawler. I grab some lunch and find a quiet spot to look out at the ocean before we bring in the catch.

If I had to describe the life of a Fisher it is water, lots of fish, exhausting, physical work that is treacherous.

I was raised with my brothers on the water and wharfs, helping our parents and playing on the trawler amongst the nets and fish. As we grew older, we were taught how to maintain the nets, trawlers and clean after our time at sea. I always try to get my brothers to do the gross jobs.

We learn to unload the trawler, sort out everything, and prepare the catch ready for processing and selling at the co-op next to the wharf as well as the markets. This is our livelihood and a reliable food source. The ocean is brutal and hard but brings rewards too.

I did not finish my final years of school. My parents needed my help and as I was almost an adult I had started working on the trawlers as a full-time fisher.

The easiness of school I miss and hanging out with my mates every day. Somehow, I managed to navigate school without too much trouble with the town kids. Growing tall quickly and developing muscles helped working on the boats and lugging tubs of fish.

I enjoyed competitive sports, with the Town kids, which was a neutral battleground. They would taunt me with insults to try to gain control of the game or incite a fight, but I just did not care.

I mixed with the Town kids outside of school, at their invitation from time to time. The girls were very pretty and friendly, I went out with a few, but they were very different to the Fisher and Farmer girls.

Town girls changed boyfriends regularly and the guys the same. It was very casual and physical. Some of the Town girls were sweet and wanted a relationship but some of them pursued you until you gave in and went out with them, only to find out they just wanted your body. It was purely physical and you were a conquest.

I had plenty of opportunities to hook up with anyone I wanted. I was tempted, I had urges like anyone does but something stopped me; it seemed meaningless and a game to them for something so private.

I decided in my late teens that this type of casual dating was not for me. I realise now, watching the older guys like my brother Matt and his friends date girls from our community, shaped my view of how dating could be. I went out with a few Farmer and Fisher girls but there just was not enough interest in each other.

Our parents taught us to respect ourselves and our partners, and they also shaped my ideas of relationships too - friendship, love, commitment, and fun. I guess that is why I broke off relationships early rather than dragging it out being polite.

As a kid I had been out on the trawlers on short trips, which was okay hanging out with my Dad and older brother. It was kind of fun, but nothing got me ready for the long days and weeks at sea fishing. Endless exhaustion.

The first few times I could not decide which part of my body hurt the most, hands, shoulders or back. The sunburn was terrible. The storms and rough seas challenged any good fisher to keep breakfast down, stay dry and alive. If I could catch short moments to sleep it helped.

Bringing in the larger fish like Marlin and Yellow Fin tuna takes great skill to keep them on the line, and to use your body to brace yourself against the boat. I am always grateful to have a safety harness to stop the fish dragging me back into the ocean. I am loving the challenge, even more with my brother by my side.

Now experienced, I still get painful muscles, but they recover quickly. As is our custom, the younger Fishers change boats from time to time to learn different types of fishing and to work with a crew that's not family. I have found this helpful adjusting to Fisher life, and I get a break from my Skipper Dad, to relax and be myself, and to be taught by others who are patient and forgiving if you make small errors. Huge errors are never okay wherever you are and they are costly.

I rest when all jobs are done on the trawler, and the boat is not going out. I usually sleep in and catch up with my friends, surf if the waves are good or go into the city to visit friends who are trying to make a go of Uni. I enjoy the fast pace.

My Uni friends share a small one bedroom, one bathroom apartment. They have mastered a minimalist style and being broke. I enjoy hanging out with them, hearing about Uni life and how the world operates in the city. They crave news from home.

I am unsure when I first started noticing Esther. Growing up and being younger she hung out with her school friends and blending with the other kids. As she got older, she helped more at the markets and meetings, and we saw each other at social gatherings and celebrations for friends. She is different, not always impressed with everything in our Fisher and Farmer lives.

My younger brother Andrew is in some of her classes. He informs me that she is super smart and can keep up with the guys climbing trees and at PK. I cannot deny this made her more interesting and attractive.

When I thought no one was looking, I would watch her, realising I was attracted to her looks, not sure what in particular, but was drawn to her far more than any other girl in the room. She is very pretty. I would look at her, trying to work her out, wondering what she is thinking. I often observe her standing deep in thought, a look of determination on her face, frowning at times.

Seeing her laughing out loud with friends is another cute side to her. I found myself staying back more often at meetings with other friends helping to pack up just to be near her, work alongside her, chat and learn what she was like. We seemed to talk easily together, which was encouraging.

It was hard to move from childhood friends to more; it's a common problem with Fishers and Farmers, as everyone knows everyone.

Esther was almost inseparable from her close friend Sarah, which made it difficult to interact casually and stay under the radar.

I noticed recently she looks at me more often and averts her eyes quickly when she thinks I might notice. James, my best mate, had even mentioned that she seemed to look at me as much as I looked at her. He is a good friend; I needed someone to confirm I was not imagining it.

I was motivated to act as it appeared Jonah was trying to make moves on her, which took me by surprise as I think of my younger brother's friends as kids when in fact, they are almost my age. Andrew would mention stuff that happened in school, and in the past, I would dismiss it. I started listening more and realising from these conversations that Jonah was after Esther.

Unexpectedly, on the day of the meeting, I had been delayed at the wharf, arriving minutes before the meeting started. Esther's family kitchen was empty and silent, the kids were outside, and the adults in the lounge room were talking, then I saw her. Esther was hanging around in the kitchen, looking at the group in the lounge from the kitchen. I vainly hoped she was looking for me.

I decided to take the next step, but was terrified. I was either going to be okay or totally rejected; at least nobody would see it. It all turned out okay. Now is the challenge to not mess it up. She is amazing.

The night of Jonah's party on the trawler was incredible. Esther transformed from a school kid into a gorgeous woman. That shiny dress was so tight, hugging her body, that I had to contain myself. I have wanted to be near her, touch and kiss her from the moment I had feelings for her but kept myself in check.

The moment sitting at the back of the trawler seemed perfect and private. I was shocked when I discovered she had not been kissed before, immediately feeling I should have waited and talked to her about it first, but thankfully she responded with the same feelings I have for her.

Feeling constant pain in my guts all the time and such strong feelings for Esther is starting to feel like torture and my head is not right most of the time. I try to focus but my mind drifts back to her. This is utterly ridiculous. Other people seem to cope okay.

The time out on the water has always helped me clear my head and get life into perspective. Like today. It is the time I feel closer to God, no distractions, even if it is just sitting looking out at the ocean and listening.

It is customary during longer trips, that the Skipper shares over a meal any safety issues and chats about some aspect of being healthy adults, inputting their experience and wisdom into it. It is usually short. It is a safe small group, made up of males and females, the majority being male Fishers. We are encouraged to chat about anything on our mind, no judgement. It is called trawler talk and the unwritten rule is that nothing leaves the trawler after the trawler talk.

When it is just Fishers the talk is about our faith and how to grow it through prayer and study. Abstinence before marriage comes up occasionally and it is helpful to hear how it is God's plan and why it works in building healthy relationships.

I noticed that when we have Town citizens on our crew the talks are modified with no faith mentioned. However, they listen intently to talks about relationships - maybe a different perspective to what they are used to.

When there are only Fishers on board and we have a longer time at sea, we learn from God's ancient writing smuggled onboard. We pray together and have teaching on Christian living, which is incredibly freeing as we cannot be so bold at home.

The bond between the Fishers on those trips is incredibly strong and positive. I often wonder if Jesus experienced this kind of mateship with his disciples. I always look forward to those trips; the atmosphere is light.

When I was a little younger it seemed awkward and uncomfortable to hear about safety, health, and relationships from your Skipper Dad or friends' Dads in a group. As time has gone on, I found listening to the talks helpful and comforting, especially as my feelings for girls shifted from friendship to more physical attraction.

Some of the older Fisher guys are blunt and admit how challenging it is to abstain from sex when all you want to do is be close to your girlfriend and sleep with them.

I have now arrived at a new crossroad. I am unsure what to do about my growing physical and romantic attraction to Esther and not stuff it up. I decide to seek out my older brother Matt who is really a mate; we have worked together for so long, so it is less awkward to talk to him about this stuff. He has been dating a Fisher girl, Elizabeth for ages.

After lunch, I find time on our current trip to lay out my situation. Matt is sworn to secrecy, no telling our parents or friends. We are teamed up at the back of the trawler for hours, the water washing over us every so often and the sea is rough today. In between busy moments I fill Matt in on my dilemma. As he pauses in his work, he grins widely, laughing loudly into the wind.

"Man, you are in *trouble,* you are in *love* and you have got it bad bro." He slaps me on the shoulder in a sympathetic understanding way.

"What am I supposed to do Matt? I'm *not* asking Dad."

"Simple, talk to her, she might feel the same. You decide together how the relationship is going to go; if you cannot agree, then you break up. Knowing how both our families look at relationships the answer is simple." Matt yells, over the noise of the ocean and trawler.

"Did you and Elizabeth do that?"

"Yep, *man* it was uncomfortable but at least we know what each of us is thinking and wants, it's all out in the open," Matt informs me.

"So, what did you decide Matt?"

"None of your dammed business bro, its private. Seriously, I get it, if your feelings are out of control, focus on work, hang out with Fisher guys more. Spend time focusing on God, not yourself. Be accountable and when that does not work jump into the ocean to cool off," Matt says, smiling good-naturedly.

That ended the conversation on a light note, even though it was tough.

It was surprisingly helpful and I suspect maybe like talking to my Dad. I am glad he deals with this stuff too; he is just older and ahead of me when it came to dating girls seriously. I suspect he may be talking from first-hand experience and had spoken to our Dad already to share such good advice. I never thought of Matt as a wise grown up.

For the rest of the trip, I think about my life and how I can be a guy who follows Jesus but still manage all these feelings for Esther, which I know are totally normal, challenging, and at times selfish too.

I am ready to commit my life to Jesus in front of our community, and I think a lot about what Esther and I talked about on the beach and what we had started talking about in her garden.

I am grateful for the time out here on the water. I needed space and have come to my decision after much thought and prayer, for when Esther and I meet up for dinner soon.

One thing I know for sure is that following Jesus is good, but it will take a lot of work and self-control impacting every part of my life.

CHAPTER 16

Searching for a restaurant on my slate that is not too fancy and affordable, I settle on a small Italian place, and it looks romantic. How would I know? I have never been to a restaurant.

I send Simon the details telling him I have missed him terribly. I have had many days to reflect on our relationship.

We have varied interests and work. We talk about God when I want to, and Simon patiently listens and answers my questions.

Our conversation seems to flow naturally. Simon listens mostly, which he seems happy with, and has shown he can cope when I am broken, especially when Paul passed.

Simon has revealed so much of himself and his character as our love has grown. Maybe I have not shared enough of myself?

I am snapped out of my reverie by Simon's message that he has missed me too. He just got off the trawler, and he writes he cannot wait to see me and eat something besides fish. He adds, "How fancy is this place?"

I reply, "Not that fancy, just wear something you can get pasta sauce on."

I head outside and water our huge garden and pull a few weeds enjoying the few moments in the morning sun. I shower quickly and rush to the bus riding to work hoping the day will go quickly. I am fortunately based at the local Medical Precinct today. No alerts for courier work yet.

Happily, I top up supplies, smiling at the patients and staff, knowing I will see Simon soon.

The staff have looks of disgust but at times they smile back despite themselves, happiness can be contagious. I even cruise on the back of the supply trolley up and down the corridors when no one is looking and stop suddenly remembering the security cameras are always watching.

I change water in the vases, which is truly disgusting, and it's a job left for me. Nothing is ruining my day, even stinky flower water. I return the flowers refreshed to the patients' delight.

"Hi, Esther, what's with the smile?" My mother notes my goofy smile.

"I'm taking Simon on a date tonight."

"Have fun, don't be too late," she says smiling

My day ends at lunch time. Taking the bus home conserves my energy, allowing me time to think about tonight. I rest my head on the window rehearsing my words in my head. I hear my name, realising it is James, he sits next to me.

"How's work going?" he asks kindly, noting my scrubs.

"Okay I guess, it's just work." He nods.

"Yep, same here, just finished another crappy half day. Would love some full days. Are you okay Esther? You seemed far away when I was calling you."

"Totally, I've got a date with Simon tonight."

"*Oh*, that's right Simon's been going on about it. Simon messaged me about what to wear. What's with that? He even got a haircut!" James laughs making me realise he is happy for us.

"Wow, he is taking this date very seriously, James."

"Esther, he is nuts about you, I've never seen him care so much about what a girl thinks." He indicates to the driver, waves, and jumps off.

Heading home from the bus I study until it's time to shower and dress for dinner. I select a medium length blue sleeveless dress that falls just below my knees. A simple design with hand stitched beads and sequins that forms a swirling pattern, almost like water, that shimmers in the light.

I dry my hair and leave it down, adding just a little makeup to my eyes and a touch of light pink lip gloss. The look is complete. Pulling on a white cropped cardigan I head out the door early to enjoy the night.

Stepping onto the bus, nobody lets me sit next to them, so I stand for the short trip heading to the town precinct, not caring. Wandering around the shops I stop for a freshly squeezed juice at a pop-up cart. Finding a quiet place to sit, I sip and observe the Town citizens come and go. I study my map to locate the restaurant and head off towards it, placing my keep cup in the collection station.

I walk carefully towards the restaurant along the narrow street with its old, cracked pavement. I follow my slate for directions then put it away as I glimpse its soft outside lighting. I approach the ornate door, and a tall man rushes to open the door for me. I look up and realise its Simon, like I have never seen him before. His new hair cut is very short, and on trend, and his tight black shirt and tailored charcoal black pants with a matching fitted jacket have transformed him into an even more handsome man.

"Hi Simon," I whisper, trying to hide my shock. He is hot!

We enter the small dark restaurant together, greeted by the aroma of baking bread and home cooking. A friendly middle-aged woman of Italian descent who seems to own the place immediately offers to take Simon's jacket. He gratefully rolls his sleeves up his forearms; she observed this and stares at his muscled tanned arms and calloused hands revealing he is not a Town or Elite member of the community.

Her demeanour changes from friendly to the warmth of a family member and leans towards Simon.

"Fisher or Farmer?" she whispers.

"Fisher," Simon whispers mirroring her.

She steps back with hands on her hips and looks hard at Simon for a moment.

"I know your Pappa Andrew, and your Mumma Rachael. You look just like him, you are not the serious one, Matthew, *no.* You are Simon, the charming cheeky one. You grow up. I am Mataya, you know me when you were little boy. I get my husband, Mario." She shouts out towards the kitchen across the tiny restaurant.

A smiling man wanders out casually wiping his hands on a small towel and looks expectantly at Mataya. She indicates Simon with her head.

"This is Fisher Andrew's boy, Simon." His face breaks out into an even wider smile and without the customary permission to touch he embraces Simon.

"Welcome to our little slice of paradise," Mario says, gesturing wildly at their cosy restaurant, which time passed it by in a charming way. Simon recovers quickly from his shock at being hugged by strangers, and he thanks them for having us.

"This is Esther." Simon quickly introduces me. I nod.

Mario puts his arm around Simon's shoulders and whispers loudly, "So, is this beautiful creature, your girlfriend? Is this a date?"

"Yes." Is all Simon can manage with increasing embarrassment turning red up to his blonde roots. The other guests have now turned to observe the commotion.

"Mataya, they go to our special table, *no* booth for Andrew's boy."

We are quickly ushered through the cluttered kitchen out back. We are then relieved of our slates and belongings, which are dropped immediately into a metal lidded box disguised as a basket and led into to a beautiful private walled garden away from prying eyes and ears and seated at a delightful round mosaic topped table set for two.

We are speechless, it's like we are caught up in an Italian tornado. Mario and Mataya stand back look at us smiling indulgently then look at each other and sigh, "Young love."

They leave us to browse the menu slates. Finally, we are alone. We sit, looking at each other, unsure of what to do. We have never experienced anything like it and not out in public.

Acceptance.

Simon reaches for my hands across the small table and looks at me smiling.

"I missed you, Esther."

"I missed you so much Simon. I cannot believe this place. It is so beautiful, it is kind of perfect." I squeeze his hand back.

I look around, taking in the vintage climbing roses, perfume just detectable, covering the walls on trellises carefully grown in pots, and a few herbs too. Fairy lights twinkle through the leaves and are strung above our heads creating a magical canopy of soft light.

We sit awkwardly again, then I ask about his latest fishing trip, and suddenly we are ourselves again, laughing about the silly things that happen in our work. We order; the young server keeps smiling at us like we are sweet puppies. Annoying!

We make our choices and the server finally leaves and I bravely dive in and bring up the discussion we planned. I blurt out to Simon, "I can't help it, I really like you, love you, want to be with you, but not *with you, with you* yet, I've never been with anyone and I want to be totally sure."

It tumbles out awkwardly. My face feels red hot and I feel nervous trembles take over my body. I look at him, Simon looks at me and listening intently, I see his shoulders relax and he breaths out slowly then smiles. Was that relief?

He moves his chair close to mine, looking into my eyes like he does, and reaches for my hands again.

"Me too, I'm here, to be completely honest too. I was so terrified you were going to break up with me, Esther. I know it is probably too early, maybe a bit scary to know how I feel but I want to be with you for a long time and get to know you more."

Simon reveals a small velvet bag from his trouser pocket retrieving a shiny intricately designed silver ring.

"Would you accept this commitment ring, Esther?" He asks nervously, his hands are trembling.

I just nod. He slides the ring on my right hand and holds it in place, running his thumb over the design, looking at it.

"If you look really close you will see a fish in the pattern, a secret symbol of early Christians. It's engraved there to remind you I'm committed to us and want to be kept accountable of how I treat you. I want to get it right, Esther. I don't want to stuff this up, I've never loved anyone before, it's totally new to me," he says quietly, in my ear.

I am sure my heartbeat changes its rhythm momentarily, witnessing Simon's vulnerability, his character, not just words. This is the deepest most serious discussion I have had in my life.

Terrified and exhilarated at the same time I hold my hand up to Simon to wait. I get up and open the hidden basket, search my bag, and retrieve a black leather band and come back and reach for Simon's hand, open it, and place it on his palm.

"This gift is my commitment to you, if you can put up with me."

Simon is visibly moved; it looks like three individual carefully braided leather straps separate but in fact it is woven together three into one strong band. I have seen many Farmers and Fishers wearing them and researched where to get one. Without hesitation, he carefully pulls it over his hand, gently stretching it until it gives and rests on his left wrist, knowing it is virtually impossible to remove as time and water tighten it to a perfect, permanent fit.

"Esther, thank you, this is such an incredibly personal gift. Do you know why we wear these?" I shake my head.

"I only know it's significant if you are a Christian."

"God the Father, God Son and God the Holy Spirit, three in one. It also symbolises God is our alpha and Omega, there is no beginning or end on this band," he whispers and points to each band.

"You're sure about us?" Simon asks. I nod, happy with my decision.

"I want to sit my exams, be free to share my life with you and see where it takes us."

We sit side by side holding hands lost in the moment. Simon embraces me tightly and whispers such sweet words of adoration in my ear. He releases his strong embrace then kisses me with great intensity and emotion, not caring that we are in public. I happily respond; I have missed his strong protective arms and touch.

Our meals arrive. We separate, embarrassed, realising the young server has been standing there for a few moments, fidgeting, unsure what to do, holding loaded plates with a young couple all over each other in the restaurant!

Mataya bustles past the server and puts the plates on the table, shooing the girl away.

"What would these silly Town kids know about romance, hey Simon?" She looks at him smiling and nodding approval of our public display.

Simon quickly agrees with her nodding, while discreetly trying to wipe my pink lip gloss off with a napkin. It is hilarious and embarrassing.

Alone again we laugh about the hot public moment and sample each other's meals, while enjoying the delicious creamy sauces and crusty bread. Simon happily wipes his plate clean with a crust of bread. We share a very rich chocolate desert, which ensures we are full.

We reluctantly gather our belongings, leave our garden oasis and head to the counter. Mario appears and I pay him, thanking him for their hospitality, adding that I love his garden. He tilts his head, looking at me.

"You are Farmer Mark and Ruth's, Esther. Yours and Simon's parents supply our restaurant. The best fresh food always!" He claps his hands.

We say goodbye to Mario and Mataya who embrace us like family. Mataya nudges me. "So handsome."

"*Too handsome,*" I reply. She nods, agreeing, laughing loudly.

We enter the street wanting to savour each other's company a little longer. We walk hand in hand very slowly under the fairy lights that zig zag across the narrow street towards a beautiful fountain in the centre of the restaurant precinct.

I talk, Simon listens, nodding occasionally and enjoying my chatter.

A Town guy walks directly up to us, *Jason*. He aggressively addresses me millimetres from my face. "What are you doing *here,* Farmer girl? Are you lost?" He does not stop, letting a trail of profane words spew out of his mouth.

Jason's obvious hatred of me is terrifying and openly displayed. Town citizens and several Law Enforcers do not react as they pass; they pause to watch the spectacle unfold. They hate us and do not intervene.

Jason looks at me, then Simon, who has remained perfectly still, but the tension in his body is visible.

"Good luck with that Farmer virgin, *Simon.* "His tone is harsh. I am in shock.

Simon straightens his broad shoulders, towering over Jason, arms stiffly by his sides and eyeballing him. Simon suddenly leans forward, whispers something to Jason and straights up again.

Surprisingly, Jason turns and walks away. Quickly.

"Coward," Simon mutters under his breath, smiling. Simon wraps his arms protectively around me.

"Are you okay baby?" he whispers. I nod; I surprise myself by not crying.

"Was that Jason the jerk from school, Esther?" Simon asks, containing his anger. Just.

"He's nobody."

I walk quickly towards the fountain, pulling Simon along. We stop and stare at the abstract fountain for a long moment.

"You're so strong," Simon says looking at me, running a hand gently down the length of my hair then resting it gently on my shoulder.

I insist on taking a candid photo of us in front of the sparkling, illuminated fountain to remember the special night and one when Simon dressed up. I am secretly glad I do not have to share him tonight. He looks gorgeous. We walk reluctantly towards the private transport hub. Simon directs me to a bench seat.

"Esther, we need to talk about what just happened back there with that jerk." He holds both my hands firmly.

"No, we don't." I avert my eyes.

"Yes, we do. How that guy behaved and spoke to you, and even me, was so disgusting and disrespectful, it burns me up. When you are ready will you tell me about that guy?"

Simon looks serious. I look down at my shoes listening - he really is fired up.

"I love you, all of you - the whole Esther package. I'm here to be with you. I respect your decisions, every decision, that's one of the things I love about you. You are strong and make hard decisions. You helped me realise that's important. I deal with that kind of Town crap all the time; all of us younger Fisher and Farmer guys do.

"The Town guys, their talk on the wharf is disgusting. They deliberately humiliate us in front of everyone about waiting and being virgins. We Fishers stick together at work and when we go out, it is easier. The older Fisher guys keep an eye on us, telling us those Town guys will never know the love of a truly good woman. Their loss. They say it like being with their wives is the best thing in the world, which is encouraging."

I look up at him and see his face relax again, such gentleness in his face looking back at me and feeling the weight of his words. He puts his arm around me, pulling me close.

"Jason is from school, he beat us all up regularly, me mainly. Remember my bruises months ago at the river? How come you can talk about this hard stuff, Simon?"

He looks shocked but relieved that I shared this with him.

"I don't usually talk about personal stuff, but *everything good* is worth fighting for."

I get up, reluctant to head home via private transport, as I head towards a waiting transport. I hold his hand and gently tug him towards me.

"Simon, come with me." Simon is unsure, resisting.

"You are all in, aren't you?"

"*Yes,*" he says slowly.

"Then it's time to tell my parents together. They do not want to be the last to know about our commitment."

As we sit in the back of the transport, Simon entwines his fingers with mine.

"I haven't been with anyone," Simon whispers in my ear.

I turn and look right at him, surprised at his revelation. My heart skips.

"Esther, it's true, but can I be honest, I can't wait."

I look at his cheeky grin and realise this is a whole lot of honesty that I was not prepared for and have no clue what to do with. We exit the transport walking down the driveway to find a familiar truck in the driveway.

"Oh *crap!*" Simon mutters under his breath.

I laugh. As we open the door, we immediately hear our parents chatting in the lounge room. We stand quietly in the kitchen feeling awkward, as we are unsure what to do when my mother appears.

"Here they are, two of you, what a lovely surprise!" my mother exclaims.

We look at each other. We are invited in and made to squish in the middle of them. Surrounded, they ask about the fancy restaurant. The mothers fuss and get excited about how good we look together and wanting to know what we ate, what the restaurant was like and did we take a lot of close-up pictures. We tell them we met Mataya and Mario; they look happy that we supported their friends' little business.

Simon manages to get a word in when there is a natural lull. "We have something to tell you, we made a commitment, to each other, not a commitment to a union," he points out very clearly.

There is a short silence as they process the revelation then they erupt into a scene of great joy, our parents are so happy for us. I show my parents the ring and his parents too. They are impressed by his leather wrist band. They can see we had both really thought about it, and this seems to have impressed them the most.

As it is late it's decided Simon will ride home with his parents. He grabs my hand and drags me into the pantry He kicks the door shut, and I stop still laughing and see him standing with his eyes closed leaning back, his head resting on a shelf breathing slowly. I stop laughing, he opens his eyes and wraps his arms tightly around me, his chin gently resting on my head. We stand still. After a long, quiet moment, he kisses me slowly, not wanting to end it, then looks down at me.

"I wanted this night to end as perfectly as it started, not like there's a carnival in town," Simon says disappointedly.

I nod, understanding why he was disappointed that everyone is here; he had wanted to savour our special night. We move back into the kitchen and head out to the driveway to say goodbye. He kisses me on the cheek and gives me one of his long looks before jumping in the back.

My parents say very little, choosing to remain in the cool air, holding hands, and chatting to each other as I say goodnight, heading for bed.

I carefully hang up my beautiful dress, running my hands over the detail and smiling, recalling when Simon slipped the ring on my finger in the garden. I climb into bed, kick my pink bunny off and look closely at the design on my ring and get excited when I find the fish hidden in the swish and swirl of the engraving. A treasure worth searching for. I switch off my light.

These are precious memories I do not want to share. Not yet anyway.

CHAPTER 17

My slate beeps. I scroll. There are no new laws today, no shifts until next week. What is this! The HSC exam timetable and confirmation required.

I forward the dates to the roster manager and HR; they reply quickly and have approved the dates for the exams. I am grateful that part of my childhood will be over soon.

"Hey anyone want to head into the city tomorrow for an overnighter and crash with the guys?" An incoming message from Simon, and James is included.

"I'm in, chat later?" I reply drifting off to sleep again.

"Simon invited James and I to stay in the city with Lizzy, Isaiah and Mark at their place." I inform my mother who has awakened me stroking my hair. I am smart enough to mention Lizzy.

"Esther, remember you are the youngest, it will be a nice break. I am so proud of you sitting the exams. Can you help me sort food for hungry Uni students and with a few chores before you go to the city?" I nod, waking fully, rise making a big coffee and green smoothy.

Enjoying a rare day together, we put on a good mix of music, which lifts the mood. We work well as a team, dividing up the chores.

We pack fresh veggies, fermented, and pickled also, as they last longer. Loading up the cooking pot we set it to reduce a mountain of veggies into a delicious sauce that can make any meal come alive.

After sanitising our family's clothes, we have tea and chocolate slice then pack my bag, time to have fun.

Calling Sarah and Ruby, I beg them to come over and help me pack after school. They agree and appear at my door looking excited. Throwing up my hands I admit I need guidance what to pack, Simon sent a list. Ruby scans it, throwing my slate on the bed with a wicked grin.

"I know exactly what to pack for an awesome city escape." We laugh; Ruby is in her element. She flings open my wardrobe, moves the hangers around, and presents Sarah and me with her final selections to decide on.

"Esther, day one, commuting and hanging out."

Ruby points to my Town style jeans, cute pink t-shirt, and white hoodie with silver details I keep for city travel. She points to my slip-on joggers in near new condition. Giving Ruby a thumbs up she hangs the clothes on the front of the wardrobe.

"Every girl needs a fabulous outfit if the opportunity arises to party!" Ruby holds my hidden black jeans with a hint of shimmer that I have saved for a special occasion. Sarah pounces on them.

"Esther! These are gorgeous, put them on."

I grudgingly put them on.

"Ruby, hurry up." Sarah insists that Ruby choose a top.

My mother pokes her head around the door at the commotion and surveys the room. Leaving a medium sized wheely bag just inside the door, and satisfied she moves on.

Ruby holds a silky black sleeveless top that exposes my shoulders, insisting I try it on. It slides over my body skimming my hips and teamed with my jeans it elevates the look to chic perfect for going out in the city. Looking at my feet, she holds a pair of flat black strappy sandals encrusted with tiny rhinestones I got on sale. Sarah hits me with a pillow.

"Esther, you secretive beast. Ruby, why not heels, Esther's got a pair?"

"Who knows how far she may have to walk, It's not great if you can't walk because your feet hurt and your man has to carry you." Sarah and I nod taking in these tips.

Ruby digs through my jewellery box producing a silver bracelet that wraps around your arm in a long spiral. She slides it up my arm and pulls my hair out of the messy ponytail instructing, 'shake.' My dark brown hair falls softly, resting on my shoulders.

Looking in the mirror, I see how skintight the jeans are. The top skimming my hips brings the outfit back to modest and classy. I nod at the mirror satisfied.

"Okay change, Esther." I pull on my sweats again, hugging Ruby gratefully. I complete my packing while chatting to Sarah and Ruby who are desperate to get details about the date.

Waggling my ring causes them to go crazy. "This is *huge* Esther," Sarah whispers in awe.

"It's just a friendship ring." Ruby looks puzzled. Sarah grabs Ruby's arm.

"*No,* this is Simon making a move, saying he is totally committed to Esther, it is like a promise. Guys only give a ring like this when they are totally in love with you and are seriously *courting* you…"

Sarah looks at me, seeing tears in my eyes. "He's in love with you Esther…" Sarah says slowly.

"I'm in love with him too," I tell them emotionally.

My friends head home to study insisting I keep them updated. I am excited about tomorrow. This is the break I have needed.

* * *

Waking early, I shower, dress, and eat a huge breakfast of eggs on toast and a green smoothy. I scroll on my slate, lots of new petty laws, but none to concern me thankfully - lots about pets though.

The bus arrives promptly; a guy jumps out in a black hoodie, it's James. "I thought you may need help, so I got on earlier." I am grateful as he easily carries my bag for me. So thoughtful.

We fill the aisle with our bags. The town citizens throw angry insults the whole trip. James is a great example of how you can be angry on the inside but look perfectly unaffected on the outside.

James wears a mask of indifference, looking out the window. He is practiced at handling abuse on the bus. I am not. I see tensed muscles in his hands as I smile to myself. You cannot hide emotions completely.

Thankfully, we arrive at the station intact. James lifts my bag in one effortless movement. We roll along to the gate and hover our slates, looking for Simon who is waiting on the Sydney City side platform. He kisses my cheek shyly, whispering, "Good morning beautiful."

Simon thanks James for helping me, and he just shrugs. The train arrives, and we sit near the entrance away from other citizens, our large bags on luggage racks. Simon and James sit next to each other and compete for the worst job ever. Simon always wins with the phrase fish guts; we groan in disgust.

I read Emily the Zombie Slayer book on my slate. She is really a badass, currently chasing zombies along the top of the Sydney City harbour bridge slaying them, then tossing them into the harbour from great heights. I look out the window as the towns pass in blurred colour, knowing we will travel over the real harbour bridge soon.

Law Enforcers appear in full uniform, their eyes only visible through their protective glasses as they work their way through the carriage checking slates for fares and trouble. Their terrifying presence fills the carriage.

Two heavily armed male Enforcers stand uncomfortably close to James and Simon, demanding they pull back their hoodies. They are ordered to show paid fares - not satisfied, they order them to stand up. They do obediently, keeping their eyes down, the Enforcers demand to know their destination and the contents of their bags. Simon and James, answer honestly.

Their faces show indifference. The Enforcers, still not satisfied, pull their bags off the luggage racks, lay them down on the floor and open them in front of a few citizens watching. The Enforcers examine every item thoroughly, even the linings of the bags, every conceivable part.

Their humiliating search is unsuccessful. Grabbing Simon and James, they throw them with all their strength against the steel wall that their faces impact so loudly. I hear the bang and overhear whispers of vile expletives including words Fishers and Farmers as they roughly search them.

Simon and James receive a final shove into the wall as the Enforcers walk off. My heart is racing, I feel nauseous; this is such a jolt into reality snapping me out of my naivety. I have never witnessed this level of prejudice before, never so violent, so public. I have miraculously evaded this treatment delivering my packages for the CEOs.

James and Simon shake off the event, smooth their hair and clothing, rub their faces, and look at each other grimly. Jumping up I help them repack quickly.

"Are you okay?" I whisper.

They nod, putting a finger on their lips. You cannot complain or the surveillance cameras will notify the law, or AI will hear through our slates. We sit and all the citizens move immediately deeper into the carriage.

I throw my arms around Simon's neck, he pulls me onto his lap and holds me close, and I rest my head on his shoulder trying not to cry. His body is rigid, despite his outward indifference, he is very, very angry.

James appears the same. I slip off Simon's lap, as it is not appropriate, and sit next to him, reaching for his hand. We all sit lost in our own thoughts.

The city is announced. We shift into the present, once clear of Sydney City Terminal without a stop and search, Simon audibly exhales. "Let's go and hang out with decent people, I'm sick of this crap." We grab donuts and coffee to share, a treat for broke Uni students.

We walk the long blocks into the older part of Sydney City. We arrive at the apartment building via the elevator to the tenth floor, revealing a long corridor of dull grey concrete.

We are greeted by our friends erupting noisily from the end unit, eagerly assisting with the coffee and donuts, and chatting the whole time.

We are recharged with their positive energy as we enter the small unit. Lizzy shows me where we will sleep in the loungeroom. Their only bedroom is a study/ storage room stacked with clothing racks, suitcases, boxes, and cushions.

Simon and James unpack, handing over food and clothing. Lizzy asks me to help her store the food in their tiny kitchen.

Lizzy sees me looking at the clothing, she explains that it is exchanged amongst them, so when they go to Uni, it looks like they have new clothes. This helps them blend on campus. Their hair styles are conservative Town styles, like mine, just enough to fly under the radar.

Observing this and the events on the train remind me this is our life. At any moment we can be discovered, endangering our communities and ourselves.

"What's with the frowny face? It's going to be okay Esther. I will keep you safe." Simon says smiling as he wraps his arms around me tightly and kisses me like we are the only ones in the room.

There is cheering from the friends - how embarrassing. Simon shrugs it off, grabs my hand, and pulls me out the door running down the corridor dragging me along, I laugh at his spontaneity. He kicks open the door to the stairs dramatically and pulls me inside.

Simon gently presses me against the wall, his hands gently cupping my face and proceeds to kiss me slowly with great emotion. His hands sliding slowly down my arms to my hips wrapping them around my waist pulling me close. I willingly submit, my heart is racing, and I redirect his lips that are moving down my neck back to mine, then slowly breaking the moment before more heat, moving his hands to hold mine.

Simon looks at me with so much intensity. It is hard to break this moment, but I want to. I am *not* going to be intimate in a stair well, and *not* at this moment in our relationship.

"*Simon.* Communicate with me, when you are kissing me like *that* it felt like you want to go further …*do you*?" I ask gently to break the moment and cool down.

"Thank you, Esther, you are right. I need to communicate, and yes, I *do* want to be with you *one* day. You know how I feel about you. In that moment I wanted to be close to you," he whispers.

Simon leads me by the hand down the stairs to the basement carpark. He has regained control after descending ten floors.

Simon opens the door that leads into the basement and stands in front of a locked garage. He punches in a code, the automatic door rolls up to reveal two double transport vehicles charging, and four sets of leathers hanging neatly with rows of boots lined up underneath. In the corner swags are stacked.

"Simon how come you have a code?"

He answers by jumping onto the sleek black transport next to a shiny blue one smiling. "Because James and I bought this second hand. Nobody knows except our friends, who use it and store it, the other one they own together."

I look at Simon, surprised and so attracted to him. I walk over and turn his face to me and ask, "Okay?" He nods and I kiss him with heat. He thankfully acts as a grown up this time jumping off and wraps me in his arms nuzzling into my hair.

"*Man*, it is getting harder to resist you, Esther."

"I know how you feel."

"Really! do you feel a bit tortured like me?"

"Yes, I am human, you looked so *fine* sitting on that transport. Let's have a word or a sign so we can be fully in control of our *feelings*." I laugh, trying to break the tension.

Simon stands back, looking at me smiling, with his arms crossed. "Hmm, great plan, like tapping out when you wrestle your brothers."

"Exactly, how about two taps or the word…"

Simon jumps in, "anchor."

"Done, seems very appropriate for a Fisher." I shake his hand like closing a deal.

"How about I take you for a ride later, you and Lizzy are similar in size. I am sure she would lend her gear to you."

"Sure." I smile to myself, it will not be long, and I will be able to ride too.

"Esther, let's take the elevator this time, there's no way I'm walking up all those stairs."

We arrive back and stow the swags in the bedroom. Everyone is sitting on cushions scattered on the floor chatting in a circle.

"Now you have returned, *apparently* getting swags," Isaiah says, grinning.

"We are discussing the party we're having here tonight with our Uni friends. We can use the space outside our door too…" Isaiah continues his conversation.

"What food have we got to spare for tonight?" He turns to Lizzy.

Lizzy looks at her slate, and I see a list of food and quantities.

"I think Mexican is the go. We can make food go further thanks to these guys saving the day with lettuce, tomatoes, cauliflower and chillis."

"Awesome," Isaiah says.

"Mark, you can sort the music and lights. Simon and James, you can come with me to get the keg I ordered, it is getting dropped off soon. Esther, none for you, you are underage." He is suddenly serious.

"Us three," indicating Lizzy Mark and himself. "Will, take turns being bouncer and look after the drinks out front as we know the crowd coming.

Everyone must help Lizzy and Esther with food prep, purely to prove we are not useless mammas' boys. Party kicks off at 6pm, let's get prepping," Isaiah says, like a game show host.

Lizzy and I make a list of anything we need from the downstairs market, I decide to make it my contribution to crashing at their place - Lizzy graciously accepts.

"We have a study meeting here tomorrow at ten too so we can double prep today and get the guys doing most of the work, then we can sleep in," Lizzy says with a wink.

I have always liked Lizzy's fun spirit. She is a genius making food stretch.

"Simon mentioned you know about study groups, so are you okay to stay for our study group?" She looks at me intently. I catch on.

"Totally, prepping for my final exams so any help would be great." She smiles, glad her message was clear; someone is always listening.

Lizzy directs the guys on how to food prep in the kitchen, which they are delighted with, as it involves using knives.

In between imaginary sword fights with knives and tea towels with intermittent yelps of pain, we assemble bowls of shredded salads, salsas, and cauliflower for spicy cauliflower rice.

We store it in the cooler, then we lay out bowls of shredded vegetables ready for when Lizzy and I return from the market downstairs to prepare the rice paper rolls.

I grab my slate, throwing the strap across my body. We leave the unit with shopping bags filled with our keep containers and repurpose bags. The elevator shudders down the ten floors to the market next door.

We enter the tiny space. It is the only way to buy food if you do not order meals or grow it yourself in the city, as so few people cook. Lizzy guides us to corn chips and is undecided.

"The price per kilo is so high today!" She is exasperated.

"Don't worry, I got a bonus last week. I'm happy to share my good fortune."

I scoop up enough to fill a large repurpose bag we have. Wow, the lie just popped out of my mouth.

"You're sure, Esther?"

"Yep, positive."

I head to fresh food and see cooked shredded chicken in the deli. I ask for several kilos passing over one of Lizzy's keep containers marked *meat-chicken.* There will be enough for another day.

I look carefully for what is on sale or marked down. Spotting brownie mixes marked down big time I grab some. I send Lizzy off to grab us a sneaky treat; I want to hide my generosity.

Paying for the items I carry the bags outside and see her waiting with two single chocolate ice-creams. We sit on a bench away from the crowds.

She asks me how work is going and I ask Lizzy about Uni. She is studying science, a three-year course. Lizzy asks me how Simon and I are going like a big sister, nudging my shoulder with hers.

I pause to think of a response and lick my melting treat.

"Really great," I say, smiling, showing her my ring. She nods.

"If he doesn't treat you right, he knows we will kill him." She laughs.

"So, how is the *romance*?" she asks, looking at me unblinking. I feel trapped, blushing.

"Mm, *that* good. Must be as if he has given you a commitment ring. This is huge Esther!"

"I know Lizzy," I sigh, grateful to talk to an older girl who has dated.

"Have you guys done it?" Lizzy asks casually. I almost choke.

"That's so personal!"

"Not really, particularly if you need some guidance on the matter. Looking at your face and how obsessed Simon is, I say not. That is good." She pats me on the arm.

She sits back and finishes her ice cream in silence for a moment then shares.

"Waiting to build your relationship is good, abstaining long term though, that is a challenge. Trust me, the longer you go out, you will realise there is only two paths and sadly I took the easy one briefly, ages ago and regretted it. That ended the relationship. No respect, he just wanted sex. I am waiting for the right one. You need to set boundaries, like using the app."

I just sit eating my ice-cream digesting what she said, so little and so much. I have never heard any girl speak so directly about intimacy in relationships. I needed this.

Lizzy talks about the party and friends. Some are Farmer and Fisher, but it will be hard to tell; the rest are an eclectic mix. She expands a little on the types of relationships some of her Uni friends are in. I just listen, taking in all this new information trying to digest it.

"Esther, our friends are easy going. Some of them may want to hook up with you, but just say you're with Simon, then they'll back off, they're totally cool." I am positive I have entered unknown territory.

"Esther, stop daydreaming, time to get prepping. Well, the guys anyway, Ha ha."

We arrive back, producing chicken to add to the rice paper rolls. I offer to make brownies in their cooker while they make the rolls.

Everyone sits around the table talking and rolling while I busily make a huge slab of brownies. I put the extra chicken for tonight's dinner in the fridge; we need to add some protein to this Mexican feast.

While the brownies are cooking, I sit on a comfy cushion next to Simon.

"Esther, I am so glad you got chicken, I love fish, but man do I get tired of it," Simon whispers.

We sit happily working side by side, enjoying the closeness and the ease of being with adult friends. Being here I realise I am wanting to go to Uni.

The cooker beeps, and I grab the brownies out; they are bubbling.

"How did they turn out?" Simon calls out.

"Hot, gooey and so, so sweet like you." Simon is so embarrassed, especially when everyone makes a puking sound.

I sit down again, and Simon leans over and gives me a peck on the cheek. We pack the rice paper rolls away ready for tomorrow. Lizzy stands with her hands on her hips declaring, "If anyone eats any before the study group, they are truly dead."

CHAPTER 18

Isaiah flings open the door. BANG! He is breathless.

"*Crap*, the law is coming to our floor. I did the stairs. Lizzy. Mark we good?" he whispers.

"GOOD," they reply. Almost rehearsed.

He gives a thumbs up, bending over, hands on his knees, trying to quickly regain his breath. We stand frozen.

Mark calmly deals out a deck of cards quickly around the coffee table, and he points for us to sit and play.

We sit playing, not questioning. We hear the commotion. Door after door in the corridor is pounded on, entry is forced and the occupants plead their innocence, including the elderly on this floor. Everyone is treated equally, of course, some are dragged into the corridor.

Words echo down the corridor. It is terrifying and excruciating to listen to. Our group keeps playing and we jump as we hear the pounding on each door, which intensifies as the Enforcers come closer. Simon holds me tight.

"Follow my lead okay," he whispers. I try to remain calm.

Isaiah stands behind the door waiting to open it, and he indicates with his hands to pray. Our door is pounded like the others. This time it is deafening.

Isaiah takes a breath, opens the door calmly and waits for orders.

Enforcers demand immediate entry and have authority to enter on a slate shoved into Isaiah's face. He opens the door fully to reveal a room full of young adults playing cards and the room smells like brownies. He steps back to allow them to enter with no expression on his face.

The four Law Enforcers enter. They are heavily armed in full combat gear with rifles filling the space, their faces are concealed except for their piercing eyes through full face shields.

Two proceed to forcibly drag us out into the corridor. They shove our faces hard against the wall, while yelling at us. The leader reads out some long-complicated order from their slate and announces, "We will search you and your property."

Two remain with rifles covering us. The other two aggressively search the flat, revealing nothing to their utter frustration.

I look at everyone lined up, their heads resting against the wall. I get a sense this happens regularly, which sickens and terrifies me. I see their lips moving soundlessly. They are all praying. Incredible. So strong in their faith despite this nightmare going on around us.

The Law Enforcers reappear and proceed to question each of us: "Who are you? Show your identity." They turn each of us around one at time and undertake detailed body searches.

Simon and I will be last. Simon senses my terror.

"Look at your ring, focus on it," he says gently, then rests his forehead against the wall and is still looking down, except for praying.

I slide my ring off and stare at it, turning it in the light marvelling at the detailed engraving. I just manage to capture in the dim light of the corridor an inscription inside, faith-love-hope; I slide it back on and search for the fish, feeling calmer, focused.

The Enforcers approach Simon, ordering him to turn around. He turns, indicating to me with his head, speaking in a tone that is cold and hard, "Don't touch her, she's a minor." I stand with my head still against the wall not moving a muscle. They tell him to shut up and proceed to search Simon roughly then they move onto me and tell me to turn around.

They check my slate to confirm my details, nod, and keep moving. We all stand in a row waiting and looking down. I see the neighbours peeking out to see what is taking the Enforcers so long to leave.

The captain of the Enforcers vomits lines of expletives screaming, "Just another stupid group of broke kids. Where is this bloody group holed up? I am gunner find those religious freaks if it literally kills me." He looks at Isaiah.

"Isaiah, I'm watching you, slippery snake. Don't think for one minute that fancy law degree will ever save you, if you ever get it, *Fisher*."

With his head, he indicates to the team sharply to leave. They follow in his angry wake single file to the end of the corridor; the leader angrily punches the elevator button waiting. They have left a monstrous mess in the unit. Nothing has been left in its place, including food.

Isaiah looks shaken but okay. We follow him into the unit, and he grabs an Esky bag and shuts the door. He indicates for us to put our slates in it, then he zips it up and puts it in the bathroom and turns on the exhaust fan and shuts the door.

He returns and turns on the exhaust fan in the kitchen too and proceeds to whisper quickly to Lizzy and Mark. "Well, that was terrifying. We are so close to being locked up it's crazy." He runs his hands through his short hair agitated. Pacing.

Lizzy looks upset and goes to the bedroom to tidy up - James follows. I hear them packing everything away; we all clean up. Mark shuts off the exhaust fans now the discussion is over.

Simon puts his arms out, I gratefully sink into them, strong and steady. He checks I am okay.

"I'm a bit shaky, thank you for helping me, Simon," I whisper.

"We're stronger together," he reassures me.

"Are we still having this hang out?" Mark asks Isaiah.

"You better believe it! I'm gunner get so drunk tonight, I'm sick of this crap and constantly being violated by some ugly Enforcer. They touch me up so much they should buy me dinner first," he rants.

Isaiah's rant goes on for several minutes, using a string of disgusting crass phrases that would make our *mammas mad.* We all stand and watch him vent, his arms flailing about wildly, he is so crass and I wince at every word, but it strangely fits the situation. The language is truly disgusting.

Simon has been standing quietly, leaning against the kitchen counter, arms folded and watching this ridiculous scene with a small smile dancing on his lips. He starts to laugh out loud without restraint.

"So let me get this right, Isaiah, you're going to get drunk on the smallest keg in the world - good luck mate." It is so unexpected that we all laugh too.

"*Man,* you are hilarious when you are scared and angry. If we were back home on the trawler, I would have chucked you overboard to cool off by now," Simon continues.

Isaiah relaxes, throws his hands up, laughing so hard he runs to the balcony door, flings it wide open and is sick over the railing. He keeps laughing so hard it happens again, and again.

"How is your aim Isaiah, did you get those evil Enforcers? Is there any carrot?" Mark yells out laughing.

We are all laughing now with tears in our eyes.

He staggers back in from the balcony, weak from the emotional and physical roller-coaster. He lays on a pile of cushions and wipes his streaming eyes and his mouth on the back of his hand.

"I need water, water, all I can taste is spew," he calls out like a pampered prince.

"That's what you said first time on our family trawler, one minute out, at sixteen," Simon shoots back.

Everyone loses it again, knowing its true.

"Shut up, Allen, that is a big fat lie. I lasted at least an hour." Isaiah holds his sides. I grab a glass of water and I bring it over to him. He sips it gratefully, smiling.

"Thanks, Esther, at least you care."

I look for Lizzy and James in the bedroom, ready to help clean up and then back away quickly from the doorway. She and James are kissing against the wall, like they know each other, very, very well. There is heat in that room. I am in shock. I have never seen James show any attraction to any local girls; this explains a lot.

Back in the kitchen I offer brownies in a loud voice. James and Lizzy appear minutes later with armfuls of cushions, informing us they have sorted the bedroom and the bathroom. They smoothly sail into the lounge room, casually stacking the cushions in a corner.

"Right, I messaged my mate Pete and he's on his way to fix the cooling unit."

Isaiah indicates talk carefully with his finger on his lips and waves his hands, indicating the whole flat could be listening now.

We hear a gentle knock on the door half an hour later. Isaiah greets a young guy in overalls carrying a toolbox. They embrace and Pete gets more details about the cooling unit.

"So, when did it start making a noise?"

"About half an hour ago, I didn't want it to disturb us as it's annoying," Isaiah informs him.

"Righto," Pete mutters, then proceeds to shoo us out of the unit.

Isaiah leads us down to the basement via the elevator. We are silent until we arrive and stand waiting for Isaiah to speak. He whispers that he has been informed if they do a full raid on your house, Enforcers usually plant listening devices too. Apparently five is the maximum in a small place. We all look alarmed at Isaiah. He shrugs.

"I'm studying law. It comes up in conversations at Uni and I listen, trying to work out what's going on in the government so I can stay safe, so we can stay safe. Some of the Elite and Town students are so dumb that they shoot their mouths off sharing stuff they hear at home from their parents.

They have no idea what is really going on out there. So, we have Pete, I met him at a study group across town. He is studying technology and has rigged up devices to pick up listening and recording devices copying the government's design. Hopefully he is successful. Lizzy, we must pay him in food and goods, can you sort it?" She nods.

We stand for a while in silence, not moving, then see a head pop out of the basement door. Pete wanders over.

"Your cooling unit had five issues. I've sorted them out. Every room in your place had an issue, but the lounge room has the most."

We just listen to this shorthand and pick up very quickly that five devices were found. Isaiah directs us all back upstairs; Lizzy makes up a container of food and finds several other items, such as new toiletries. Pete says goodbye and quietly closes the door behind him.

"We must be super careful, say nothing stupid, just talk about our usual crap, especially around our Uni friends, they are a mixed bunch." We all respond like replying to a sports coach.

"James, Simon come with me, the keg is arriving any minute downstairs. Let's go."

They head out, the rest of us rearrange the coffee tables for snacks and dinner against the wall, and Lizzy grabs another small table to put in the hall for the drinks and the keg. She stands back happy, there's plenty of room for dancing.

We arrange our bowls of food. Our Mexican buffet is ready, the room feels cosy and the aroma of spices fills the air.

I put some brownies out for tonight on a plate and store the rest in the bedroom ready for the study group. I also grab the party outfit I packed. Showering quickly, I dress and brush my hair, smoothing it into a dark, silky sheet.

Lizzy looks stunning in a dress that shimmers and hugs her body like a second skin. Her hair is swept up high in a messy bun which highlights her dramatic makeup. She is transformed. She admires my bracelet and loans me long silver earrings that match perfectly.

"Now you're ready," she grins.

The keg arrives with Simon carrying it. They disappear, shower, and change quickly, reappearing in Town style attire too. Looking incredible. Lizzy and I look at each other, impressed.

Mark turns the music on, tests the lights he has temporarily set up and opens the front door to greet the colourful, loud friends arriving. They are just like us, either working, studying or doing both.

We only have a small keg; it is obvious our group does not need much alcohol. The noise is rising and the room is alive with laughing, and dancing bodies moving to beats that have everyone on the floor, forgetting their troubles. I am enjoying this vibe; we are free from the law for a moment to have fun.

I head to the bathroom after waiting ages. It is a moment's respite from the noise. As I am washing my hands and running a brush through my hair, I notice a basket on the bench full of colourful packets of condoms.

I pause my brushing, confronted with the reality of the world, and realise I am in fact in the world. I exit quickly for the next person waiting.

Moving with difficulty back into the noisy swirling space I grab a cool drink from the balcony, leaning on the rail as I sip. I cool down in the evening breeze while observing Simon's friends, Mark, and Isaiah, hot and heavy with some girls in the shadows. I see James and Lizzy slip away for brief moments, and covertly return and separate.

I wander back inside. While I am dancing with a group, I observe Simon, who is gorgeous, leaning against the wall. He is chatting to some town friends with a beer in his hand looking totally relaxed and at ease. I see him searching, he finds my eyes, smiles, looks directly at me, holding his gaze with those piecing, blue eyes and inclining his head. It is evident he is not listening but totally focused on me. I smile back at him, enjoying the flirtation.

We are transfixed.

We eventually break our gaze, and I turn my attention back to the people around me. They invite me to eat with them in a corner sitting on cushions. I chat and dance with Lizzy and her friends; there is barely room to move, which makes the atmosphere come alive. We sing at the top of our lungs, bumping into each other, which is hilarious. Everyone is laughing, some a little drunk or high, I suspect.

Several of Lizzy's friends whisper in my ear that they like me and want to hook up. I tell them I am exclusively with Simon, pointing to him across the room. They nod, smiling, it's totally okay.

"*Damm girl*, he's fine," some say far too enthusiastically.

I am sure Simon gets hit on, all the time.

Mark has dropped the volume of his mix as we edge closer to noise curfew, the soft lights illuminate this tiny space. He is very talented; his mixes transform the atmosphere. Everyone's dancing or cooling off on the balcony.

I dance with my arms above my head, my eyes closed, lost in the moment, swaying to the music. Free!

I feel strong familiar hands slide slowly down my arms all the way down to my waist giving me goosebumps. Simon's arms wrap around my waist, pulling me close. I lower my hands, resting them on top of his, and we sway to the music. His signature cologne just detectable in this crowded space.

Simon leans over my shoulder and whispers in my ear. "Help me, Esther, call the fire brigade, you are so, so hot. I'm burning up!"

I laugh out loud, yelling as he kisses my exposed neck and shoulders. "Anchor, Anchor, Anchor."

CHAPTER 19

The party clean up involves many bowls and cups to wash up. I am envious of the previous generations who had disposable ones.

Disposable, one-use items are forbidden unless for medical purposes. We must reuse or recycle everything. Any waste is tracked and charged heavily for by the government.

We head for bed very late. Lizzy sets us up on the opposite side of the room to the guys.

Simon sweetly kisses me good night and falls asleep in his clothes quickly on top of his swag, all the guys do. Lizzy and I shower removing our makeup and then change, whispering in the bathroom like sisters.

We snuggle deep into our swags and sleep until Lizzy's alarm wakes us.

"Up, study group in one hour."

We arrange the lounge area. I watch fascinated as everyone sets up the cushions for maximum capacity in a crescent, even Simon and James. I wonder how often they come here.

The coffee table remains on the balcony for food. A small space in front of the balcony door has been reserved for the study leader to talk.

Mark leaves the unit for reconnaissance and reports no sign of the law, returning with four sets of transport boots in hand. He sits calmly on the floor removes socks from the tops of each pair and proceeds to pull out paper packaging and flattens it out. The others jump in and help, as they smooth out the bundles of bound paper, revealing pages of carefully handwritten notes in ink compiled into small notebooks. They stack them, placing heavy bowls on top to flatten them. I am a spectator, unsure of what is going on. I feel scared, deeply uncomfortable knowing it is illegal ancient writings about God.

Lizzy asks Isaiah who the study leader is today.

"We never know until they show up. Who wants to grab some study before the others come?" Isaiah asks.

There is a quiet knock on the door, and Isaiah opens it slowly, letting two girls in. One heads straight to Mark who embraces her, and they sit sharing a book. I barely recognise her and the other girl from last night who were wrapped around the guys. Today they are dressed in jeans, t-shirts, and old joggers.

Isaiah hugs his girl tightly at the door and kisses her so gently. Everyone teases them as they are so sweet together. They separate and find a corner to read in together.

They all reach for different notebooks, Simon grabs a notebook that says 'Romans', and takes my hand and settles us in a corner on cushions. He puts his finger on his lips.

"Let's study together." Simon proceeds to open the notebook.

We start reading quietly together. This small book of the ancient writings was handwritten in ink by a very patient and neat writer. I struggle a little to read it as I have only ever read typed text on a slate and the occasional note from Paul.

There is a sacred hush over the room. Everyone is totally engrossed in their reading about God brought to life on repurposed paper packaging.

Reading quickly, I drink up the words, especially learning so much about this guy Jesus and his friends. It becomes clearer the more I read, how thirsty I have been for clear answers about who he is and what he was like.

My parents and Simon have relayed their knowledge, but these words fascinate me how it reads like it was freshly written for me, today, not recorded thousands of years before.

Lizzy signals that time is up. The books are stacked in an order everyone seems to understand and placed carefully near the balcony door in a basket. They place a fake planter on it to cover them from sight.

The front door is left ajar, and citizens slip in, arriving in small numbers and sit quietly on cushions. Some take a notebook and sit out of sight of the door to read. Some sit with their eyes closed. Some from the party last night. Isaiah and Marks girlfriend's stand by them chatting quietly, Mark introduces me to them.

"Esther, this is my gorgeous Phoebe and Isaiah's sweetheart Deborah." I incline my head.

"This is Simon's Esther. She turned Simon into the lovesick puppy he is today."

Both say. *"Oh,"* like it is a revelation of who I am. I look at Simon pointedly who is now bright red. What does Simon say to his friends? He leads me quickly to some cushions.

The room has a respectful hush. A gentle knock rouses the group, as an older member picks their way through the crowd to stand in front of the balcony door. Isaiah closes the front door and locks it. Mark stands quietly and holds up his hand; everyone does something on their slate or puts them in the esky bag.

Simon switches his onto sleep mode, puts mine on study mode then puts them on the floor in front of us face down. Mark surveys the room to check everyone has done the same and gives the older member a thumbs up.

It is Ruby's father Peter! Simon reaches for my hand to steady me. This is my first meeting and its being led by someone I did not know was part of our community.

Peter lifts the planter and looks through the notebooks, chooses one and proceeds to pray briefly over the group then talks about the Sower and the seed from a book called Matthew. Apparently, it is something Jesus taught through storytelling called parables, Peter explains.

What Peter shares about the parable is enlightening. It is so easy to understand, perfect for me, I am like a child. Peter challenges us to consider what part of the parable represents us personally.

I find myself leaning forward, trying to catch every word. Many others lean in listening intently, after all, they do not have ancient writings to read either.

Peter concludes his retelling of the parable. He asks if there are any questions or insights into what Jesus was saying. Many ask good questions I had not even thought of. Some share what it meant to them following Jesus and the challenges the parable had for them living in our society.

I feel myself nodding with others agreeing, acknowledging the same struggles. Peter pauses while Mark stands up raises his hand and everyone changes their slate settings again. I realise if a cluster of people have turned off their slates at the same time in the same location it raises suspicion with the law.

Peter invites citizens who need prayer to stand. I observe them standing and Peter talking to them quietly, putting his hand on their shoulder. They have their eyes closed.

"Are you okay?" Simon whispers.

"I don't understand, Simon."

He pulls me close with his arms around me.

"They are talking to God and asking for his help; it's called prayer."

"Does he respond?" I whisper back.

"That's God's choosing," Simon sighs to himself.

As Peter prays some look emotional, happy, or overwhelmed. Does God have the power to change citizens like that? Peter moves to the front again.

"I know some of you are really struggling. Can everyone bow their heads and close your eyes. I want you to raise your hands."

We follow his instruction hearing footsteps quietly moving to the front of the room. We are asked to open our eyes. James is standing in front of Peter. Peter addresses us. "James has told me he believes in Jesus but struggles to fully accept Jesus as his Saviour; he thinks he's not good enough."

Simon quietly gets up and stands a respectful space behind James. Peter nods and Simon gently puts his hands on James' shoulders.

"James, do you accept Jesus has taken away your sin through his death on the cross?" Peter asks James. James answers yes. Peter lays his hand on James' arm.

"Do you acknowledge you haven't acted as you should? Are you willing to turn away from sin and accept Jesus as your Saviour?" James nods.

"Yes, I accept Jesus as my Saviour, I just wasn't prepared to take the next step before, but I want to change." Tears roll down his cheeks with Simon steadying him.

The room is silent but the emotional current moving through the room is like nothing I have ever experienced. Powerful as the ocean. Peter embraces him and James just sobs without caring. I look around the room, and everyone sits respectfully; some are quietly tearful. James is ushered to the bedroom to sit with Simon.

Peter turns to the group, whispering, "Let us pray the same prayer to remind us Jesus came to saves us. If any of you have never said this prayer before and accept Jesus as your Saviour today, please come and speak to me or Isaiah."

He quietly takes the group through the prayer. I choose not to say the prayer but to listen. I acknowledge there is a Creator called God, but my secret work life is a lie, which I struggle with, since my encounter with the Holy Spirit, calling me on the cliff top.

James and Simon reappear. James looks at peace. Everyone rushes to encircle them and hug James cheering. He is now smiling as everyone welcomes him into the family of Christ. Such a celebration!

I realise this is what has been happening in my home and our community's homes, just in covert language. It's so dangerous to acknowledge our faith, but I see it is vitally important to honour it and live it out daily despite our circumstances.

Our society comes sharply into focus. Every aspect of our lives is orchestrated by the law. We cannot think or act freely - the suppression of faith and religion is just wrong.

We change our slates again; the notebooks are stashed into a new hiding place and lunch is served. Peter prays over the food, giving thanks.

"Looks like you are going to get dunked with me now." Simon approaches James and pulls him into a headlock, ruffling his hair.

"Yeah, but you're going first." James laughs.

Simon and I sit on the floor eating our rice paper rolls.

"Simon, what's happening?" I ask, concerned.

"Next weekend down at the river we are having a picnic for anyone who is ready to publicly acknowledge their decision to follow Jesus; it's called baptism. We only have adults present; water baptism is a deeply personal and spiritual experience. It represents the break from your old life choices and your new commitment to live following Jesus and studying the ancient writings. It is the beginning of a new life.

One of the older members lays us backwards in the water, fully submerged, and raises us up again. Like a guy John the Baptist did. Even Jesus got baptised."

"I wonder if your Dad is going to baptise me? Simon muses.

"It sounds dangerous," I admit, desperately trying to understand it all.

Simon smiles, leading me out to the quiet balcony, gathering me again in his arms. We are so cosy, and I rest my head on his chest - it feels like home.

"I can't imagine life without my faith, and for you not to experience it. I pray you encounter Jesus one day like James and I have and truly understand how life changing it is," Simon whispers.

"I had an experience near the cliff, when I heard my name being called on the wind repeatedly. Do you remember when I was at your place after your fishing trip? Your Mum invited me in. I did not know what to do, Rachael helped me." I look up at him, I see Simon's eyes widen and his heartbeat quicken then slows again.

He pulls me tighter into his arms and rests his chin on my head, then stands quietly looking into the distance. "Esther that is incredible. I'm here when you're ready to take the next step, I'm glad you will be there for me when I do," he whispers again.

We remain standing quietly reflecting. Peter approaches us, apologising for the interruption. "Can I pray for your both?" Simon and I nod.

We bow our heads. He prays over us, asking God to truly reveal himself to us, to be the centre of our relationship and that we look to him for guidance on how we should love one another. We all say, "Amen."

Simon shakes his hand and thanks him. Peter embraces him and holds him firmly for a long moment, a silent communication, then they separate.

I have observed how Farmer and Fishers are comfortable with their instincts when it is okay to touch each other. Nobody touches in our society without it being essential or given permission, especially romantically. Hence, the custom of inclining our heads, acknowledging each other. Our society strictly adheres to respecting each other's physical and mental wellbeing. It is the law.

"Esther, we can never speak of this in public okay." I nod, wondering what does he tell everyone at home?

Everyone slowly disperses until we are our small group again. Phoebe and Deborah remain.

"So, Simon and James it's going to be awesome hanging out back home. Just wait Esther, when we all get together, we have a great time," Isaiah enthuses, Phoebe and Deborah nod too.

"Can we borrow your leathers? I want to take Esther for a ride and show her the city. We might grab dinner out too," Simon asks Lizzy.

"Sure, have fun," she says, smiling.

Simon grabs my hand and we head to the basement, get changed, discreetly turning our backs to each other, in the lock up. He unplugs the charger, starts up the transport, puts on my helmet, and tightens it. He lifts me like a feather and sits me on the back of the transport. Simon jumps on in front of me, and I wrap my arms tightly around him. We head to the automatic doors leading into the city and take off. It is exhilarating. Everything I thought it would be, but better.

We zig zag across the city and see all the beautiful inner-city sights, the high-rise buildings, and the blue sky reflecting off them. Everything is so clean and well ordered.

Simon takes us towards the harbour, and I see impressive leisure craft bobbing quietly on the water.

We tour through the different precincts, some of which I have never seen, neatly organised for each of their purposes. So much to see, so many domestic units in such a small space. He pulls smoothly up to the huge parkour park, which we have previously visited.

Hopping off the transport we buy coffee and muffins from a cart watching the very skilled locals work their way around the course - cheering them on. I secretly take mental notes of new moves to try.

"I love the atmosphere here in the city, Simon. There is a real energy as people go about their day. I don't see any poor or homeless here. Where are they or doesn't the city have any?" I ask, looking around.

"You just have to know where to look," he says simply.

I realise I have been naïve again. We finish our muffins, place our keep cups in the collection station for cleaning, and head to the transport again.

We take off in another direction I am not familiar with. I notice the beautiful shimmering buildings disappearing, and older ones appearing as Simon weaves the transport around them. Many of them unused and in disrepair.

Simon turns another corner taking us deeper into the older city precinct with solid grey concrete buildings. It looks abandoned a little like the outskirts of our town.

The concrete structures feel like they are leaning inwards, creating illusions of narrow tunnels; light is only visible at the ends of streets. Simon slows and parks his transport in an isolated street. He helps me down, zipping my jacket up tight. We pack our helmets and slates away.

Simon tells me he wants to show me something. Grabbing my hands he walks backward guiding me down the street, as strong gusts of cold air blast us. Simon's body buffers me from most of it, which is so sweet. I stare at his short blonde hair, which is not affected by its force and his serious, clear blue eyes staring back at me, not revealing anything, realising I would follow those eyes anywhere.

I keep asking him where we are going, excited and scared at the same time, He is not smiling, he is neutral and grabs my right hand and turns left. We jog along an old, broken footpath and see a shop front in the distance, a warm light glowing from within.

There is an eclectic mix of citizens milling outside on the cracked footpath and unused road. We slow to a walk, passing citizens with their children playing at their feet. They stop talking and stare, but they are not smiling and laughing. Some acknowledge Simon by inclining their head. I realise this is the government's help centre for the poor. Just one help centre for all these people? Surely not!

My mind is scrambling to work out where do all these people live and how do they survive in the city? Most importantly, how do they know Simon? The young Fisher guy from up the North Coast.

The mood suddenly shifts, rippling through the group as they scatter deeper into the shadows or look down, shielding their faces as two surveillance drones glide very low down the nearby streets, their red lights cutting through the dark interior of the back streets.

I realise these citizens waiting for assistance are vulnerable. Simon quickly pulls me into the shop through the group and away from the drones now hovering scanning everyone on the street.

He is immediately intercepted and hugged by a young woman wearing a dirty apron who has been ladling something hot and steaming into huge jugs and loading baskets with sliced bread. The familiar aroma of spices fills the shop tingling my nose, mmm, spiced pumpkin soup. She sees Simon and smiles warmly while greeting us.

"Don't worry about them, they check us out about the same time every day, sometimes I wave to make their day." She indicates the drones with her head.

Simon smiles finally at her cheeky approach to the law and introduces me to Lydia who appears to be in her mid-twenties.

"This is Lydia, a family friend who came to the city and never left. This is Esther my girlfriend, the love of my life." Simon smiles, looking at me sweetly.

I am overwhelmed by his public declaration of love, my face burns.

"Ahh, I finally get to meet your Esther. The truth is I'm studying at Uni and help out here." She hugs me and looks happy for us.

"Did you want me to show you around?" she asks.

I nod, following her. She takes us for a short tour around the shop, and I see a few old chairs and tables adorned with clumsily potted plants to brighten the space. She shows me the spotless commercial kitchen where she preps meals with others who wave and say, Hi. "They are simple, cheap meals for the needy usually soups that can be sipped, they're easy to cook and serve," Lydia informs me.

"How do you fund the centre? It looks like only volunteers work here."

"Yep, a small handout from the government, mostly donations of points or produce from others. A lot of our city Uni students help when they can. The law leaves us alone if we follow their laws and there is no fighting. As you can see, we are under constant surveillance; fortunately, the citizens still come."

I am speechless. This is a huge voluntary operation, much better than back home. I look around at the happy volunteers cooking and chatting to the visitors, many seem like regulars. The warmth is inviting. Judgement free.

"Since you're here, want to help out?" Lydia asks Simon and me.

"Are you okay to serve one of the groups?"

"Absolutely," Simon replies enthusiastically.

Simon grabs a basket of bread and hands it to me with a stack of keep cups, and he carries a jug of soup that looks heavy and very hot. I continue to look at him, amazed at this private side of him.

We step outside and walk carefully along the cracked footpath to an empty warehouse next door that has been carefully swept and temporary lights hung.

Citizens start filing in, and I see something like a beautiful dance; everyone gathers quietly in large circles. Then each of the servers enter the circles - someone offers to hand out the cups for me.

I follow Simon's lead, as he pours steaming spiced pumpkin soup in the citizens' mugs and indicates I offer the basket to them to take a slice. At each person, he stops, inclines his head, and they offer their name, and he thanks them for coming by name. Some of the people he knows.

Each person smiles or softens at the interaction; he turns and whispers that I do the same. I find myself smiling the more I speak to the citizens and they smile back. Internally I'm way out of my comfort zone. We finish serving and everyone is holding their food, not eating. I wonder if something is wrong - I see all the circles are perfectly still.

"We give thanks for the food provided and the hands that prepared it. May we eat and be satisfied," Lydia says quietly.

Everyone is about to sit and eat when two citizens run up to our group late. The circle smoothly accommodates them, cups are thrust into their hands and many of those around share their own soup into the late comers' cups and break their bread to share. I have tears in my eyes; these are such simple acts of generosity. Everyone is now happy; they sit and chat in smaller groups.

I turn to Simon whose face is shining with happiness and he sees I have been moved. He smiles nudging me.

"Amazing isn't it," he enthuses.

We walk together in silence back to the kitchen and are promptly handed tubs to collect the keep cups in and any scraps into baskets. We return to our new friends collecting the cups and bread chatting to a few of the citizens. Some are studying or are the working poor, barely earning enough to house themselves; food is a bonus.

Simon tells Lydia we have to go. We thank her for her time and walk slowly back to the transport past the citizens. We think about them; it is heartbreaking to see the need.

We glide away on Simon's transport, back into the shiny part of the city past the impressive arts precinct with museums and galleries I have never visited.

My heart is heavy with what Simon showed me. The city could easily fool you into believing it is all light and fun. Suddenly the city seems like a cheaply veneered version of our Town. The shiny illusion distracts the city citizens from the struggle out of sight, and it sickens me.

CHAPTER 20

Simon parks the transport at a high observation point overlooking the city's harbour near a small park. It is a beautiful sunset in rich oranges and pinks. We remove our helmets and jackets, then sit on the wooden seat looking out over the stunning city. We take it all in, thinking about our day while holding hands. So comfortable in the silence. Simon turns to me, looking down at me gripping both my hands tightly.

"Esther, I cannot imagine experiencing today without you. It has confirmed my feelings; I am totally in love with you. Would you be willing to spend the rest of your life with me knowing it won't be easy? Esther, will you marry me? I never planned to ask you like this, but I am committed to you forever if you will have me."

I am in shock. I feel his whole body trembling and hear his heart beating so loudly after letting his unrehearsed but heartfelt words tumble out in one continuous stream, it's very unlike Simon.

I look up and see love, strong and certain. I nod smiling, reaching up and wrapping my arms around his neck. I reply with a kiss that is gentle but confirms my love for him. I feel a definite shift between us; we are leaving behind unrestrained attraction to a love not fully acknowledged until now.

Simon looks in my eyes again resting his forehead on mine whispering, "Are you sure Esther? It's a very fast courtship. I just dumped all my thoughts and feelings on you."

"I'm sure," and I smile feeling euphoric.

He holds my hands again slipping my ring off my right hand and slides it onto my left hand. His finger rests on it like in the restaurant, tracing the pattern and lost in thought. I look at him. "Simon where are you?" He looks like his mind is kilometres away.

He refocuses on me. "I'm imagining waking up next to you every day. I want to make you happy," he says sweetly.

Simon scoops me up in his arms and sits me on the transport sideways. He inclines his head, and I nod yes, then he kisses me so confidently I do not feel worried about the future. We break without the safety word.

"That ring has magical powers over me; I don't need the safety word," Simon laughs. "Hmm, we'll see." I am unsure.

He opens the storage box on the transport, pulling out a blanket, leaving our slates inside. Simon leads me to the little park with beautifully curated lawns and gardens. He spreads the blanket out then takes me on a tour of the illuminated garden paths. The solar lights create a magical place; it is so beautiful and fragrant.

We pause at a magnificently manicured tree, located in the centre of the garden. It's protected by an ornate iron fence circling it, and the tree is covered in bright red berries.

Attached to the fence is a simple sign, DO NOT EAT THE BERRIES. We look at this laughing.

"Simon, who would eat berries they don't know anything about? You would have to be a total idiot to not follow the instruction." Simon agrees.

He leads me back to our blanket and lays on his back with his arms behind his head, looking up, the stars becoming visible, and I join him.

I remind Simon of Jonah's party and how beautiful the stars were. He smiles, still looking up at the stars, whispering, "So were you."

"I have ruined you, Simon, you are now so soft, sweet and *romantic,*" I say smiling, leaning on my elbow looking at him. I poke his stomach. In a flash he has me on my back gently pinned down like on a wrestling mat.

"What about now?" He laughs,

I challenge him, saying he is weak against my Esther powers. I cannot move.

"What about now?" he asks.

"Definitely soft and weak." I challenge him again, twisting and flipping him over easily, onto his back, powerless like a turtle.

I straddle him, which is not easy in leathers, pinning his arms down with my legs and boots. Simon forgets I have a brother too; we wrestle all the time trying to overpower each other. I am super strong from working in the garden and Parkour. Simon is powerless. He stops fighting, he laughs, enjoying a new challenge.

"Oh man, I cannot tell the guys you pinned me down. Can I tap out?" he pleads.

"No, I am the victor of this match."

"Okay," he says not caring. Simon is not worried about surrendering to his girl, well, that is his take on the story anyway he tells me.

"What am I going to do to you?" I tap my chin dramatically.

"Bring it on, I can beat you." He grins.

Simon quickly realises, as I lean over him, that he is powerless under my Esther spell. I hover over his lips but do not kiss him.

"No, you are truly evil," he groans.

I laugh, pinning his arms to his side tighter with my strong legs and boots. I kiss him once.

He laughs while yelling anchor, then flips me unsuspecting onto my back and then we try to gain dominance over each other. He is naturally strong but is shocked how I match him being so petite, realising I am all muscle and strategy.

Simon pants with exertion and frustration being beaten by his new fiancé. He lays down on his back and tries to catch his breath; I lay on the blanket rubbing my arms and legs.

"You never fail to surprise me," he says, turning to me in between breaths, with admiration. We look at each other talking quietly.

"Thoughts?" Simon asks me about last night. I just look at him. "It's a lot if you're not used to it," he says simply.

"A lot of everything," I confess.

"Esther we are hiding in plain sight. We are in this crazy world, but we chose not to be of it. Esther, you can ask me *anything...*" he says and looks at me steadily,

I admit I had only glimpses at school of how citizens act with one another but nothing like this, especially when I went into the bathroom and... I am so nervous to bring it up.

Simon nods gently saying, "Don't you think it's better that protection is readily available rather than...the alternatives. Most citizens carry them, but some forget."

"Do you?" He looks shocked at my direct question, then acknowledges that is a fair question.

"Yes," he says simply. He pulls his wallet from his pocket and opens it, pulls out a condom grinning.

"What's so funny?" I feel even more nervous.

"I realised a while ago I should throw it away."

"Why?"

"Because its expired, and since meeting you I'm in no rush to replace it until the time is right." He groans, "Oh *no*, my Dad is in my head. Better to be safe than sorry, always carry protection. I should replace it."

I smile, thinking of what a cringy conversation that must have been. My mum had spoken to me about relationships and being prepared last year but

I had parked that conversation like an immature kid, thinking, that is for the future. Way into the future.

Simon wants to know what I am smiling about.

"I'm trying to picture the scene where your Dad's having a chat about sex stuff with you."

He puts his head down and shakes it.

"You know… *he is* really chilled about it all. He gets straight to the point. No embarrassment. It was more about respecting your partner and how good God's purpose for sex is," I nod, I know Andrew does not talk much, like Simon.

"Simon, what do think about sex, being with someone?"

He is quiet for a long time, looking into the distance, then his eyes find mine again. He reaches for my hand, looking a little nervous. It is such a personal, intimate question.

"Esther, this is a huge question; I am trying to think how to put my thoughts into words. Well, this is what I know. God created our bodies; we honour him with how we treat them. Having babies and sex is good; it is his plan for a couple to be intimately connected not just physically but maybe spiritually too, building a bond. A couple should please each other."

Realising I have not breathed or blinked for that moment, I suddenly take a breath.

"Do you really believe what you said?" I am still processing such a beautiful, deep personal response.

"I never used to, when I was younger, I just wanted the physical stuff, but as I went out with a few girls I realised that something was holding me back. Then with my parents' chats, watching other Fisher's date and at the meetings it was explained in such a such a respectful way it changed what I thought, and then going out with you, it made sense not to rush.

"Naturally I have *feelings* for you. Forget about all that serious stuff and chill, we are out in the city, free." We lie looking at each other, chatting quietly. Simon reaches for my left hand and kisses it intermittently as we talk.

"Esther, I promise I will find us a home we can afford that is perfect. I have saved so many points. I could sell my share of the transport to James to provide for us if we need to."

I am so moved by his concern for us and wanting to contribute that I hold up my hand as if to say wait here, then I go to the transport and retrieve my slate, open it and come back to Simon.

"I can help too." I sit cross legged on the blanket. He sits next to me, his chin on my shoulder looking at my slate with me.

He looks at it, then at me and stands up quickly, running his hands through his hair and then swears under his breath, agitated, pacing back and forth.

"*Seriously* Esther!" He swears under his breath; he has never sworn at me or even raised his voice before; he is now breathing hard, containing his feelings.

All he can say is, "How?"

Simon is coming to terms with how many points I have on my slate already; in our world it is an indecently large amount for the short time I have been working. I shut my slate off and put it in reflection mode. I now clearly realise it really is an outrageous number of points for a Farmer girl who cleans the Medical Precinct.

He looks at me, crouches down, and holds my face in his hands, looking in my eyes unblinking with visibly great restraint.

"How can someone your age, not finished school, a Farmer, earn so many points? It is crazy, no *insane!*"

I am not afraid of his intensity and scrutiny; I'm more terrified of the depth of deception I will have to continue.

I quickly formulate a feasible reason.

"The Precinct has chosen me to be on call, travel between all the Medical Precincts to help as I am a quick learner, fast, smart and they are providing me with lots of training and shifts in different roles, each pays a different number of points. Soon I will get my single transport licence so I can travel between the Medical Precincts quicker to fill in if someone is away or not available. I'm not telling my parents they will freak out," I mumble leaving out I am a covert courier of who knows what?

He sits, puts his hands in his lap, nods but I see he cannot work it out. He is smart.

"Esther, we can't splash this amount around, it will be suspicious."

"I know, I'm so glad I can talk to someone about it. I see everyone struggling but I cannot help," I moan.

He picks up my slate and puts it back in the transport carrier, to ensure our conversation is private. He returns, sitting for a moment, then I see the full realisation on his face.

"I didn't pick up on it before, the new clothes, dinner out and generous grocery shopping while you've been here."

"Please don't be angry with me Simon. I am trying to be honest with you about everything. I do not know what to do. I am so happy I can survive and not be poor."

Simon pulls me close to him, wrapping his arms protectively around me. I lean my head against his chest, slumped and despondent.

"Baby, listen to me, do not ever worry about being poor, God will provide for our needs. We can handle it, we always have. What is important, is us," he whispers and squeezes me tightly.

"We need to love each other honestly and trust entirely on God no matter how hard and crappy this life gets," he says, with such adult authority. Like a strong protective husband.

"You're sure?" I stare into those determined blue eyes.

He nods and gently lays me down, looking at me intensely, wiping away my tears. I nod, and he kisses me slowly; the intensity of our moment becomes too much.

I break it quickly, jumping up, standing, knowing this moment is about to get even hotter. I reach for Simon pulling him to his feet and tell him to go and walk it off; I will find a place to have dinner. He gets my very clear message while I fold up the blanket and head to my slate to look for a restaurant.

I observe Simon in the distance jogging a few laps of the park. He takes a drink from the water fountain every lap, splashes water on himself and appears to be having an animated conversation, alone. He comes back looking tired and damp.

"You, okay?" I ask, handing him his jacket and helmet and putting my slate in the carrier.

"Let's go get pizza." We do not discuss what just happened between us, but I cannot resist asking,

"Who were you talking to back there?"

"I told Satan the evil one, to get behind me and leave us alone. Then I prayed and asked God to help me control myself, I keep having *thoughts* Esther, about you all the time, and *you know*," he whispers in my ear,colouring.

I stop for a moment and think he is being so honest with me. Incredibly awkward, *man* that took some guts.

"It's okay, Simon, we are in this together. Remember, we are playing the long game. Not the short one. If we are going to get married, we must be honest about everything, even the personal stuff. It is as much my responsibility as yours to cool it. Agreed?" He agrees whole heartedly, relieved.

We find a gourmet pizza restaurant, which is what we need to chill out. We choose our favourites, Simon orders a beer, the server looks at me, "She's underage," he says, and she just nods. I order a soft drink and she moves on.

"Not long now and you can have a glass of bubbles to celebrate your birthday!" Simon reminds me.

We sit over dinner in our cosy booth talking over what we saw today, the sights we want to visit together and the homeless people. We start formulating when we will celebrate our union and everything that needs to happen leading up to it.

"This is such an important week, I am now engaged, going on a picnic next weekend and you start your intense exam prep for the next two weeks. It is going to be a lonely two weeks," he says ruefully,

"You can message me, Simon."

"It is not the same," he says, looking forlorn, reaching for my hand.

We head back to the unit, happy having toured the city, admiring the sights, and full of pizza. We park the transport, plug it into the charging bank, and hang up the leathers.

I run my hands over Lizzy's leathers, thinking I will own my own soon. Simon brushes my hair away from my neck and gently kisses it.

"What are you thinking about baby?"

I turn smiling. "I'm so happy."

"Good," he whispers, grabbing my hand.

We enter the unit where our friends look up from lounging on cushions. "Hey guys, what have you been up to?" they ask. Simon lifts my left hand to show them where my ring is. They stop, pause then yell out together, "You're engaged!"

Simon looks down at me smiling like he has won the best prize in the world and kisses me in front of his friends who are cheering. I wrap my arms around his neck not caring one bit.

CHAPTER 21

We farewell our friends, it is early walking to the train. The city is silent, except for few joggers. We step onto the empty train carriage heading home and sit lost in thought. Our luggage is stacked, we look out at the pink blur sunrise as the bullet train flies out of the city over 300 kilometers an hour.

Simon kicks James' jogger, sitting across from him.

"What?" James grunts.

"Did you meet anyone? Plenty of hot girls?"

"Don't talk like that!" I punch Simon.

"You are right, Esther. James did you meet anyone that sparked your interest?"

"Now you are being a jerk. Leave him alone. Everything okay, James?" James leans against the window looking out.

"Yeah, lots to think about." I just nod.

I am bursting to tell Simon about Lizzy and James, but I contain it. The relationship could be new.

Have I put James in a pigeonhole as shy and introverted?

I snuggle into Simon, tucking my feet under my long yellow dress and scroll through my slate; Simon snoops at my screen occasionally. I add some pictures to my social page from the city, a few cute ones of Simon and me, much to his feigned horror, saying I am ruining his reputation with his mates then kisses my cheek telling me I look beautiful today.

Messaging Sarah and Ruby our news, I tell them it is private until our parents are informed. Reaching for my wheely bag, Simon assists me with a flourish.

"No, you are my queen," he says.

"What an idiot. My idiot. Wait, that makes you my future king?" He smiles.

"Yep, I knew you would catch on." He gives me a cheeky kiss on the cheek.

We arrive at our home station. There is no sign of any Law Enforcers, thankfully just a single drone doing its usual rounds of our Town above us.

We grab a waiting private transport, my treat, I insist. We drop James off and proceed to my home to tell my parents of our engagement. It is market day, I know they will be up.

We need to help our families with the markets. Pausing outside in the garden Simon calls his parents and tells them we are engaged, they are absolutely delighted, saying they will see us soon. I am sure Rachael was crying. Andrew was just smiling through the screen.

We wander in to see my parents hastily having breakfast. They pause when they see both of us. My mother looks straight at me, and I nod and she runs and embraces me then Simon.

My father stands in the same place like there is a glitch in the slate. He looks at Simon then me then my mother. "What am I missing?" My mother jumps in saying, "They're engaged silly," grabbing my left hand to prove she is right.

Dad reanimates and gives me a tight hug, shakes Simon's hand, then says,

"Right, son- in -law, outside and help me load the truck. We will see you at the lot," he says looking at Mum and me.

"I am sure you have plenty to talk about."

I guess that is his way of saying he is happy, especially when I observe he and Simon walking out to the garden, my father's arm around Simon's shoulders in a natural fatherly way.

Luke wanders out of his room disheveled, "What's going on, so noisy?"

"I'm engaged to Simon."

"Cool, I've always wanted a brother and my own media room," Luke says pulling on his boots and punches my arm on the way out the door yelling, "Wait up bro."

We laugh suspecting he has been waiting to say that for a long time and planning my exit too. My mother is desperate to know the proposal details. I relay a little and she sheds a tear.

"Esther, I am so pleased you have Simon; you have known each other all your lives, now you will spend the rest of your life with him. I know you are young, it will be hard, but you can build a wonderful life together."

We walk to the lot and set up side by side. I wonder which stall I will work on when we are married? Or will I share my time?

Sarah races across the lot and throws herself at me. I catch her.

"Easy Sarah."

"Esther, I am so happy for you. I read your message and had to contain myself."

I look at my mother who nods, meaning you are released. We run off laughing and walk towards Simon's family stall, stopping to visit Simon's parents. Rachael embraces me with tears in her eyes.

"I'm so happy for you both. You are a beautiful match for Simon; he truly adores you. I know he's in good hands." She indicates Simon being shown the finer points of bundling and weighing vegetables on our ancient scales and how to handle the cabbages by my Dad and we laugh.

Andrew comes over whispering, "Welcome to our family Esther, you are the daughter we always prayed for," he says shyly, giving me a gentle side hug.

Matt stops momentarily, then continues his work smiling filleting fish for an early customer, and pauses again when he hears Simon come over saying, "Easy old man, she's taken." Simon sweeps me up in his arms, twirls me around, kisses me and puts me back where I was and wanders back to my Dad, grinning.

Matt has finished his transaction and is washing up and drying his hands. He indicates with his head to come over.

"Esther, I am so happy you are going to be a part of our family. I could not imagine Simon being with anyone else. You are good together. I can't believe he is going to get married!" I smile and throw my arms around him.

"One day you will marry the one." Matt looks pleased but not used to girls throwing their arms around him. I cannot see his longtime girlfriend, Elizabeth, today.

Sarah and I find a shady spot under a large gum tree. I share basic details about our engagement then move onto details about the city, which Sarah enthuses over every detail.

We agree to study after I share a few pictures of the city until our parents need us. Our school friends join us; I inform them of our engagement. They share their happiness for Simon and me, and bluntly raise the question of marrying so young, asking, if I'm sure. Our group decides to work on the same subjects and share notes and food, like at school.

Ruby calls, blowing kisses of congratulations. She invites us all to her place to stay and study for the next two weeks, to keep us focused and have the weekends to rest.

Peter has given Krystal, two weeks away at a retreat and he has employed a married Fisher woman to be a live in chaperone for the two weeks to feed us.

We have study camp! I am thrilled. I have a chance to get a reasonable grade with this intense study plan. I have been studying conscientiously at home and completed the assignments, but it is not the same. We will not goof off; this is our way out of this life.

I message work for study leave. They reply quickly. Affirmative. I update the CEO too; he wishes me well in my exams. I am now set to study.

The markets finish at midday. I help my parents pack up and Simon returned reluctantly to his parents' market stall to help.

Updating Simon of Ruby's invitation to study at her place, he looks sad, holding my hands.

"I'm going to miss you, my queen." I remind him he will be working and I will be studying.

"I guess, we can see each other at the picnic."

"I would not miss it. This is a huge step Simon, for you and James."

"I know, no turning back."

We walk towards home to collect Simon's bag, chatting when a drone tracks us.

Simon pulls me into his arms, looking into my eyes, and proceeds to waltz me down the road home. Leading me strongly, his footwork is impeccable for a guy dancing those vintage steps in joggers. My dress swirls around us as we dance as if the drone is not there, and it tires of us after scanning our faces and shoots off again. Simon ends the dance at the gate, smiling and bows.

"Thank you for the dance, Simon. You are full of surprises; it has been ages since I have been to a vintage dance. Stay with me today. I want to hang out together before the next two crazy weeks."

"Okay," He messages his parents, so respectful.

We agree to change our status to 'in a relationship' with each other to keep the law happy. They are tracking us anyway, might as well keep it clear and out in the open.

The law prompts us to complete the iRESPECT dating app. We decline. We sit on the veranda chatting about the weekend with our slates inside, comparing city life to ours.

My parents join us. They sit with their lunch mentioning that they, along with Sarah's parents, have chosen a date for our eighteenth birthday party - the Saturday following exams. Our actual birthday! The location and theme are a surprise. I am happy with the plan.

"Can I find out?" Simon asks.

My father laughs, "Absolutely, I'm counting on you strong guys to help."

"*Okay,*" Simon says slowly, realising the parent network is in full operation.

This is turning out to be a good year. We update my parents on our city visit and James' decision, and they are pleased, having seen his struggle too.

"So, what did you think about your first meeting Esther?" my mother asks, my face gives it away, she nods. "It is a lot. Just listen and ask if you do not understand."

I mention the booklets they had, "Do we have some for our meetings too? Simon and my parents look cornered.

"What's going on?" I demand.

Simon leans in whispering, "You know how I bring your Dad fish guts; it is really squid for him to extract the ink and mix with a medium to write in the booklets, your mother also. There are a few in our group who make the booklets, we call them scribes. There are a few others up and down the east coast. You need a master copy, so Paul's Bible was a bonus. We now have a few master copies to use." My parents nod.

I look at Simon. "Is that the last secret between us?" He smirks, "I think so, besides your birthday party."

"This is a very, very dangerous secret." They all look at each other, then me. "Well actually there's more."

I grab Simon's hand tightly. "What?"

"We um, write ancient words about Jesus on rice paper tucked into cabbages and share with citizens we trust at the markets."

"Yep, it all makes sense now, rice paper, and strange goings on at the markets." I now realise this is what Peter and Paul were talking about, the harvest. My parents and others are planting the seed about God.

Sitting back, I digest this information, like eating a whole whale one bite at a time. They excuse themselves and leave me with Simon to make sense of it.

Simon's slate beeps inside. It's a message, he checks it and returns a missed call from a Fisher. He returns smiling and leading me into the garden so we can talk freely.

"That was Zach," he is Simon's close Fisher mate. "He and Hannah have invited us to have dinner weekly with them until we get married, to help us prepare. I accepted, I hope that is, okay? I thought it would be good to hang out with them as they are a little older, chilled and have not been married that long . . ." He looks at me hopefully.

"That sounds perfect. I think we need that as I have no idea how to be Fisher's wife."

I sit on the bench looking out over the flourishing garden. Simon sits on the ground in front of me stretching out his long legs. I wrap my arms around his neck, and hug him cheek to cheek, and he sits staring out into the garden too, stroking my arm gently. Peace. I slide down and sit next to him; he puts his arm around me drawing me to his side.

"Let's get married New Year's Eve, Esther."

"I love it."

Simon turns holding my face in his hands for a moment saying quietly, "I want us to have a small group for our vows, just us, our parents, and brothers. I want it to feel special, our private moment."

Simon is so thoughtful that it makes me fall in love even more with him. I nod, I imagine it now, just us, isolated somewhere with our family at a discreet distance, the two of us sharing our promises.

"I know where to exchange our vows. On the cliff top in the pine reserve looking over the ocean, you know I love it there." He smiles, knowing.

He leans over, looking at me, and I barely nod as he starts kissing me slowly. I'm totally caught up in the romance of our wedding plans.

I whisper, "*Anchor, anchor.*"

Simon immediately stops. "Are you okay? Feeling, okay?" He pauses, looking into my eyes, unsure what is happening, looking awkward.

"Feel like you need to walk it off?"

I nod, feeling wobbly and energized all at the same time.

"I'm so sorry, Esther, I just couldn't help myself in the moment, we just felt so…connected."

Simon gets up quickly to cool the moment, dusts himself off, and helps me to my feet.

"I need to head home because I have work tomorrow -shorter trips thank goodness, now we are in the restricted season. Can l message you while you are studying?" he asks.

Simon puts his arms out. I walk happily into them, rest my head on his chest, feeling that strong, steady heartbeat that is now beating very fast.

"Of course," I whisper.

I will miss him, I enjoyed being with him over the weekend. I order a private transport for him despite his protests, respecting the hard work he does and wanting him rested.

We stand chatting while we wait, agreeing to tell our parents our plans for the wedding. We are enjoying being together, are comfortable, and realising the fire we felt for each other in the city still burns and needs containing.

Holding each other, Simon runs his hands down my long hair playing with it free from its band. "I love your hair, well everything about you. How about we exchange our vows at sunset on the cliff top?" he says, smiling awkwardly.

"Promise to waltz with me at our wedding, my handsome fiancé?"

"I will dance with you for the rest of my life, if it makes you happy, he laughs.

"You seem at peace," I observe.

"I am ready to take the next big steps in my life; maybe my desperate prayer in the park helped." He laughs, colouring right to his blonde roots. "That was a such a humiliating moment in every possible way last night."

"I am no better than you just a moment ago in the garden. Our private moments. It is kind of flattering to know I stir this emotion in you."

He whispers in my ear again, acutely aware of AI. "You and me. What we feel is good, God's plan means when we wait, we only want each other. I only want you, and to make you happy, Esther." He has a point. I do not desire anyone else.

"Maybe you're right. I kind of get why the Town kids do whatever they want, they take the easy path." Simon agrees wholehearted then laughs to himself, "They certainly don't go and walk off all their *feelings*."

His transport arrives and we embrace promising to chat.

As I pull our gate shut, I see our house number hand carved into the centre of the gate. The number eight has been carved into two small perfect circles with eight spokes on each like antique bicycle.

I trace my fingers over it, so precise. I have never noticed it before.

My mother sits on my bed watching me repack. She pats the bed for me to sit next to her putting her arms around me tight. Her head rests on my shoulder, her familiar perfume just detectable.

"It won't be long and you'll be eighteen and packing to leave home to start your new life." She sighs, braiding my hair and asking if Simon and I are okay with getting ready for our marriage.

"I thought you guys may have courted longer; I could have prepared you for everything much better. We still have time, I need to make sure you can cook more than salads and cakes," she says smiling.

"Mum, you forget I have been trailing you all my life. I know how to clean, cook, manage points, shop, and sanitise laundry. Can you teach me how to care for Simon like you do with Dad? I have no idea how to look after a grown man and what to expect."

My mother stands up and kisses me on the head.

"I think you just gave me the best job. I will leave gutting fish to Rachael." We both grimace!

"What have I got myself into?" She shrugs.

"You're the one who fell in love with a Fisher."

I groan, "I should have fallen for an accountant."

We chat briefly about setting up a home. My mother asks me if it is okay with Simon and me that she and Rachael organise a wedding register with our community to share surplus home wares that are in good order for our new home. It is a generous Farmer and Fisher tradition that I am happy to continue and gratefully accept.

I inform her Simon and I have had been preparing for marriage by having honest discussions about *everything,* which she is impressed with. I said that Hannah and Zach have invited us to have a meal each week with them until our wedding day to chat about life and marriage. Mum looks especially pleased that we will have their input.

Farmer and Fisher families do not spend many points on a wedding; we set the date within three months. We go to the Union office like everyone else, then meet up with friends and family at another location and share our own vows then enjoy a relaxed meal in someone's home. There's lots of dancing and music. We put our hard-earned points into renting a home.

My mother suggests that maybe Simon and our fathers could find somewhere for us to live as I will be occupied with exams and work. I smile, wondering if they will look for the place with the biggest garage first?

I inform her that Simon and I have set a date for our wedding - New Year's Eve, sunset on the cliff top. We will go to the union office then straight there.

"Esther, it's perfect. You guys really understand how special this is."

She shakes her head, overwhelmed, reaching for my hands, squeezing them tight. I look at her gold wedding band running my finger over its intricate design, realising I have never really studied it.

She slides it off, handing it to me, putting her finger on her lips. I look inside, there is an inscription 1 Corinthians 13:7. Mum whispers the verse in my ear with great emotion,

"The verse says love never gives up, never loses faith, is always hopeful, and endures through every circumstance. Your father chose that and surprised me on our wedding day."

She places her warm hands on my face, looking deep into my eyes, full of love and a tear.

"Esther, you are truly blessed with Simon. His transition into adulthood seems so natural, and he wants to please you; he doesn't take his eyes off you."

I inform my father and Luke of the wedding plans over dinner. My parents ask me if they can they arrange the wedding meal after the vows with Simon's parents. I thank them, telling them it is a beautiful gift. They smile saying, "You study and pass the exams, and we will plan the best wedding ever."

I relay my decision to buy my own dress, not borrow one. I can afford it and desire to buy one in the city. My parents look at me, and I am unsure whether they are disappointed or proud of my decision; I think the latter.

We enjoy our family dinner; Dad and Luke clean up. Luke informs me from the kitchen he will be wearing his basketball gear to the wedding, and my father snaps him with a tea towel. "Not if we have any say over it. I am sure Simon's brothers will have a suit you can borrow."

I lay in bed realising I am going to miss my family and have no idea what to expect being in a Fisher family.

"Simon, can I come out on the trawler tomorrow? I want to understand your work. Can you ask your Dad?" I message.

Simon calls, he is concerned. "Baby, are you sure? It's hard dirty work. If you think you can handle being a Fisher, Dad says it's ok. Me, I am unsure…because you shower, brush your teeth and smell *so nice.*"

I cannot help laughing, despite my seriousness.

"*Simon*, I want to see everything, otherwise I won't really understand when you talk about your work."

"Okay, I hope you aren't going to be a mermaid and distract me out there." He laughs. I assure him I will.

Informing my parents of the plan, they worry for me.

My father sternly says, "You follow Skipper Andrews' safety rules, never take off your safety vest, you never know when the sea will turn against you. Use the harnesses and safety points all the time, that is what they are for." I promise faithfully to do that.

My mother's face says it all. She is terrified.

I message Ruby, updating her I will come one day later. She replies, 'Totally fine. Be safe, see you soon.' She signs off with lots of icons, hugs, mermaids, fish, and me throwing up. Ruby is funny and encouraging.

I pack my bag and order a transport to pick me up for an early start.

As I drift off to sleep, I give thanks for all the people in my life and am thankful they love me, unconditionally. I realise I just prayed my first real personal prayer today.

CHAPTER 22

Weaving my way amongst the noisy crews on the dimly lit wharf I find the trawler, called 'Shalom,' and wait to be welcomed on.

Simon sees me and jumps onto the wharf - a practised manoeuvre. He gathers me in his arms tightly and briefly kisses me. Everyone on the wharf has stopped working, and stares unaccustomed to crew kissing each other.

Simon smiles broadly. "Back to work, it's like you've never see a hot girl before."

He assists me across; I do not look down at the dark swirling water. The familiar smell of fuel, fish, and the sea fills my nose, it's strong and pungent. I am shown where to stow my bag, and a set of smaller high visibility wet weather bib and brace has been laid out for me to change into. Simon throws me a pair of his woollen socks from his locker.

"You can thank me later," he tells me mischievously. I pull them on and see there are heavy duty rubber work boots for me too. I pull them on, the socks help make them fit tight, realising now this clothing can be waterproof and warm.

Pulling on my woollen hat I tuck my long plait under it so my hair does not get caught in any machinery. I emerge and am welcomed with a cheer from the small all male crew today and I am promptly handed a bright sky-blue knitted woollen hat with three-dimensional coloured knitted fish sewn onto it, and I change hats, laughing.

Skipper Andrew calls order, as it is time to pray. We move inside and everyone bows their heads.

Skipper Andrew asks for God's protection out on the water, to provide enough to feed us for another day and to cover the trawler with his protection to get us home. It is said with great conviction. I realise it must only be a Christian crew, otherwise the prayer would have been silent.

I am immediately fitted with a life jacket by Matt, who is first mate. He is trying not to touch me out of respect. I look him in the eye and say, "Matt, I'm crew."

Matt relaxes and tightens the straps. He shows me where all the safety harness points are; these protect us if the sea gets rough. He instructs me to quickly move to the very next one when moving around and anchor myself properly, as I am not used to the ocean and not a strong swimmer. I nod, conscious that I should do what is right and not embarrass Simon or his family.

Matt excuses himself as he must instruct the crew. I feel the engines roar to life and the trawler moving away from the wharf. I have been instructed to work alongside the youngest crew member, Ezra, who is sixteen and strong already. It feels good to be on the water.

Ezra tells me we will prepare the bait to reload the traps retrieved in an hour and a half that were set yesterday. He informs me they use GPS to track the traps again to pick them up.

I ask him what we are catching. "We're hoping for snapper and leather jacket; you're never quite sure what else ends up in the trap."

Ezra sets me up with long rubber gloves and a plastic apron to wear. We stand at a bench with a gentle breeze on our backs, with an overhead light illuminating our space. He begins to roughly cut up large fish pieces reserved from yesterday, and I pack it into tubs ready for reloading traps.

The smell and textures are utterly disgusting and squishy. I remind myself that Simon would have done this when he was younger.

We scrub down our workspace and gear, hang it up and move onto breakfast prep for the crew. Once they start bringing in the traps there will be no break for hours.

The crew appear and devour a huge, cooked breakfast of scrambled eggs, crispy bacon and grilled vegetables prepared by Ezra, impressive.

I am permitted to serve and sit next to Simon who eats steadily, occasionally stopping to chat. I suspect this is normal. He keeps smiling and leans against me in a cosy way; he even holds my hand under the table when everyone is distracted.

Skipper Andrew looks happy too; the weather and tides will be in our favour, so he is hoping for a good haul today. He excuses himself after thanking Ezra and me for the food, as he heads off to track the GPS signal.

Andrew yells out informing us how long until we are expected to pull in the first trap. The guys gobble the remaining food and head back to prepare for picking up the traps.

Ezra and I quickly clean up, and throw the food scraps overboard. The seagulls following us, gratefully swooping. Ezra shows me what is going to happen next and how to stay out of the Fishers' way and not get caught in the ropes. Apparently, they get angry as it is costly if they miss a trap and must go back, or worst, leave it and the catch inside.

We dress again into aprons and gloves, Ezra passes me a hard hat. My stomach is okay if it is not fish guts all the time. I stare out at the water as the sun rises, seeing Simon's photos come to life. It is stunning, the sky is clear and the water reasonably calm, but there's no land in sight now.

Simon wanders down, putting his arm around me, and asking Ezra how the new crew member is going. Ezra gives a cheeky thumbs down. "We will see how she goes," Simon says, kissing my cheek; Ezra looks away for a moment respectfully. Simon smiles and says, "It's okay, Ezra, don't be embarrassed, mate."

Ezra teaches me that what we do as a trap is pulled in by the crew, we are to quickly sort the fish by size and throw back what is not correct. He passes me a piece of flat stainless steel, telling me I will need to quickly measure, throw, or put them into tubs, for sale. If we are not fast enough, we get behind as they pull in another trap. He assures me I will work out size by eye and measure the rest quickly.

We are told the first trap is coming up. We stand at the ready as the skipper adjusts the trawler speed, I watch Simon, his brother and crew all work without talking, knowing their roles. It is noisy as the winches heave up the full trap.

Suddenly they move into action as the trap is caught and winched up onto a rack. I watch Ezra and crew quickly sort the fish tipped out of the trap, it's checked and stored ready for later. I am amazed how quickly they sort, throw, and stack the fish.

I learn quickly, finding the measure a great help, and get into a rhythm of - measure, throw, keep, repeat, breathe, ready for the next trap. I stop for a moment watching the seagulls following us. I keep moving, not wanting to be the weakest link.

Ezra heads off to prep food for everyone to eat when they can. I stand next to Simon who starts prepping the catch on the deck bench, the tubs are stacked ready.

Simon grabs the pretty yellow shiny fish, deftly cut behind its head through to the spine. Then to my horror, he pulls it apart throwing the head into a tub, rips out what he informs me, is the female's egg sack, and throws that in another tub with the body of the fish.

I bolt to the side of the trawler and throw up everything I ate, I suspect, for the last five years.

Simon laughs hard, not stopping as I retch until I cannot bring up anymore. Everyone cheers like it is a rite of passage. Simon, without looking up, passes me a bottle of water and says to rinse; I promptly swish and spit over the side, and stand up and face the crew who are clapping. Apparently, I have broken the time record for a new crew member before they spewed.

"Get Esther a beer," Simon yells to Ezra over his shoulder. The thought of smelling a yeasty beer makes me throw up again over the side. I slide down the side of the trawler and sit and Ezra arrives quickly with a ginger beer, passing it to me.

Simon says, while still working and not stopping, "Have a few sips then get back to work."

Ezra jumps in next to Simon, pulls on his gloves, and starts packing the tubs of fish, quickly and neatly ready for sale at the co-op.

Getting up, I realise the ginger beer settled my stomach quickly and the sugar has pepped me up.

I watch Ezra work. "I've got it, if you are needed somewhere else." He nods gratefully and moves to help finish empty the final traps. He packs the bait into the small baskets ready for the traps to be dropped again. I cannot look; it is another horrible job, and I have nothing left to throw up.

I enjoy the fast pace and challenge to keep up with Simon's cutting. He nudges me with his elbow. "We make a pretty good team don't you think?" Agreeing, I nudge him back.

We work silently, completely happy out in the ocean. Occasionally water washes over us from the side, drenching the deck, which is annoying and refreshing as the sun heats us up. I have been given a sun hat now, that covers my face and neck. I do not need my hard hat as I am out of danger. My sunglasses reflect the glare. Simon looks out at the ocean from time to time; despite the hard work he seems happy out here.

Skipper Andrew looks around the trawler and observes Simon, the crew and me from time to time. He pauses watching me work. He just nods and smiles and goes back to his Skipper work, keeping the boat moving and logging the catch for the authorities.

Once all the traps have been brought in, the fish are sorted and everyone jumps in and helps prep and stack the catch in the hold underneath. We wash and scrub down everything. We pack away what is not required for the rest of the trip.

All cleaned up we sit and have a moment to rest. The Skipper hands over the trawler to Matt so he can update us and have a coffee and a sandwich. Apparently, it was a good haul especially as some of the fish were a really good size, which will earn lots of points.

Skipper Andrew has plotted our next drop for the traps from intel and chats with the other Fishers who share the good spots. We can rest for half an hour, drop the traps, then go home. He acknowledges me in front of the crew.

"Esther, I underestimated you; I had no idea you were so strong and determined. You are one of the best novice crew I have ever had." He looks at Ezra. "Nearly as proficient as Ezra."

Simon finally speaks after many hours of working silently, "Dad! Esther is really fit and strong especially wrestling her fiancé," he declares proudly.

"Well, whatever she does, she has proven she can handle it. She was born to be a Fisher. Here you had better wear this then as a qualified Shalom crew member." As he walks away, he tosses me a shalom woollen hat with their logo on it and whispers, "and a Fisher's wife."

We all sit outside enjoying the calm water, and Simon pulls me to my feet and holds my hand, like I might blow away. We sit on the side of the trawler on a narrow seat out of everyone's sight and hearing. Simon and I kiss for a moment then sit quietly looking out at the waves and I'm wrapped in his arms. I am so excited when I see a small pod of dolphins swimming alongside us. I make Simon film us and the dolphins in the background. I am on a high; this day is tiring and exhilarating.

Simon puts his arm around me and tells me this is the seat where he encountered the Holy Spirit in the middle of the ocean, looking out just like this. He told me about attending the meetings being younger than some of the others as he had started working on the trawlers when he was sixteen.

He was introduced at this age by his parents to God our Creator, the ancient writings, and clear instructions on how to live. They instructed him how our whole community communicates using fishing and farming parables to teach the ancient writings of God and how to apply it in everyday life. He went to the meetings but did not feel connected at all.

One day he was sitting alone around the age of eighteen, staring at the ocean, feeling frustrated having to work when he was so young. He felt lonely, helpless, and exhausted, particularly that day.

It ran through his head in a constant loop, feeling miserable and suddenly felt, for a moment, peace wash over him. He heard a voice in the distance, which he could not understand. Thinking it was the crew, he looked around but they were all inside eating. He sat down again and looked at the ocean again, seeing it as for the first time, shimmering and bright.

His Dad came looking for him and saw his face, asking him if he was, okay? He told his Dad, "I think so."

His father sat down next to him and said, "Talk to me about what is going on in your head." I told him everything, all my worries and then suddenly it stopped.

His father hugged him, telling him, "I am pretty sure you just encountered the Holy Spirit out here; God spoke to you." I was shocked. He told me to stay where I was and wait, and if I felt someone's presence or voice that was not the crew I should say, 'Here I am Lord.'"

Gripped by his personal story I cannot wait to find out what happened. Simon continues as I hold his hand, squeezing it hard. He tells me he sat on the seat looking at the ocean. "I felt so overwhelmed by my life that I figured I have got nowhere else to be. I will sit here and if the moment is right, I would say the words.

"I sat there feeling a change come over me, then a voice in my head was saying my name. I could not help it. I said, 'Here I am Lord,' and suddenly all my sadness and stress disappeared, my body felt light; it was like I had just awakened from a good night's sleep. I had tears in my eyes, which I could not explain." He says it so simply. It was a bit like James in the city.

Simon looks at me, seeing I am moved by his experience. "Simon that is amazing, remember I had that moment on the cliff near the reserve too. I am still trying to work it all out."

He just squeezes my hand while gazing at me. "Esther, you are like James and I were, you are seeking what a personal relationship with God means to *you* and *your life* after he reveals himself to you. I am so proud of you Esther; you took on today like a Fisher would. Has it helped coming out on the trawler today?"

"Yes, very much. Simon, I need to understand what you do so I can fully support you and share the struggles." He shakes his head, overwhelmed.

"How did I get so lucky?" He embraces me, kissing me with sweet affection fuelled by our connection today. I feel it too and respond, feeling his heart racing like it does when we are close. I feel breathless, overwhelmed with my love for him then it is over as a huge ice-cold bucket of sea water washes over us.

Matt stands there, arms crossed with a mixture of amusement and irritation on his face. A bossy big brother face. "Right! Now you two are cooled off, back to work, time to drop the traps." He flings Simon his hard hat and heavy-duty gloves.

"Why did you do that, *JERK?*" Simon asks aggressively to his brother and gives him a huge shoulder barge as he walks past Matt who says with an edge in his voice, "*You know,*" and walks off to set up the traps and lines.

We shake off the water, knowing we will dry off quickly. Simon kisses me softly on the cheek and pulls his gloves and hard hat on. As he walks away, he looks at me with a look of 'I will continue later' look on his face. I suddenly feel grateful for the bucket cold water. I feel a deeper connection to Simon the more he shares with me.

The crew prepare and co-ordinate the traps being dropped in the new location. It is loud with a beep each time they need to drop, and its fast, hard, and heavy work.

I see how there is real danger, especially as there is a swell and that makes it more challenging for the crew to keep their balance while working quickly with the heavy traps. The deck is often a wash with water as the trawler pushes through the swell.

Looking for a safer, drier place, I sit with Skipper Andrew who is very focused on his GPS, tracking a neat line that he has set up on the screen, managing speed and when to drop the traps. It is intense to watch and impressive how precise it must be. Hard work in every possible way.

Despite being so focused, Andrew seems happy to have me here. He lets me hit the button for the beep to alert the crew; he just nods, and I enjoy helping him. I have rarely spent much time with any of the adult community men to get to know them.

The older men all seem like father figures, which is good. I have never observed or experienced the camaraderie of men and how they interact with each other before, which is different and new. It has been helpful to observe why Simon, and other guys behave the way they do. They are different. They do not talk much.

I watch Andrew announce over the speaker that it is 'pack down.' Everyone packs up the gear in between dodging the water spray continually washing over them. Andrew asks me to help enter data from the trip as it will save time.

He realises quickly what a wise decision it was - I am very adept as it is like math at school. Once satisfied with the data entry, he releases me and gives me a quick side hug, which seems natural. I suspect he is looking forward to having another female around in the family, not just loud alpha males.

Skipper Andrew suggests I could get changed out of my gear and maybe have a nap downstairs. "You've earned it, the crew have too much energy and testosterone, they can burn it off cleaning up and can rest later."

I thank him, happy to get changed, realising the exhaustion is setting in. Once back in my own clothes I find bedding and lay down.

Awakened with a gentle kiss on my cheek, I feel strong familiar arms around me. It is almost dark. Simon is carefully carrying me off the trawler and heading to my Dad's truck. I wake up properly but am tired and feel the lactic acid in my muscles building. I allow him to carry me, happy to rest my head on his strong shoulders and feeling safe.

Simon places me in the front seat of the truck; my Dad asks how I went out there.

"Esther was incredible, strong, and worked hard like any crew member; I could not be more attracted to her Mark. Today confirmed everything, I feel about her. I am not worthy of Esther, yet she loves me."

I see my father slap him on the shoulder. "None of us are mate, yet they love us. Amazing. Maybe you could use that in your vows."

I give Simon a quick hug and kiss, thanked him for today, and promising to message him during the week. He says goodbye and turns and jogs back to the crew.

Arriving home, I shower and pull-on my long cotton pink pyjamas, so comfy. I consume a huge dinner then curl up on the lounge with peppermint tea as my mother massages my sore shoulders and back with a soothing liniment, which is helping to stop my muscles from cramping. I share my day at sea; she listens and is shocked saying, "I now see why the Fisher women worry while their family are at sea."

She sits looking at me differently, maybe as an adult.

"Esther, you are on the most wonderful adventure. Enjoy it, it will not be easy. You are my bright shining star, that is what your name means, as well as being aligned with many strong women, of course. Esther, go out into this world knowing you will shine in whatever you do." I sit with this for a moment - my name means star.

Unlocking my mind's vault of treasured memories. I place my day at sea with my strong future husband. I am humbled he does not think he is worthy of me, when in fact I am unworthy of him. He is so confident of his future, his faith and works incredibly hard.

Is that how we should be? Humbled in each other's presence, knowing we are loved despite our imperfections.

That is exactly what they said at the meeting, about our relationship with God. We are made perfect only through Jesus, *if* we accept him. They used a word 'Grace,' which means underserved favour.

With great clarity I see that is what James and Simon struggled with. Maybe everyone does, including me.

It is clear to me that attending meetings and reading God's ancient writings does not change my relationship with him, only that he is revealed to me. I must examine my life and what I am seeking, then make the decision whether to surrender my old life completely and be renewed by following Jesus, or remain as I am.

Feeling very uncomfortable in my own skin, and reflection on myself is confronting. I am not proud of compartmentalising my life and hiding secrets, but I am not ready to share them with anyone, let alone God. Should I accept that some of my life needs to remain a secret?

I lay hoping to fall asleep peacefully. Unfortunately, it is as rough as a day on the ocean with unrelenting high seas.

CHAPTER 23

My slate beeps intermittently at five am. I check my slate, several messages from Simon and an alert for a delivery to another Medical Precinct. Luckily, it is not the city so a short trip and I will get paid. I hit accept, rise, and dress for work and play today. Ordering a private transport is my only option as my muscles are stiff and painful from new movements yesterday.

Waiting at the curb for my transport, I browse today's laws and messages. To my delight a single transport manual has arrived for me to study, and I'm feeling a flutter of excitement.

I open one of the many messages from Simon. It has been less than a day and I already desperately desire his strong arms around me again. It is full of photos from yesterday, so sweet.

Simon took sneaky candid pictures of me working on the trawler. They are well taken, with the ocean and sky setting the scene. I forward them to my mother; she will treasure these seeing me out there as an independent woman at sea.

Opening the next message truly melts my heart. Simon has recorded himself sitting on the back of the trawler at sea yesterday when I was asleep at dusk on the water. He reveals the things he loves most about me, how he is looking forward to our wedding day at the cliff top so he can tell me how much he loves me. He blows me a kiss at the end.

I close the message and store it in my file safely to look at again later. My eyes are misted up from that beautiful private message.

Arriving at the Medical Precinct's back entrance, I hover my slate and move towards a locker to put my luggage bag in. I may be in time to catch up with everyone at breakfast. I smoothly move to the next locker and retrieve a small satchel, throw it across my body and slip out again. It's great being here in between the shift change, and as it's early, there are only skeleton staff members on duty.

I double check my location standing outside and see the CEO approaching. I play it cool like we hardly know each other. I incline my head, he says good morning to me neutrally, keeping up the charade in case we are observed. He notes how early I am at the Medical Precinct and the satchel across my body for delivery.

"I couldn't sleep and I will be doing intensive study for the next few weeks for my exams."

He nods. "I appreciated your update. I'm impressed you are pushing yourself; we need more high achievers like you." He pauses, looking past me and says awkwardly, "HR tells me your union is at the end of the year…." His voice trails off; I know the polite condescending tone so well. It really indicates: aren't you too young for a union and why bother?

"Yes, I'm looking forward to my union with Simon." I slip easily into town talk.

"What are your plans for study and work?" he asks, concerned.

I suspect that he is worried I may have lots of babies and lose one of his best couriers. I assure the CEO I am planning to study. Not completely settled on law, paralegal, or law enforcement yet.

He looks genuinely shocked. "You are going into law? *Really*!"

I nod like it is the most natural thing in the world to me. "I'm not *dumb* you know," I blurt out, biting my lip. That was rude.

He looks at the ground, realising he has been a huge judgmental jerk. He apologises profusely, his face changes into all shades of red, and his humiliation burning. Town citizens believe so strongly in not offending anyone and equality.

"I am so sorry I misjudged you, I know you are bright, but your academic ability is hidden here. Please come and talk to me after you get your exam results, who knows I may have an internship for a rising star." He smiles briefly, looking at me.

He checks I received my single transport manual to study adding, "Do not open it until you finish your exams. I don't want you distracted."

As he is about to enter, he adds, "I wish you future happiness. I hope this bloke Simon is worthy of you."

"I tell Simon I'm worried that I'm not worthy of him."

"Oh Esther," the CEO says shaking his head, "you are the rising star that everyone sees, but won't acknowledge." With that unexpected boost of praise and insight. I head to the transport hub travelling north today.

The shuttle train transports me quickly to the Medical Precinct. I alight and make my delivery easily and see there is a return satchel for my Medical Precinct, I head back to town to drop the delivery and retrieve my bag.

Entering the back entrance staff are milling around chatting before the next shift. I incline my head to those around me, pretending to get ready, and slip the newly acquired satchel into the CEO's locker like it is my own.

I panic as I realise I have never encountered so many staff in the back entrance before. To go to another locker would be suspicious so I head to the coffee shop for a strong coffee and muffin and wait until the crowd disperses.

As I am walking away from the café, the CEO, who is drinking his coffee nearby, makes a point of calling me to his office sternly. He never usually speaks, only messages - I look genuinely shocked.

As expected, the other staff relish the Farmer girl getting into trouble by the big boss, hoping I will get sacked. They continue to stare at him. Ruby informs me Town people call attractive people eye candy. It is unsettling to observe this behaviour.

I am ushered into his sleek office, observing my surroundings properly for the first time. It is entirely glass, with frosted glass that affords some privacy. The two huge wall screens are switched off, which create a peaceful space. I rest my hand on a soft black leather chair. There is a discreet glass shelf displaying two personal items, an ornate vintage pocket watch and a vintage motorbike toy on a stand, a replica of yesteryear's transport. Totally out of character for this sparsely furnished office and its occupant.

The CEO closes the door with a wave of his wrist whispering, "Sorry about the charade, I must keep up appearances that I'm a little scary." I'm surprised, accepting maybe he is a regular guy when he is not here.

"I saw you in the café and I wanted to give you this gift for your union; I know it is early, but it might help in your planning." The CEO taps his slate, and a message appears from him; I open it and find a three-night accommodation certificate at a fancy hotel in the middle of the city with open ended dates.

I look at him shocked. He says quickly, "After speaking to you earlier I realise I have been a huge judgmental jerk. I do not want to be one of those bitter single citizens ruining other citizen's happiness."

I note he is single, so that might explain the attention from staff. Remembering my manners I thank him.

"This is very generous, CEO Ward, thank you; I could use this for my honeymoon!" He inclines his head, looking at the carpet.

Without thinking I throw my arms around him and give him a brief hug. He is so shocked by this personal interaction that he freezes. I step back and apologise profusely that I invaded his person. He regains his professional persona, smooths his suit, opens the door and waves me out the door, saying loudly for the staff milling around snooping, "I will be watching your work closely Williams and expect only your best."

As he closes the door, I see him smiling. I am unaccustomed to the big boss talking, let alone smiling. Or any Elite.

I rush to return my keep cup to the café, grabbing my bag from the locker and shoving my muffin into my bag. I cannot eat, I am too exited today. Exiting through the rear of the building I walk towards Ruby's place. She really is a town Elite, everything is handy.

Arriving outside her security gate in minutes, I message Simon, hoping to catch him before he is out of range at sea and lean against the beautiful sandstone wall. I trace my finger over a design in the stone absent mindedly. It is a circle with lines through it like a wheel with a P at the top, and I trace around it while I wait for Simon to answer, thinking this seems familiar.

"Good morning love of my life, how's the muscles?" I tell him not too bad considering, he nods, "Everything *okay*?" he asks quickly as he was not expecting me to call so soon.

"Yep." I try not to cry but the dam bursts, and tears are everywhere. I cannot help it and Simon looks crushed. "What's wrong? Do you need me?"

I shake my head as the ugly cry erupts.

"I'm so happy Simon, your message was so beautiful" He waits patiently watching me cry on screen looking very uncomfortable and helpless.

"How can you love me so much?"

"Esther, it's easy to love you, stop crying," he says firmly. "You are getting too worked up, I can't handle seeing you cry, it hurts my heart."

After this sweet sentiment I calmly tell him about the gift we received. Simon cannot believe it.

"You hardly know the CEO, he's your boss." I tell him about our conversation and how I think he felt like a big jerk. I cannot tell him I have met the CEO on several occasions at his bidding to check in on the courier work.

"Can you thank him for the generous gift. I cannot wait to take my hot wife there," he says with far too much enthusiasm out in the open.

I realise he is not on his family trawler. "Simon, where are you?" He looks guilty.

"Um, I am on Zach's trawler doing maintenance today." He looks around whispering, "Secret fiancé business. Zach invited me to hang out with him and some of his married Fisher crew since we will not meet with him and Hannah for two weeks. He thought it would be good to have a break from fishing today."

"Okay have fun, I'm off to Ruby's to study."

"I will. Hannah is your chaperone, so I will keep Zach entertained until she is home again. I love you Esther, you remember that," he says very quietly but seriously.

"Me too," I say, blowing him a kiss.

I pass through the gate and into the house, which is alive with housemates who have woken up eating a stack of scrambled eggs, grilled tomatoes and can I smell bacon?

They all cheer when they see me. Jonah, Andrew, Thomas, and a few other Fisher guys run and gather around me - I look at them.

"Are you guys okay?" they laugh.

Jonah says, "We heard you totally rocked it, out fishing yesterday, we are impressed."

I start laughing and tell them huge respect to you Fishers going out to sea, then I look at young Andrew. "I'm so glad you will be there to help them soon." He nods, pulling me into a headlock. "Good to see you, sis."

We all laugh and settle down as Peter wanders into the kitchen looking pleased there is real food in front of him.

"Can I?" he asks Hannah.

"Of course," she says, loading his plate. He looks at Ruby and all of us saying, "Not a word to Krystal about any of this," indicating the food he is about to consume and the bench heaving with fresh produce ready for food prep. The kitchen is on its maiden voyage of cooking not reheating.

We all nod, sworn to secrecy. Peter announces he will be heading out for the day and will not be home for dinner. Leaving the kitchen he kisses Ruby on the cheek affectionally, heading to his study.

Hannah comes around the bench and gives me a long sisterly hug. "I'm so pleased for you and Simon. Maybe we can catch up during the week over a coffee in the garden."

"Okay, thanks Hannah," I say pleased.

She breaks the hug saying, "I believe that our men are hanging out together today."

"Apparently, I don't know how much work they will actually do."

We laugh thinking about young guys with some time on their hands supposedly maintaining a trawler.

I turn to everyone. "So what have I missed?"

They all groan, saying Hannah is brutal making them study and has even set up an annoying song as an alert to change activities. I get the feeling they secretly love the routine.

The food is amazing they all inform me. I look around and see that all the families appear to have sent some food along. I offer to buy pizza one night to give Hannah a break, which she happily agrees to.

Ruby and Sarah practically carry me to Ruby's room, where they have set up camp, no different from any other time we sleep over. I unpack my bag pulling out Bunny and throwing him onto my bed.

Sarah lays on my bed picking up Bunny saying, "I think you should be called Simon, cause you're *so* cute." We all laugh.

Sarah sighs. "Hannah is hypervigilant, I cannot even get close to Josh without her keeping us on task."

Ruby nods, smiling. "Me too. Jonah is hopeless; he tries to sneak over to be with me. She immediately has him taking the rubbish out."

Sarah smiles, "We are all so lucky to have totally hot, sexy Fisher boyfriends and fiancé."

Hannah sticks her head in the door, "Study time. Sarah, speak more respectfully about the guys."

"Okay," we say, and as she leaves the room, she says quietly so no one else can hear except us, "Yep, especially Fisher husbands," We all laugh. Hannah has revealed she really is human and is totally in love with Zach.

I smile thinking that will be me soon. The others see that smile and tease me saying we will never see you when you are in a union with Simon.

"Yes, you will," I say defiantly.

They shake their heads smiling mischievously laughing. "No we won't."

The sudden realisation that Simon and I will be intimate soon makes my heart race a little. I'm not sure if I am excited or nervous about the unknown and fulfilling my desire to be with my new husband. I wonder if he feels the same? My face feels warm; I dismiss the image quickly, hiding my thoughts.

"Right, study time, what's on today's plan?" I look at my slate and Hannah has emailed me the timetable for the week and a link to a study tracker app. She is determined we are all going to pass these exams and not stray with our boyfriends.

Hannah has reset the kitchen, dining, and lounge room with areas to study in; anyone in a romantic relationship is separated to stay focused. She has set up the open plan kitchen bench as a healthy snack and drink station.

The first bars of the silly song start, and everyone finds a quiet place to study, those already integrated into Hannah's routine, which strangely seems calming and welcoming. I notice she has set herself up at the kitchen bench with large and smaller slates on stands. She sees me admiring the large slate.

"I'm studying for my final exams in medicine." I nod, it helps that she is studying too. She is disciplined herself, especially getting through a medical degree. Wow, a Fisher doctor, that is cool.

I download the study app and get into my study rhythm, feeling good. I work through practice exams. I look around for a moment and see everyone is quiet, and focused.

Hannah's song starts and everyone places their slates on charge and head outside. Apparently its yoga now, led by Ruby's yoga teacher who has been hired to come in through the week. We all head outside, there are brightly coloured mats laid outside on the soft grass. All I can think of is a nap would be so nice as I am still tired from yesterday and sore.

Sky, our instructor, assigns us a mat, including Hannah, taking us through the gentle movements. She walks among us; Sarah, Ruby, and I try not to laugh at our poor efforts. Ruby is downplaying how flexible she is. Sky notices my stiff reluctant movements and asks if I have had an injury, and everyone laughs.

Andrew says, "Nah, she was out deep-sea fishing yesterday, gutting fish."

Sky processes the whole disgusting image of me out at sea fishing. To her credit, she keeps a neutral demeanor and says, "Right, let's work on stretching to get rid of all that lactic acid."

I follow her instructions and she continues the class, reappearing later with a spray that apparently soothes and heals sore muscles. I thank her after the class, spraying it on all my sore muscles and I feel relief quickly; it is amazing. It must be a town Elite product. I am grateful, as the burn grows in every limb.

We are encouraged to change rooms to keep focused. I curl up on cushions in the lounge room and start on my next task, to download more past exams. I might as well face what is to come. I am pleasantly surprised that they are not too difficult, which means over the last six months I have managed to study enough alone while working essentially two jobs as well as the garden, to have a real chance.

We have lunch together and then have some free time until three pm to resume more study. Everyone swims. I choose to rest in the shade of a huge umbrella slathered in sunscreen. Hannah joins me, sipping on a green smoothie.

She settles in the shade too, supervising of course; she really does care about us and is trying to keep everyone from getting carried away in every possible way. She seems to be respected, maybe because of her younger age, but a responsible adult too.

Hannah tells me that Zach thought it could be helpful to Simon to have some trustworthy guys work together and chat casually about how to be a good husband and preparing to run a home.

Zach is a cool surfer guy. I do not see him as a serious Fisher who runs his own trawler and supports his wife in full time study. I wonder what that conversation would be like. She reads my mind.

"I know what you are thinking. How could he get guys to sit and talk? They don't, but he assures me that it gets them working alongside each other and the conversations flow. Apparently, that is what the guys did for him and he was totally grateful, so am I." She pauses and smiles to herself.

I look at her surprised. "Hannah, are you thinking about *you know*?" She nods in agreement.

"Sorry I got sidetracked; I miss him already you know. You get used to having them around, in your bed, tripping on boots and fishing gear."

I wonder what the guys will talk about...my expression causes her to clarify.

"Esther, it is totally wholesome, nothing disrespectful, and very general. Wouldn't you prefer Simon to hear about marriage from good guys in our community, not from citizens at the wharf who do not respect their partners? Like us talking, I hope you trust me Esther, to ask any question you have. I am also going to be a doctor so technically I know stuff," she says, raising her left eyebrow a little and smiling.

She pats me on the arm and closes her eyes under her sunglasses. She's glad of a break from studying too.

At least, training to be a doctor, she is used to explaining things to people, especially awkward stuff. Maybe I will take up her offer. I drift off to sleep, unable to fight the exhaustion.

CHAPTER 24

Study week at Ruby's is occupied with study schedules keeping us on track. It is a sweet moment floating between childhood and adulthood.

Friday, the end of our week, finally arrives. Hannah has arranged for some Uni students to drop in tonight and chat about life after leaving school. Hannah asks if pizza is okay tonight and can I arrange it.

Hannah has organised for us to collaborate today. We break for lunch and Hannah asks us to message her some meal suggestions for next week so she can arrange supplies.

Ruby looks happy and not just because she and Jonah are holding hands covertly under the table. She tells us she has never eaten so well, and her stomach pain is gone; she usually has issues with town food.

Hannah asks slowly, "Do you think the fancy meals are making you sick?"

Ruby shrugs. Sarah and I smile. Our friend seems to be thriving with home-style cooking, which we have taken for granted. Ruby is asked to choose a few of her favorites so they can be provided.

"Jonah, any suggestions?" Hannah asks sweetly.

"Nope, just lots of it and less fish." We laugh at his honesty.

After lunch, we sit scrolling our slates and see pictures of James and Simon riding a single transport. To our surprise, James is on Simon's family trawler, Shalom, dressed as a Fisher. My friends are delighted, laughing and punching the air celebrating.

"Yes! we got another to turn Fisher, Esther's next." I groan to their amusement.

James looks content in his new occupation. I smile thinking about my fishing trip as the most inexperienced, he will be too, working with Simon.

Opening my messages from Simon, I slip away to savour them. He has left a message that he cannot wait to see me at the picnic and is missing me.

I open another message and to my delight, he has sent three pictures of properties to visit together. He went to the trouble of travelling to each and taking a picture of himself out the front posing as the occupant. Even Zeb features in one of them. I am touched by his dedication of finding us our first home.

I open another message from Simon. It's a photo diary of his week, plenty of photos with the guys, and lastly a beautiful photo of Simon on the trawler in his casual clothes at dusk, smiling making the heart shape with his hands over his heart, and blue eyes looking directly at me. Pow! That stopped my heart for a moment. I sit looking at my fiancés picture for a long time, sigh, and save it as my cover screen.

Ruby and Sarah discover me staring at the picture of Simon and go crazy. They hit me with cushions 'whack, whack' saying, how dare I be so happy. The guys come in and I show them the picture; Andrew makes a puking sound and shakes his head.

The guys laugh, "You have destroyed Simon; he used to be cool." Hannah reins in the noise and sends us outside to burn off all our energy.

After many rounds of aggressive pool volleyball we are summoned to study again. Every day my confidence grows approaching the exams. We settle down for several hours of study, changing locations every hour. I see Hannah totally engrossed in her study too, with two slates open and slumped over them. We all must work hard to get ahead. Opening more past exams I test myself; I cannot wait for this to end and have a life.

My study app tracks my study and accuracy - this is incredible. I receive helpful feedback too; it lists specific tasks to work on. My study ends quickly as the noise of the front door banging open announces Isaiah, Lizzy and Mark arriving, followed by a grinning Zach. Hannah flies into his arms; they embrace for a long time, briefly kiss and separate.

We gather in the lounge room, and the three students sit on the floor. I smile to myself, reminiscent of them in their own place.

Isaiah enthusiastically starts the conversation, regaling memories of his first experiences at Uni, waving his arms around to punctuate his points. He's not only a Fisher kid but trying to make it in the city.

He tells us they are very different to everyone in the city and decided if they could blend just enough, they may survive but trying not to lose their identity. He shares with us the high cost to live near Uni.

Isaiah shares with us how they swap clothing with Simon and James, so it looks like they are not poor. My friends hang off his words like tickets to a new world.

Mark speaks quietly about his courses in tech which is interesting and how he navigates the campus and the other students who tolerate him, some accept he is just like them. His friends nod, agreeing this is their experience too.

Mark finishes saying something that stings. "We must make a choice of which path we are going to travel as adults; we cannot travel on two paths at the same time." He looks around the room and deliberately points to each of us.

"You will have to decide, are you going to keep the values you were raised with and the struggles it poses or totally abandon it for the easy life? These are choices we need to make alone, without parents or community telling us."

The room is silent; the weight of his words resting on us.

Lizzy, after a moment, says that the others have covered everything, except that they put her in charge of managing their food budget. She invites everyone to ask questions, which they are happy to answer.

Hannah and Zach separate us into male and female groups and send the guys to hang out in the garage with him and the visitors. Hannah and Lizzy stay with the females.

Lizzy and Hannah talk directly to us about Uni and being female adults, free from school and how they imagined it was going to be. They stress that even if you do not study, you will be exposed to the cruel and harsh treatment from town and city people, and must be prepared for that, as Mark mentioned. Make decisions ahead of time, so you know how to respond when situations arise.

They talk about sex. I cringe inwardly. They are so cool and relaxed saying we were created to enjoy it but there are many stages of intimacy. However, the world jumps to the last stage first, where our community encourages strong foundations built on trust and friendship *first.*

"We need to accept that we are young and want to have fun. That is why guys do crazy dangerous stuff, and girls do too," Lizzy says, asking for questions.

Sarah asks, "What's the night life like Lizzy?"

Lizzy says without hesitation, "Loud, scary, and fun. Sometimes dangerous, depending on where you go and who you are with. Usually, too much alcohol and drugs are the problem; it makes people feel free and confident."

She retells of a few scary nights in the city where guys or girls have made unwelcome aggressive moves on her and she did not feel safe. The worst is seeing people you know under the influence of these chemicals with no inhibitions.

It can be dangerous because everyone freely shares themselves around and expects others to behave the same. If someone says no, they get violent and angry.

One of our friends asks, "Do Farmer and Fisher students choose to have sex, casual sex?"

We all sit feeling uncomfortable, looking at Lizzy and Hannah intently. Lizzy and Hannah say at the same time without hesitation, "Sometimes."

Lizzy adds, "It is usually not in their plans, it just happens due to the moment and quite often followed by regret, or in some cases they choose to be sexually active. If they are not careful, they may become pregnant or contract an STI."

Hannah agrees that she has seen a lot of casual hook ups and was tempted when dating but chose not to. She adds there is a real health risk of having multiple partners or even the danger of abuse.

The doorbell alerts us that the pizza has arrived. We thank our visitors for their insights and Hannah for helping us get through the first week. The students leave to head off to catch up with friends at a local bar.

Zach wraps his arms around Hannah. "I'm going to steal my gorgeous girl away for the weekend." He asks us to clean up for her. We promise to clean up the whole house before heading home, noting how cute Zach and Hannah are together. They leave hand in hand.

Finally free, everyone runs around chasing each other and having wild battles with pool noodles.

Ruby, Sarah, and I sit at the kitchen bench laughing at everyone's antics. We freeze when we see dark silent figures moving through the house with hand guns and beams of red light sweeping every room - the Law Enforcers.

I grab my friends' hands telling them quietly to follow my lead, to answer questions honestly and to keep their eyes down. I see Ruby covertly touch her slate under the bench, putting her finger to her lips.

We are immediately rounded up like cattle into the lounge room and told to lie face down and shut up. I can feel the terror and fear in the air; it makes me angry not fearful, trying to work out why an Elite house would be under suspicion.

The faceless captain demands to know what is going on. His eyes are dark and liquid, he informs us they were alerted to this house because it has Farmers and Fishers squatting, having wild parties and wrecking the place.

"Anyone prepared to talk?" he barks out.

I turn my head and shoot a look at Jonah that clearly says not a word. I raise my hand.

"Stand up, speak," he barks.

I stand, my arms at my side and my eyes on the floor. They keep their weapons focused on me and the group.

"We are Ruby's friends, she lives here. We are studying for our HSC exams and were blowing off steam. Our chaperone has just left, and we will all be going home after dinner." I indicate with my head at the mountain of hot pizza stacked on the bench.

We hear someone bursting through the front door smashing it against the wall, and their feet stomping down the hallway. I am pleased to see Peter with Town Elite officials following; he looks rabid. I try not to laugh at this scene.

He marches straight up to the Enforcers and identifies himself as the owner, revealing a very long official title, and confirming it with his slate.

"Show your faces, cowards. If you are going to pick on school kids at least have the guts to show your faces." He points at their captain. "Come with me." The captain tells the Enforcers to lower their weapons but not to move.

We see Peter, Elite officials and the captain move down the hallway to Peter's study, which was a waste of time. We hear every delicious morsel of Peter's verbal assault on the Law Enforcers' invasion. We cannot hear what the officials are saying but it would be polite. Elites do not shout or even raise their voices except for Peter tonight.

There is a long silence.

We remain perfectly still. Even the Enforcers, who have uncovered their faces, which reveal they feel like idiots, but need to keep up the charade of being in control.

Peter, the officials, and the captain reappear. The subdued captain apologises for the intrusion, saying they had been alerted and had to respond. Hardly an apology but the humiliation was satisfying enough.

He jerks his head and the Enforcers leave silently in single file. He follows and must yank the front door, now embedded into the wall, to close it. My friends stand up, some cry, some express anger or are in shock.

The officials check if we are okay. Satisfied, they excuse themselves and leave. Peter holds Ruby tight. "I am so proud of you, you did everything right, just like we practiced. This is a nightmare I never want to experience again." He looks at us all pale and shaken.

"You all did well. Get used to this crap, the more you go out into this world the more hate you will experience."

Jonah says with admiration, "Peter you could have totally kicked his ass. You should have seen Esther, she stood up and did not flinch, even when that giant gorilla was barking out orders."

"Well, Jonah, some of us are equipped for the job," he says, giving me a subtle nod.

"I have to confess Jonah, I was afraid I was going to totally lose control, and yeah I was so fired up I could have kicked his ass," Peter says laughing. "Hey, pizza, there is no way I am going back to work now," he says excitedly.

We chat about how we felt after the Enforcers' invasion; everyone is okay but shaken. Peter messages our families to inform them what happened and reassures them everything is okay.

After finishing the pizza, Peter invites us to stay and make some noise since the neighbors have already complained. He tells everyone his chill-out zone is available downstairs too if we want to game on his big screen.

As I am helping myself to a drink in the quiet pantry, Peter approaches me asking, "Have you got a minute to pop down and check out the chill zone?"

I look at his face, and I get the clear message he wants to talk about today without the law listening in.

"Sure, it's been ages, I haven't seen all your new gaming technology."

I leave my slate behind following Peter downstairs and shudder a little; the temperature is significantly lower. I slip past the wild activity of interactive gaming that everyone is engrossed in.

Peter ushers me into what looks like a home gym. He bends down to release a secret panel manually at the base of decorative wall to reveal a private office and storage area. He closes the door.

"Peter, what is this place?"

He says simply, "This room, if discovered, will have me killed and cause a huge problem out in the community."

It is confusing, all I can see is a desk and a wall of storage drawers, nothing to change the world. He asks me to sit at the desk then manually unlocks drawer after drawer, which springs open. Peter proceeds to explain quickly that our community has our faith and many other groups have their own, different to ours, but the law has forbidden it - made it disappear.

Those who have defied the law are locked up and he suspects some have been silenced. Permanently. He opens a drawer and pulls out a bag carefully labelled with a name on it, GOLD, I hold my breath, my neighbors' items.

He informs me, "This belongs to a local family who's hidden faith is Judaism. This prayer shawl is significant to their faith and to them."

"There are so many people being controlled. How have you got *their* shawl?"

Peter confesses he is responsible for checking, recording, and destroying confiscated belongings from the communities, but he cannot do it. He decided to have this room built and he completed the final stages with a few trusted people. He looks at me.

"Like your Dad." I look in the drawers and there are hundreds of bags carefully labelled and packed.

"What are you going to do with all of this?" I am perplexed.

"I am planning to give these items back to their owners when peace and freedom to practice religion returns." He looks at my terrified face.

"I am telling you because I believe you can be a part of the change to this stupid closeminded thinking."

I lower my eyes. "Why *me*? I am only just coming to grips with all this God stuff."

"Because you can," he says simply.

"I will help you, you are going into law, right? You will need to immerse yourself in their world and know the laws so intimately that you can help all these people."

He gestures to the drawers. "I am very fluent in them too. That is why I can get people out of trouble knowing the laws and use it with my knowledge of history. I want Ruby to help me one day when I think she is ready to understand our life and help change it for the better."

"*No, no, no,* I'm marrying Simon and going to Uni. Ask someone else in our community to help you." I plead.

"They already are, but in different ways. We deserve independent thoughts and freedom to express of our faith," Peter says quietly.

"NO! I can't lie to Simon. We promised complete honesty."

"Esther…" Peter holds my hand gently.

"Haven't you realised he is already involved? He will help you. You are both strong and smart and can withstand the laws and brutality."

I think of the conversation with my parents and Simon about being scribes, covertly writing God's word using the resources they have. It is clear now that anyone over eighteen in our group could be involved, even if they have not realised it.

I tell Peter *NO* again, firmly feeling the flip-flop in my stomach and slip away, not looking back, trying to erase what I just heard and saw.

We farewell Ruby with big hugs who looks sad that we are leaving.

Jonah kisses her, saying, "Don't worry Rubes, we will be back next week to trash your place." This makes her smile.

I order a transport for Sarah and me - happy to head home. Sarah asks me what my plans are and I reply truthfully, “Hanging out with Simon, I miss him.”

“I’m going to hang out with Josh without Hannah patrolling us,” Sarah says.

“Do you really think that Hannah wants to be like that? She knows we do dumb stuff at our age and get distracted.”

She agrees, saying, “Honestly, I don’t think I would have studied, as Josh can’t keep his hands off me.”

“Sarah, be careful, it’s a challenge to stop when it’s like that, I know.”

She looks at me surprised. “*Really!*”

“Yep,” is all I can muster looking out the window heading home, thinking about picnic day, and seeing my Simon start his new life.

CHAPTER 25

My parents awaken me early to avoid detection at the river. We dress quickly and slip out of the house. Luke will not be coming as it is only those who attend meetings.

We walk briskly through the bush, keeping our slates on sleep mode, and arriving at our destination where the water is shallow, waist height and almost still. I observe men and women dotted in the bush acting as guardians to protect this sacred moment. They nod to us as we pass, another reminder that we are never safe.

We settle near the riverbank with everyone already seated quietly on blankets. I see Simon and James in the distance with their fathers getting ready.

Friends from the city sit right on the riverbank, with their feet dangling in the water. I sit, taking all this in. There have been so many things I have been omitted from knowing and now it is all available to me; it is overwhelming.

Simon and James quickly change into long white cotton shirts that cover them. They bow their heads, praying with their families then enter the cold water with their fathers. Each of their fathers has elected to baptise them. They stand side by side. Peter appears and addresses us from the riverbank and the group in the cool swirling river.

"Simon and James have met with me during the week and have confirmed they are committed to turning their lives around to follow Christ. They have confessed their weaknesses and failure to do what is right.

"They accept the Lord Jesus as their Lord and Saviour and ask that we support them daily in our prayers on their new journey as followers and defenders of the faith. Will you support them?"

"We will," everyone replies.

Peter sits down lost in the crowd again; I wonder what they talked about? I turn my attention to the river where the fathers stand next to their sons, Simon, and James, talking quietly. They stand facing us.

James goes first. His father supports his body, praying over him as he leans him back fully immersing him in the cool river water and brings him up slowly. James stands for a moment quietly clearing the water from his face and beams looking so happy, then turns and embraces his father for a long moment. His father pats him on the back when they separate and I see tears in James' eyes and a huge smile I've never seen before. They move several steps sideways respectfully.

Andrew prays over Simon and lowers him into the water supported, and fully immersed, which seems so long to me. I hold my breath for a few seconds and his father brings him up. He too stands quietly for a moment. He seems to be taking in this precious moment then turns to his father smiling and they embrace warmly and Simon even lets out a cheer with tears at the same time. He looks exhilarated and energised.

They climb out of the river and their families embrace them.

I run to Simon through the groups of people now standing, feeling completely connected to him, sharing in this intimate part of his life while his family discreetly stands back. He holds out his arms as I throw myself at him wrapping my arms around his neck. I kiss him and we embrace. Holding each other tightly, he and I stand embracing and talking quietly, our foreheads touching. He speaks such beautiful words of love and promises of his commitment to me to be a better person every day, and he has silent tears running down his cheeks. I nod with tears running down my cheeks and say, "Me too."

We are transported to a private moment reflecting on Simon's baptism, and the profound meaning it will have on his life. I acknowledge to him I am a beneficiary of his decision today. I, in turn, will try to be worthy of it, knowing I have a lot of work to do in my own life.

We eventually break the special moment, which transfixes everyone. Our love is strong.

Our community is a witness to Simon and James' public declaration to turn to Christ. They are moved by the experience too; everyone is quietly sitting and reflecting.

Simon and I separate. He removes his long, wet, white shirt and hands it to his mother, who quickly wraps it up and puts it into her basket. Simon quickly pulls a casual t-shirt back on while smiling down at me, "Sorry you're all wet." I shrug, I will dry.

Rachael invites my family to sit with them and share breakfast. We lay out our blankets and food in the centre and we all sit around the edge. Andrew asks everyone to join hands and give thanks for God's blessing on this day and the food he has provided.

He continues to pray a heartfelt thankfulness that their son has given his life fully to Christ and God has provided a partner for life who will soon be a part of their family, my parents and Luke too. Everyone says, "Amen," happily agreeing. We eat a simple meal together, enjoying each other's company.

As there is a limited time, we can leave our slates switched off. Our parents farewell Simon and me as they will return home and leave the younger people to stay on and hang out at the river for the day.

Jonah, Andrew, and a few others say they are heading down further where the water is deeper. Some of us stay where we are and switch our slates back into relaxation mode near the river after a long week working or studying.

I see James approaching and throw my arms around him, squeezing him tight. "James, I am so happy for you. You seem happier, I've never seen you smile like that."

He untangles himself from me and sits with us, totally serene and happy. James tells us he has felt much happier than he has for a long time this week. He has a constant smile on his face, and his eyes are bright and he's not shy all the time. He is truly transformed and comfortable in himself.

I observe that his dark brown hair has been cut very short and he is tanned being out on the water. He suddenly has grown up. Maybe fishing is his future not laboring in construction, or is it surrounding himself with good people?

James has a leather wristband like Simon's, a gift from his parents, he tells me. I noticed he and Lizzy talked briefly, but no sign of any intimacy there; maybe it is over. I am glad I kept it to myself.

I leave Simon and James to talk to their out-of-town friends while I stretch out on my blanket in the shade of huge gum trees and read more of my zombie story and then drift off to sleep. I am suddenly awakened by loud vibrations on the ground and commotion from squawking birds getting closer. Realising I am not dreaming, this threat is real.

Simon is stretched out next to me on the blanket, also asleep. He wakes with a start, and I hear him swear under his breath and says to follow his lead.

We sit on the mat and kiss, he keeps kissing me as I observe from the corner of my eyes Law Enforcers breaking into the clearing in full combat gear, rifles out, eyes only visible. A truly terrifying image. They quickly survey what is going on; they leave two on guard, and the rest look around the surrounding bush.

Simon stops the kiss, but he holds my hand firmly, to reassure me I am okay. We sit and wait. The captain demands to know what is going on. Isaiah steps out unafraid and says we are hanging out for the day with our friends, having a picnic and swimming.

The captain indicates sharply with his head for the weapons to be lowered. He looks Isaiah in the eye, who does not blink or change his demeanor. He looks carefully around at this scene of distasteful Farmer and Fisher kids by the river appearing to be lazing about. He makes a hand signal to his crew who search all our belongings. Satisfied there is no illegal activity, they leave as nosily as they arrived. Isaiah puts his finger on his lips to say the slates are listening.

After repacking our belongings, some choose to go home, distraught, unsettled after this violation. However, many stay to enjoy the day, free and defiantly determined to not be intimidated.

We are becoming more accustomed to these invasions of privacy. Although, today was different, the authorities new something was happening, just unsure what. It makes sense now that we met early and had centuries to guard the baptism space. To disperse quickly afterwards, switching on our slates and having a picnic, reflecting exactly what our chatter online was about, meeting up for a picnic.

Isaiah suggests we all go for a swim, keeping up the charade and knowing we can talk freely in the water. We wade in and enjoy the water, and the guys go crazy tackling each other making noise.

The girls find a quiet spot in the water and chat. I have missed Lizzy, I enjoy chatting to the older girls too, as they are so relaxed about life.

I ask Lizzy how city life is. She looks sad and confesses that she and James were seeing each other and recently decided it was not working. She said she really likes him, he's so different to the city guys.

Everyone looks surprised and disappointed for her. Phoebe and Deborah ask her why she did not tell them about James; I feign surprise too. I get the sense he ended it. Shame really, but honesty is a good quality regardless of the pain. We all say we are sorry and vow to keep it private; we do not want Lizzy and James to feel awkward.

Lizzy says to Deborah, "How long have you and Isaiah been together now?" She looks embarrassed, putting her hands over her face; everyone screams, excitedly splashing her.

"Ages, we just did not want everyone knowing about us early on. The party was when we went public."

Lizzy says, "Isaiah isn't the most discreet when it comes to girls he likes; he usually tells everyone." She wades over to Deborah, pulling her hands away from her face, looking her in the eye.

"*No,* is he the one?" Lizzy asks.

Deborah nods. "I'm pretty sure he is." Everyone is silent.

Lizzy asks, "Does he act like you are his *one*?" She nods smiling, "He is so sweet, romantic and he wants me so bad. I hate to admit it, but I love him courting me."

She covers her face again. We all laugh far too hard trying to get the image of Isaiah romantically pursuing Deborah - so different to his carefree bachelor ways.

Deborah puts her finger on her lips to indicate it is our secret.

Lizzy says, "Thank goodness for this freezing river to cool these horny guys down." She really does lack tact.

"So, you feel *nothing, absolutely nothing* when you see an attractive guy at Uni or especially when we're at the beach, waxing his board, you're totally dead inside?" Phoebe challenges Lizzy.

We all erupt again into laughter, which is so liberating to talk about this real stuff in a lighthearted way.

Lizzy says to Deborah, "Seriously, don't play games with him, tell him straight how you feel." Deborah agrees, promising she will.

The girls turn to me, teasing me in a good-natured way about how handsome Simon is and the upcoming wedding. They assure me, "Don't worry, Simon's solid, he'll take care of you, after all that's what his family name means, Allen means Rock."

We swim for a while then Simon and I get out and dry off. I steal long looks at his uncovered toned torso, strong shoulders, and muscles while he is not aware. He is very modest and pulls his t-shirt on quickly. I pull my dress on over my costume as I usually do so I can continue to swim later, suspecting he has spied on me too, but too discreet to be caught.

Simon lays on the blanket and I rest my head on his chest, listening to his steady heart. We chat easily about our week as messages and photos do not convey the full story.

He opens his slate and we look at his three choices of homes to rent. I am impressed how good they are and how thoughtful he has been as he talks through each one and the considerations and what he thinks we need. A quiet area for me to study, room for a vegetable patch if I want, a garage for his fishing gear, tools and storing the transport and maybe room for Zeb.

He asks me which one I think I like the most. I roll onto my stomach and lean on my elbows looking at him. I genuinely mean it when I say, "I trust your choice, the one that you think is the best, they all look good, I just want to be with you." It sounded mushy to me, but I meant it.

"Good, because I have already put down a deposit on this one, a large two-bedroom granny flat with a shared yard. It's located at the back of an established older home and a short walk around the corner to the reserve." I see him smiling, today he looks so self-assured and certain of what to do, it is very charming.

I ask him, "What made you choose this place besides it's near the reserve that I love?" His face is bright red, and confesses the master bedroom, which is spacious, has a great view of the garden and is private.

"So, it is the view you had in mind when looking at this master bedroom?" He puts the slate down and covers his face with his hands so I cannot see him smiling and what he is thinking.

I lean over him, my hair falling over his face, and laughing.

"Look at me, Simon, confess!" He looks through his fingers at me. I pull them away and lean over closer, looking directing at him unblinking.

He says quietly, "I couldn't help it; all I could think was, this is where my hot wife and I will sleep." I cannot contain my sheer delight and laughter. We look at each other, smiling for a few moments quietly and thinking about the next step ahead of us, not just intimacy.

He leans up, kissing me so tenderly, and gathers me in his arms, sitting up and pulling me onto his lap. We stop and I rest my head on his shoulder, and he holds me as we sit looking out at the river together.

I run my fingers over the intricate woven design of his wrist band and notice a healing tattoo underneath. Simon puts his finger to my lips as he pulls back the band to reveal a strong black anchor.

"Remember this Christian symbol like on the trawler? It means hope and steadfastness in the face of adversity and persecution. I don't think today could be more perfect with my girl by my side on the day I made the biggest decision of my life," he whispers in my ear.

"How come our Dads weren't with you looking at the houses?"

"When we chatted this week Peter helped me see I want to be independent, and it was making me crazy. Peter told me, 'We are a family too, you and me.' I went looking all by myself and it helped me think about making my own decisions and how freeing it was. I really enjoyed thinking about what you might like. It helped me not miss you so much, except looking at master bedrooms…" He smiles shyly. "I'm so glad I didn't take the Dads; they would have fussed. I asked God to decide and here we are," he whispers in my ear.

I whisper back, "Thank you God, thank you Peter. It is time to head home, another busy week ahead. This day had to end eventually." Simon gets up slowly, clearly not wanting the day to end.

"How about dinner at my place? You can show my parents the place, and the details of the master bedroom, with what you said …to share with your hot wife!" I laugh as I gather my bag walking off with a bounce in my step, only to be swooped off my feet by strong arms and swung around.

"No, I think you should tell them that this is where you will share your bed with your very handsome, very hot, strong husband."

I feel heat in my face looking up at him and so comfortable in his strong safe arms. He places me carefully on the ground and I reach up and wrap my arms around his neck. We are so close, whispering so no one can hear us.

"I have no problem saying that to anyone who wants to hear it. You are the only one I want and cannot wait until I can be with you." Simon's heart beats faster and kisses me briefly.

"I will see you at the house. I want to say goodbye to the guys before they head back to the city." He jogs back.

I head for home. Lizzy calls from a distance, so I wait for her to catch up.

I nudge Lizzy, saying, "James hey!"

Lizzy tells me they had fun hanging out and riding together. She was very attracted to him, and he seemed very attracted to her, but things started to move very quickly and he was not prepared to let it go any further, so he broke it off. She concedes that their communication was okay, but it could have been a lot better and probably the main reason for the breakup.

As we walk back down the bush trail, I realise that James is committed to setting boundaries early in dating, I admire that courage. Many would stay in a mediocre relationship because it was easier than having the hard conversation to breakup or letting it go further.

Both Simon and James seem more confident and happier. Whatever they talked about with Peter was powerful enough to bring them to today - self-assured and ready to live God's way.

Saying goodbye to Lizzy at the bush reserve gate, I order a transport for her back to her parents. She is very grateful.

I reach my gate, and Simon is just behind me, so I wait for him. He comes up grabbing both my hands and looks down at my ring, tracing the pattern as he often does. He tells me he wants to be better, and that means more self-control over every part of his life.

"You're not angry with me for stopping us when it gets too much, are you, Esther?" He lifts his head up and looks into my eyes; I shake my head.

"No, I'm glad you do."

"Not by much, it is one of the things Peter challenged me on, if I could stop. I am determined to be more in control of my decisions and how I spend my time with you." He smirks, Simon releases my hands and starts tracing the number on our gate with his finger absent mindedly.

"I was thinking, on my way back, let's spend time having fun; I want to *really* date you. Let's explore the city together, go to night clubs when you are eighteen, dance with me until it's late and maybe seeing a few bands." I nod, wanting to spend quality time with him.

"Simon, I'm glad you're doing the work, I need to also. I think you're further along on that journey than me." I ask about the tattoo.

Simon says grimly, "Trust me, I am braver than I thought. Esther, I never noticed this before because the gate is always open, the number on your gate is made of two circles with line like a wheel with a P at the top, this is an ancient Christian symbol." He points to his anchor and my ring and puts his finger on my lips.

I stop for a moment and think for the first time in my life, '*Oh crap,* what scary stuff has my parents got me involved in? I have seen this symbol before….'

He holds my hand, leading me to the house. "Now it's time to start planning our life without too much interfering from parents." I laugh, knowing they love us, but we are more than ready to be independent. Or are we?

CHAPTER 26

Our final week of study begins. I am focused without distractions.

Hannah greets everyone smiling, reminding us of the goal ahead and sends her plan for the week - shorter study periods. She has assigned us all to help with cooking, called life skills. Ruby is excited about cooking. Jonah moans he is only interested in eating.

Sarah and Josh cook tonight, while they create a monstrous mess in the kitchen. I step out into the beautiful evening looking at the sunset, the birds nosily settle for the night. I open my slate, realising how clear I am in my plans moving forward, and not easily distracted.

I scroll until I find messages from Simon, a short message of encouragement. Perfect. Sweet. I message 'guess who's cooking tonight?' When I inform him; he sends back hilarious pictures illustrating vomiting. I inform him that we all will cook, even Jonah, which prompts images of a house on fire. I laugh out loud messaging back 'goodnight, missing you.'

We sit eating lasagne, laughing, and relaxing after a solid day of study. These moments are fleeting now we are finished school.

After dinner clean up, Sarah joins Ruby and me. We chat about our weekends. Sarah and Josh went into the city with Elizabeth, Andrew and Thomas and some others to look at the university, as well as sightseeing.

She enthuses about how beautiful it was. I smile, not wanting to ruin her romantic view of city life. I look at Ruby's face; I am sure she is thinking the same.

Sarah turns to Ruby and looks her in the eye. "Ruby, please give me a tiny hint about the party. Please, please," she begs sweetly. Ruby has a mischievous smile on her face.

"*No,*" is all she says firmly. Sarah moves closer, millimetres from her face. "*Please.*" Ruby replies with a complete emotionless face, "*No.*"

Sarah grabs a cushion and hugs it tightly. "I can't stand it, I hate waiting for surprises."

Jonah wanders past eating a giant chocolate chip cookie. She grabs his hand. "Jonah, can you tell me about our party, a hint?" He just shrugs. "I don't know anything, really."

Sarah looks at Ruby, "Is that true?"

"Yep," she says, driving Sarah crazy.

I smile, sipping my hot chocolate and retrieving a gooey marshmallow. This is going to be fun. I am looking forward to the surprise. I look across at Ruby.

"You can be truly evil sometimes."

"I know," she says smiling, taking another sip of her hot chocolate and munching on a big fluffy marshmallow smugly.

* * *

My turn to cook tonight. I am partnered with Andrew, so I wonder if he can cook anything? He and Thomas, his best mate, had hoped to team up but Hannah insisted I needed to know how to cook seafood. The two guys being Fishers are used to prepping fish. Much to my horror and Andrew's amusement, she produces a whole fish.

Andrew kindly fillets it, showing me how to cut down the fish quickly to utilise all the parts. We settle on making a sweet chilli fish dish with stir-fried vegetables, honing in on each of our skills. Hannah helps occasionally in between studying her slates.

Everyone cheers when the aromatic dishes appear. I realise I need to learn how to cook a whole meal quickly and economically.

Hannah shows me how to use leftovers, creating another meal. Genius! We decide on fish cakes for lunch tomorrow. I thank her for helping me, feeling more confident that maybe I can do it. I just need practise and some awesome recipes.

Our week ends, with Hannah running quizzes throughout the last day using previous exams. She even hands out candy prizes.

Everyone is excited about graduation day on Monday. A special assembly is held the day before the exams. I have taken a few days off to get set for the exam week and cheer my friends on.

Sadly, a group of us who finished school early cannot participate but we will be there in the crowd.

We pack our bags, knowing the world awaits us just beyond the next two weeks of exams.

Standing in the driveway I hug Ruby. "Thank you so much for hosting and I'm so happy you are looking well." She smiles, agreeing.

A sleek white van pulls up and a team of cleaners unpack their supplies. Ruby smiles. "Dad thought it might be necessary to remove any evidence of the last two weeks, especially the kitchen."

Ruby greets one of the cleaners, "Hi Joe, thanks for coming." He has a big smile.

"What did you do, that you need Joe?" He waggles his finger as if she is in trouble.

Ruby laughs. “Had fun and used the kitchen a lot. Mum’s been away.” He looks shocked.

“No! really! No wonder Joe is here, to clean up for M Krystal; she does not like *any* mess. She tells me, Joe, I want the house looking like new, always.” We wish him well.

Sarah and I get into a transport. “Sarah are you ready to face the exams?”

“Absolutely! Then we can party.”

Was I kidding myself that I could even pass?

* * *

I rise early for market day pulling on my boots, tightening the straps and choosing my best casual clothes, suitable for working at the stall. I take care with my intricate braid. The day is warm, summer is here.

I cannot hear Retro idling in the driveway. I have grown accustomed to it waking me on Saturdays and wander out onto the veranda to see a large shiny flat-bed tray truck in our driveway, sitting silent, fully laden, and ready for market.

My Dad jumps down from the cab smiling. “Look what I got from Dennis.” I am speechless. “Dennis thought I could use the truck for the weekends and advertise the business if I do not go crazy driving all over town.”

I nod, casting my eyes on the cab, which can hold four people. I climb up into the high cab, Mum, and Luke too. We move silently down the driveway.

James and Sarah love the new truck. James finds loading effortless with the hydraulic arm to pick up crates. Sarah simply loves that it is new. Luke happily jumps on the back with James so Sarah can be with me.

Sarah looks at me. “Esther why are you frowning again? Don’t you like the new truck? *No*, you liked the old one!” My parents laugh. Retro had character.

We arrive and my heart skips as I see Simon waiting at the curb for us. He helps my mother, Sarah, and me down from the cab. He holds me for a moment giving me a quick kiss, smiling, and looking at me for a moment, saying, "You look so pretty, I missed you."

Simon immediately helps the guys unload, joking, and teasing Luke without ceasing. Luke returns fire just as fast and strong, and loving every minute.

I am happy and content. The markets are noisy today. My mother releases me from the stall, and I seek out Simon's family, finding Rachael finalising their setup under a pop-up gazebo, like my family's in the shade.

She immediately embraces me. "Good morning beautiful."

I smile, thinking how sweet she is. I tell her I am here to learn, and that Simon and I cannot expect her and Andrew to always run the stall. She melts at my sincere offer to learn the family business.

"Oh, Esther, you are amazing, come on then." She shows me the cleaner jobs, such as topping up the ice in the tubs from huge cooler boxes, and the names of the fish, which I recognise from the trawler, looking much more palatable laid out on the ice. There are scales to weigh the items and how to operate the Shalom business app on her slate to collect the points on sales.

She pulls a bright coloured scarf from her bag and expertly covers my hair and puts her smaller apron on me and points to her petite gloves. She stands for a moment, looking at me, a little misty.

I suspect she has been waiting for one of the boys to bring a girl into the family. She just caught a glimpse.

She pats my arm. "You seem to have it all under control. I might go and hang out with your Mumma and talk about wedding plans and maybe learn about the veggie trade too."

While standing at the table Matt comes over after parking their truck, looking exactly like Simon, dressed in the same clothes, only older. He looks around for the family only finding me; he stops, then politely asks where are they? I just shrug.

"All I know is that Rachael left me in charge of sales." He stares at me dumbfounded.

"*Really?*"

"Really!" He smiles and says over his shoulder as he finalises the arrangement of tubs, "Mum never steps aside for *anyone.*"

"Maybe change is in the air, Matt."

He smiles, "Maybe, it's a good change, you being a Fisher's wife soon."

Simon arrives and sees Matt and me laughing. He, in turn, looks around for his parents, particularly his mother. "Hey Matt, where's Mum?" Matt points with a long knife towards my family's stall.

Simon says slowly, "*Damm,* you're incredible, Esther, you did it, you got her to finally leave the stall and relax." He then kneels in front of me and begs, "Esther, please teach us your secret powers of persuasion."

Matt laughs, saying, "Yes, please, please Esther, teach us your ways."

"Sorry it's a secret." Right on cue Rachael waves to me. Hilarious.

"Get up you idiot," I tell Simon while smiling.

"Remember, I'm your idiot for life," he reminds me.

I sigh looking at Matt, "Matt, what did I get myself into?" He shrugs.

"You said yes to my foolish brother, who apparently isn't planning to do any work today."

"You're wrong, I am going to stay by my beautiful Esther and run the stall, the way I want for a change," Simon informs us.

Simon grabs me by my hands, looking at me from an arm's length for a long moment with tenderness, and love.

He leans down and kisses me gently for a moment telling me he had not really envisaged me as a Fisher's wife, just as Esther. Seeing me now dressed completely like a Fisher woman, particularly the head scarf, reminded him what our future life will be like.

He tells me I look beautiful. I laugh as if he is joking, touching my scarf and he catches my hands again and says, "No, Esther, I mean it. All I see is your smiling face and beautiful eyes looking back at me." I do not want the moment to end.

Matt, unable to move from his work filleting, stops discreetly listening; I see his face, it's hard to read, but is emotional. Moved. Then he resumes his work. He really is a serious young guy.

We work side by side all morning with Rachael absent. Simon makes changes to the stall that work well. Andrew comes by to move tubs back to the truck and check in. He even looks more relaxed and happier to leave us all to the stall today and wanders about chatting to the other adults.

I learn quickly how to identify and sell the seafood, especially with the goal to sell everything, as it spoils quickly. Simon is surprisingly good at selling, bundling, and bartering.

When I praise him, he looks embarrassed. "I confess, I move the sales quickly to finish early so I can spend more time with you and go surfing."

I smile; I really have caught a big fish.

Matt's girlfriend Elizabeth, approaches, leaning over the bench to kiss Matt, which seems so natural, and then stands back at a respectable distance. I observe the gentle interaction. She chats quietly and he listens, nodding from time to time while he is working and looks up often to acknowledge her, smiling at her.

Elizabeth is from a Fisher family too, no apron, just looking gorgeous in her head scarf. Her blue eyes sparkle as she talks. I am mesmerised watching this romantic interchange take place. A gentle dance!

Simon rests his chin on my shoulder, watching this exchange and says, "Matt is in love with that girl, but he keeps the details to himself."

I nod. You can see they are madly in love with each other, but there is restraint, they are discreet. It is respectful, and mature.

Elizabeth gives Matt a kiss goodbye without breaking their gaze. She wanders off back to her family stall, walking very slowly and looking over her shoulder smiling at Matt, who smiles to himself, only breaking his gaze to continue working.

He looks up to see us staring at him. "What?" he says, looking red-faced and flustered.

"You *really, really know,*" Simon says. Matt mouths swear words to his brother smiling broadly.

It is late morning; we have sold everything and pack up. Andrew and Rachael appear. I return Rachael's apron and gloves, then I unwind the head scarf and release my braid thanking her for trusting me with the stall. She just gives me a quick squeeze and runs to the truck that is being loaded.

Simon says goodbye, "See you at the meeting tomorrow?" I nod.

"See you there." He grabs my hands and briefly kisses me asking, "Do you want to go to the beach with us all tomorrow arvo?" I nod.

I head back to help my parents, and my mother tells me, "Sit in the shade with Sarah and study."

Sitting in companiable silence we lean against a beautiful shady eucalypt. Sarah sighs looking at her slate; she has finally run out of words I muse, as I revise history dates.

It's home time. I pull Sarah to her feet saying, "Come on, not long now. Want to go to the beach tomorrow after the meeting?"

"Yep, I need sea, sand, and Josh. He is teaching me to surf you know."

I know because Simon's brother Andrew updates me on her attempts when he sees me. Apparently, it's hilarious but cute. I am not inclined to surf. I am terrified of great white sharks and swimming out deep.

We arrive home, and Luke and I unload the truck quickly, chatting as we do. "I'm going to miss this you know," he says.

He is right, as I will eventually be with my own family, unloading our own truck with Simon. I ruffle his hair saying, "We will see each other, maybe you can crash at our place sometimes."

Luke looks happy with this plan, looking at me with a poker face saying, "Only if Zeb is there."

"Absolutely, Simon has already planned where his bed will be."

We head inside for lunch only to find my parents looking worried. My father points to the garden, and we follow, leaving our slates behind.

"I just looked at the new laws; I was too busy this morning ... the law has now made hybrid fossil fuel vehicles redundant. In one month, they must be off the roads, scrapped, or restored as historical artefacts."

He suddenly looks angry and conflicted, "Dennis must have known it was coming, running such a big supply business. He really is a good guy letting me use the work truck."

We sit in this knowledge, and he says quietly, "This is a deliberate attack on the Farmers, Fishers, and anyone else who is like us. Stay vigilant, Luke, no more goofing around. You must look at those law updates every morning, study them and do not put a foot wrong. Be careful who you hang out with, what you say with your friends, especially the Town ones, AI is always listening."

He looks at me, "Esther, you already know the danger. If you do not know what to do follow Simon's lead, he is smart."

He puts his arms out; we are wrapped in his strong embrace standing together united. He looks at me and my mother, "Listen and watch what is going on around you at work; maybe we might be able to stay safe by staying ahead of any new laws."

"Lunch," Luke says, running inside. My mother and I walk towards the house. With her arm around my shoulders she says, "Those fancy Town folk can't keep their mouths shut and they are clueless."

I am surprised, as she rarely speaks badly of anyone. She simply states, "In the booklet of Romans, we are reminded, that if God is for us, who can be against us? That gives me comfort."

She stops and puts her hands firmly on my shoulders and looks me in the eye.

"This is serious, Esther, you are an adult now. Be strong and courageous, and stand alongside your husband in unity, like us, no matter the cost. God is always with us." She pulls me close into a strong embrace whispering, "Trouble is coming, my darling Esther."

She walks away quietly, leaving me standing in the garden motionless - longing for Simon's steady strong arms.

I make my lunch, grabbing snacks to take back to my room. I want to be alone, to lose myself in study, and deciding my only defence against the Elite is to succeed.

Messages continuously pop up on my slate as I work. I pause when a genuine message comes through from one of my previous teachers, offering to tutor me this week before my exams in history and legal studies.

M O'Neill mentions I can call her today if I am free, as she is busy during school hours. A wave of relief washes over me, and suddenly I do not feel quite so alone.

I message M O'Neill, who replies immediately, looking very relaxed in her t-shirt and hair down. She is a younger teacher, and easy to talk to.

"Hi Esther, how's it going?" I spill my worries about the exams and at her request, send her tests I attempted and feedback from the study app. While she uploads the data, she asks me, "Esther, how are you really? It cannot be easy working and studying, engaged too I hear. You are busy!"

"I admit at times I feel overwhelmed but nothing I can't handle."

"Right, I have reviewed the apps feedback, and it only tells half the story. Esther, your test scores on these samples are incredible. The essays are harder for the AI in the app to assess. Same as your legal studies. Leave it with me, I will read the essays in full and give you feedback from a human perspective. Esther, your future is bright, keep going. Remember the harvest is ready and the workers are few." She signs off with a wave. I am left feeling lighter and perplexed.

I realise I missed dinner; my family left me a covered plate in the cooler.

Grabbing the salad out, I wander into the lounge room where my parents are sitting sipping tea and chatting. They stop and invite me to sit. This is their signal they are listening. I notice their slates are nowhere to be seen so it is safe. I relay my afternoon of studying and chat with my teacher, raising the last thing she said to me. My mother simply says, "We are the workers and she obviously is a Farmer; she has shown her hand to you." My parents look at me and tell me this is huge; she wants to see change and acknowledges I have potential to do it.

I listen to my parents chat about the markets and how the wedding plans are progressing. They tell me that they are proud of my initiative to learn the Fisher's way of life. They have received messages from Simon's parents, grateful for my help.

Apparently, even Matt praised me. Rachael says that I will be a beautiful bride and she cannot wait for the afternoon tea with the women.

My mother laughs, "Andrew and Rachael are excited. Seeing you two working alongside each other today gave me comfort knowing you are going to be okay."

My Dad stands, stretching his legs.

"Simon's a good bloke, he is worthy of you," he says, patting me on the shoulder heading to bed.

My mother and I look at each other smiling. Dad has now shown his hand - he *really* likes Simon.

CHAPTER 27

While getting ready for bed I see a message from Simon. Watching it feels surreal, like I had just been punched in the gut so hard I cannot breathe. Simon filmed his message which makes it worse.

Simon looks terrible; he is pale, his voice is low, heavy, and shaky. He simply says he loves me but cannot handle the pressure of work, getting married and everyone in his business.

His anxiety has been getting worse. He had shared a little with me but has hidden most of it from everyone. He wants to put our union on hold until he is sure he can commit. He asks me to give him time to think. He does not want to commit to a union, then fall apart because he was not honest or ready, that would not be fair to me.

Simon looks at me through the screen. "I envy you Esther, you know who you are and where you are going. I feel like I have no idea. I get up every day going through the motions. Except for you and my trusty anchor, I do not know what I am doing or really who I am out in this world.

"I have messaged a family further up on the North Coast on my parents' recommendation, and they will take me on their crew working on their boats and have offered me their granny flat to rent. I can have my own space to clear my head; I am so grateful.

"I am about to head up the coast on my transport. Please reply to my message so I know you got it, then I ask you to respect my decision to have space and time to work out what I am doing with my life. I love you, Esther." He places his hand on his heart signing off.

Feeling completely numb and nauseas, I run to the toilet and start throwing up so violently that my mother appears at the door and rushes to hold my hair. She waits until I cannot throw up anymore. She gathers me in her arms on the floor. I am shaking, pale, and sweaty. She strokes my hair gently rocking me. She finally asks, "Are you okay, did you eat something bad?"

Shaking my head I stand up sticking my head under the tap washing my mouth out, the taste of bile lingering. I wipe my mouth with the back of my hand. My mother stands up. "Come with me." She puts water on to boil, plucks peppermint from her planter on the bench, and prepares it for steeping, then turns and says bluntly, "Out with it, I can't help if I don't know the facts."

Damm, she is smart. I love her for it. I have fully regained control of my body and thoughts. I reach for my slate and show her the message, telling her would not paint a clear picture.

She watches the message with no emotion until the end. She then is angry and not the kind that is over dirty dishes, this is next level. I can feel it and see it. She is a woman who is deeply passionate about everything in her life who brought me and my brother into this world and fiercely protects us, like a lioness.

Mum turns to me. "Esther, I'm so sorry. This is so, so wrong. He could not even come and talk to you in person or trust you enough to talk it over with him. I am calling his parents and we are going to *talk.*"

I wrap my arms around her, feeling how angry and uptight she is, like a steel rod. "No, don't. They must be gutted too. I'm sure they are fully aware of the situation, struggling to handle it. It is not about us in this moment Mum, it's about Simon, and his well-being. Clearly, he is not in a good mental space; he's a grown man, it's his choice. I just hope he will communicate with me, so I know he's okay. That is what matters."

She nods slowly, thinking it through, visibly calming down but still clearly angry and hurt for me. I make the tea and settle her in a lounge chair with a blanket.

I go to my room, breathing slowly and pacing up and down. I finally message Simon, "I'm in shock but okay. Go and do what you need to do. I love you and will wait for you. Please message me so I don't worry, I'm begging you don't do anything drastic. Call me or someone you trust if you are in a bad moment, you're not alone in this. I love you."

I sign off with a love heart over my heart showing I love him so much but also hiding my true feelings, which would be unhelpful right now, but they are *my* true raw feelings in this moment.

Hurt

Fearful

Anger

Rage…

I feel burning rage and anger at being blindsided after what I thought was a great day and the last few months together. I want to fling and smash every plate in the kitchen and scream like Emily the zombie slayer would.

I pull on my running gear and a light jacket. I grab a head lamp from the storage cupboard in the hall and a runner's satchel that hugs my body, adding a water bottle. I tell my mother I'm going for a run to clear my head. She nods, lost in thought, sipping tea.

Slipping out of the house I pull the gate closed behind me, push my ear plugs in deep and run, listening to edgy aggressive music my parents hate. It fuels my emotions and propels my body right through town and out along the single lane road winding all the way to the huge white light house, which I have always loved since I was child.

Stopping along the road, pausing for breath, I see the lighthouse bright and illuminating in the distance, while still trying to catch my breath. I feel the burn in my muscles, which has taken away any anger and reduced me to feelings of loss and helplessness. I walk the rest of the way, determined to reach the lighthouse.

Walking to the base I rest my back against its cool smooth surface, looking out to the dark ocean, intermittently illuminated by the lighthouse. The lighthouse is so solid, its foundations bedded down into rock, dependable, shining every night, keeping boats safe out in the ocean, and steering them away from danger, and crashing on perilous rocks.

I feel myself screaming, shouting, and crying out. It's raw and primal against the wind that intermittently buffers the lighthouse. "Where are you God, where are *you*. Are you real? Simon needs you. *I* need you. Are you even *there* ..."

Realising I have relied on so many people is confronting - my parents and especially Simon, to be my lighthouse when they are just ordinary citizens.

Sliding down the lighthouse, I sit on the soft grass, still resting my head against its steady surface. The ocean breeze cooling my body quickly. I sip water slowly staring out at the ocean, listening to the powerful waves crashing against the rocks, and thinking about nothing, just feeling my breath in and out, in and out. Silent salty tears roll down my cheeks, feeling very alone and heartbroken.

Refusing to go against Simon's wishes and message him again, I sit with my feelings, really feeling them in my gut. I thought I had been doing work on myself when, in fact, there is more to be done below the surface.

I thought I was independent and strong when really everyone was propping me up.

Clearly, I have missed the signs my fiancé was genuinely struggling, unhappy and deeply depressed. I feel aggrieved over that. I acknowledge I am young, but I should have noticed.

A thin band of light appears next to me, and I see a door in the lighthouse open slowly, an elderly man sticks his head out and sees me. He smiles warmly.

"Everything okay? I'm the caretaker just checking everything is in working order." He steps out the door and indicates can he sit with me. I nod too spent to move.

"Quite a set of lungs you have Esther. What has upset you? Oh, sorry, we have met before. We both know Paul. You are *angry* at God? Did I hear that right? You wouldn't be the first."

Refreshed from water and the cool breeze and the caretakers calming presence I unload on him without thinking.

"…and that's how I ended up here." He just listens looking at me and leaning against the lighthouse. When I finish my pitiful tale, he looks at me steadily and then smiles.

"So, Esther, let me get this right. Simon took off because life was so overwhelming, and he went up north so he can return, being clear in his decisions moving forward so he doesn't hurt *you*. And now you are mad at Simon, God, and *yourself*." I stare at him nodding, while I angrily brush away my tears. He is smart.

The caretaker stands up and puts his hands out and pulls me to my feet. He looks me in the eye. "What makes you think God isn't present in this very moment watching over Simon?" I shrug, realising I have no idea.

He pats me on the shoulder. "How about you let God and the citizens he sends to help take care of your Simon and you head home to rest. Maybe *talk* to God about *your* problems, he is a good listener. Take care out there. God is with you." He turns and closes the door and I am in the darkness again.

I start my descent down the hill slowly, winding my way along the dark road. My head lamp is shining ahead scattering rabbits. I'm realising I am enjoying the run, clearing my head and thinking about what the caretaker said.

I must trust Simon's decision, which in hindsight now was very much about selfcare and a selfless thing to do, to withdraw and come back when he is ready.

But I still feel helpless not being able to be with him. My guilt still lingers over being totally oblivious to his depression.

Running through the brightly lit town taking a short cut through the restaurant precinct, the tavern is full of life, laughter and music spilling out into the night. I almost run into a citizen, stumbling out the doors, not watching where they are going, directly into my path.

Matt, Simon's brother! I stop just before my body slams him mid stride. We stop and look at each other. "Esther, I'm so sorry," he puts his arms out to me as if to say, do you want a hug? I happily let him.

I look down the street over his shoulder and see his younger brother Andrew in the distance looking relieved. He runs up to us. He tells me he has been looking for Matt all over town. He has taken Simon's leaving badly, feeling personally responsible.

Andrew whispers he's terrified Simon's never coming home or worse, commit suicide. I nod, looking at Andrew's terrified face. It is confronting when someone verbalises what you have not dared to fully admit to yourself.

Matt has obviously had too much to drink but is not quite drunk. He steps back, looking down at the ground.

"I begged him not to send the message, I told him to go and talk to you, but he wouldn't listen. I begged him to stay so we could help him, but he said he had to leave." He informs me apologetically, crying.

I nod, listening to him speak, and feeling for him. He is helpless the poor guy, like all of us. I assure Andrew and him that I am okay; I just needed time to process it all. He nods, looking even more depressed, and maybe the effects of the alcohol are now fully taking effect.

Waving down a passing private transport I propel both into it to take them home. I transfer points to the driver and give directions to the Allen house.

Matt says, "Thank you, you are so good to us, Esther. Please promise to still come to our place tomorrow; do not be alone in this. We all care about you and Simon." Andrew nods in agreement.

I promise to think about it. Matt is surprisingly articulate, even after what seems like a large amount of alcohol.

Ordering a private transport for myself, I finally acknowledge my exhaustion, too tired to feel anything now. Arriving home, I slip into the house and see my mother and father just sitting in the lounge room waiting for me to come home. I put my slate in the clothes sanitiser along with theirs and sit with them. My father asks me if I'm okay. I nod and relay what happened on my run.

My parents look surprised. My father says, slowly looking at me, my mother nodding, "Esther, the lighthouse is maintained remotely. It does not have a caretaker. It has been sealed up for years. I think you were speaking to an angel, one of God's messengers. This is incredible."

I look at them a little afraid.

"*Really*? No. Not possible. I was just talking to some old guy. Is that what angels look like? Dad, he said he *knows* Paul, not *knew* him and he has met *me* before."

My father looks at me steadily and I see him trying to digest what happened himself and what I am saying. He sits next to me, holding my hands.

"Esther, few people can say they have encountered an angel knowingly. Sometimes they may have been in their presence but not recognised them. Not all of them look like the Serafin with the big wings apparently. How did you feel talking to the caretaker?"

I think for a moment, then say, "Okay, he was so calm and reassured me that God was with Simon and suggested I should *talk* to God because he was with me."

My mother looks at me. "Esther, God has revealed himself to you in your distress; think about everything that happened tonight. I hope it brings you some peace." She gets up kisses me on the cheek and my father does the same as they head to bed.

I shower and lie in bed thinking about my day and Simon. I feel comforted when I think about God and that he apparently is watching out for us, even though I am still a bit unsure about him, even more now an angel showed up. *Apparently.*

CHAPTER 28

Kookaburras awaken me early at five am and I pull my pillow over my head cursing those beautiful creatures. The cicadas are deafening too. Typical Australian summer! Waking several hours later, I think to myself, 'Happy Birthday Simon.' He is twenty-two today. I post a loving birthday message on his social page, hoping he will read it and be reminded that I love him.

Making my way into the kitchen, my parents sit at the family table. They kindly mention they would like to get to the Allens' early to speak to his parents.

"I think it's best, so we have the same narrative about where he is," I tell them.

I am hungry from burning through so many calories last night, I cook a huge breakfast of eggs on toast.

Luke looks at the mountain of food "Hungry Esther?"

"Yep, you hanging out with the kids today?" I ask.

"Nah, Zeb and I have business over in the pine forest." We all laugh. Zeb and Luke have a cute co-dependency.

We arrive at the Allens' simple two storey home and we walk up the front steps of the expansive veranda. Zeb bolts straight to Luke, bypassing me.

We leave Zeb and Luke reacquainting outside and enter the house with the familiar welcoming smell of Rachael's home cooking, the dog and an aromatic candle burning.

Rachael embraces us, grateful we can gather as family, and we all agree on Simon's story that he is up North working for friends. This gives Simon the privacy to work through whatever is going on.

My father offers to pray. We all put our slates on the outdoor table and he prays for Rachael, Andrew, Matt, and Andrew. He then pours out his heart asking for God's protection and clear direction for Simon's life. He even prays for me, asking that the Holy Spirit watch over me and guide me, whatever the outcome of Simon's time away is, and that I am given peace.

I am thankful for the prayer as we stand quietly and say Amen. We separate to set up for the meeting, and Simon's parents look exhausted. I feel for them having to pretend everything is okay.

Andrew suddenly looks panicked. He passes his slate to my Dad who reads it and shows us the message from Peter. "I would have loved to meet up for fishing today; it has been ages. I am sure the ladies can spare us blokes for another morning soon when I am better. I have a virus, which is persistent and hard to get rid of. P."

They move quickly after conferring with each other. Dad and Andrew grab Luke, Zeb and some food saying there is a change of plans. Luke just tags along with his furry buddy. I see them intercept any guys arriving and send the women and children in.

My mother informs me quickly, "Peter has just warned us the law is coming to investigate our meeting, and he is trying to get them off his tail. Our emergency plan has always been that we all separate quickly and make believe whatever we are doing is planned.

"The men have headed to the wharf and will take out boats to keep up the charade. Follow Rachael and the other older women's lead."

I look outside to see vehicles and people separating quicky in the street; it is empty in minutes. I re-enter the house to see it transformed into a women's morning tea with tablecloths teacups, cakes, and cookies.

Rachael has set up the counter with fresh food ready to be prepped and a whole fish lying on a cutting board with a filleting knife beside it. All slates are left switched on to keep us transparent and accountable.

Andrew, Simon's brother, remains behind to scout from upstairs while studying. He comes down and indicates with his hands to his mother that the law is coming down the street, searching house by house. We are next, then he bolts upstairs.

Just like in the city, they are loud, aggressive and you can hear them coming.

Rachael welcomes everyone and points to the fish and chairs set up around the counter; the women instinctively know what to do. I am fascinated by this play unfolding. They sit or stand chatting about their week, ready to be totally engrossed in what Racheal is doing and following her lead.

Rachael is heroic as the front door is almost ripped off its hinges. The Law Enforcers enter and stand in the living area, having entered uninvited and filling the room with their presence.

This is new.

She encourages everyone to watch her as she swishes her knife dramatically. "Today we are learning how to cook a whole fish using every part of it, no waste, and lots of sides to complement it."

She says so sweetly over the tops of the women's heads, "Good morning, Enforcers, can we help you?" All the women turn in unison.

The Law Enforcers shuffle a little uncomfortably, standing in front of sweet-faced Farmer and Fisher women. The captain is a robot. I suspect his tenth house in a row reads the information from his slate, stating they can search the property today.

Rachael feigns boredom, shooting the captain a firm *mum look*. "Very well, get on with it, but please be respectful of the women and children in this house; my son is studying for his exams upstairs."

She turns to the women again. "Okay, … the key to cooking a whole fish is …" She launches into a graphic commentary about gutting and filleting the enormous silvery fish in front of the intimidating Law Enforcers in full combat gear who suddenly disperse into the house the minute she starts gutting the fish like a pro. Several run outside to vomit in the garden.

Across the kitchen bench I see my mother's happy face, which exudes pride and defiance, not fear. I cannot help smiling. Simon and the men would have loved to witness this performance. Rachael would have been declared a legend.

The Enforcers look around, not really searching, but putting on a good show for the captain as they are visibly repulsed by seeing and smelling fresh fish being prepped. They prepare to leave as they have found nothing, saying a hasty, "Thank you M Allen sorry for the intrusion," as they carefully closed the damaged front door.

Rachael and the older women put their finger on their lips. There is to be no criticism of the law. We stand in shock. Then laugh a little at how weak these Town people are.

"It's like they don't know where food comes from. Rachael, are you going to finish cutting up that monster?" Sarah's mother, Miriam, asks.

"Of course not, that's what I have sons for. I'm exhausted, I am going to sit and have cake with you beautiful women." She promptly sits at the table and pours herself tea and takes a bite of cake, calmly. "My work is done for the day until those men come home hungry from fishing all morning."

Everyone stands in shock. Rachael stops mid bite and looks around the room of terrified crying women and children. She stands and looks at us, then picks up a small crying child at her feet and sits her on her hip, rocking like all mothers do.

"The Enforcers have left; follow their rules and you'll be fine." She places her finger on her lips to indicate she is speaking like the law is listening.

"Come, eat, and chat," she encourages.

Rachael sits the crying child in her lap, feeding her cookies. She reminds us, still frozen on the spot of Paul, that he faced many trials and hardships in his life before he passed. If he can do it, we can too.

I take food upstairs to Andrew; he is looking through a vintage telescope down the street. I am horrified. The street is lined with black vans and teams of Law Enforcers pouring into homes on the lookout like an ant invasion. Knocking on the door, I inform him that the Law Enforcers have left the house.

"Cake and sandwiches - I grabbed them before it was all gone."

He thanks me and lets me look through the telescope. It's impressive and a helpful vantage point; I can pan across the whole lookout.

I sit on his bed and ask him about his studies.

"Okay, I think. Are you alright?" he asks. Not a lot of words!

Andrew sits down next to me. "It's Simon's birthday today. I miss him."

"I miss him too mate. I'm so worried about him, Andrew." I put my arm around him for a moment in companiable silence. I quickly remove it, realising I have invaded his personal space.

"It's okay, is this what it is like to have a sister? I could handle that. It's different with two brothers; they are not like… you."

"Soft and fluffy?" He smiles. "Maybe, but you talk about stuff, well that's what Simon says anyway."

"Really, you guys talk about me?" I feign surprise.

Andrew stretches out on his bed. "Simon talks about you *all the time*, he talks more now he's with you." I sit thinking about this world I have entered. A house full of men.

Andrew seems to be on a roll, revealing family secrets.

"Simon talks to Mum every night while she's prepping dinner, 'Esther did this, Esther said that, would Esther like this?'" His voice trails off.

"What did you say?" He looks guilty, spilling Simon's secrets.

"Nothing, well it is a present for your birthday. Every night he has his slate open looking at stuff and showing Mum. She loves it. She adores you. The talking drives my Dad and Matt crazy. Matt complains, but Simon tells him to shut up. It's funny."

"So, back to my present, what is it?" I ask.

"Not telling."

I place him in a head lock. "How do you feel having a sister *now*?" He laughs.

"It's different having brothers." He easily escapes, standing up, brushing his blonde curly hair out of his eyes, grinning. I am struck how he looks so much like Simon, just younger. It makes my heart ache.

Andrew flops into his desk chair, swivelling side to side. "Are you thinking about that dirty rat Simon who ran away and left us?"

"I am thinking about him. I am not angry anymore; I have forgiven him. I keep wondering how did it get so bad that he had to leave us? Andrew, he is not a rat, he is very lost. I hope he can find his way back to me, to us, soon."

"I get that he had to have space, but I feel angry because of the pain it caused my parents and even Matt. You saw him, he's a mess, they're all a mess."

I assure him it is okay to feel that way, but it is not about us, it is about Simon. We need to be there for him.

He shrugs. "I guess, but I'm not ready to forgive him yet. He won't even be there for my year twelve graduation tomorrow."

"I will be there - wouldn't miss seeing you lined up like a robot solider." He smiles a little and switches on his slate opening his study notes. I leave the room a little more enlightened. I walk downstairs to Simon's room. I have never been in there and I stand respectfully in the doorway.

It is simply furnished like Andrew's room, with timber floorboards, a single bed made up with a beautiful blue hand stitched quilt and matching pillow, a woollen blanket folded neatly on the end. There is a simple timber dresser with a few toiletries on it, a worn wooden chair, and a shelf with several personal treasures on it and mainly unusual shells from the sea and a small worn teddy bear.

The wardrobe is closed; I suspect only a few pairs of shoes and a few pieces of casual clothing reside in it. Like mine used to be. I am touched by the dog bed next to his for Zeb.

I rest my head on the door frame thinking, 'Please come home Simon. I miss you.' Rachael finds me and we hold each other for a long moment.

"We need our Simon home, Esther; he is fortunate he has a family and fiancé who love him. You can go in if you want."

"It wouldn't be right, an invasion of his privacy," I tell her.

"Where did we go wrong Rachael? I feel lost in all of this, you and Andrew must be so worried." She pats me on the arm.

"I knew he would leave eventually; I was hoping it would be on his wedding day. That I can live with, not this, this is excruciating.

"When he gave his life to the Lord, I had to accept that I had done my part and leave Simon in God's hands. It is hard to wait on God's timing as I am impatient, but maybe that is my lesson in all of this." She moves towards the kitchen.

Sighing to myself, I accept I am getting stronger; I am not scared of the law anymore. I am angry. They persecute us. They not only breached our homes today, but they have also raided whole streets. Theres no stopping their escalating mission now.

Entering the kitchen, most of the women and children have left. I tell my mother I will order a large private transport for us and Sarah's family to share.

She nods and thanks me for my generosity. She asks Rachael, "Will you be okay?"

"Andrew's here."

"The men are heading back," my mother informs us from her slate.

We hug Rachael goodbye. "See you tomorrow, Esther?" She asks me, and I nod.

"I am so proud of you, Esther; you have pushed yourself to get to this point. You do not need a fancy ceremony to acknowledge your achievements." My mother agrees.

I bask in the warmth of their admiration.

I step into the private transport, happy to be heading home, which always was my fortress. Now I'm fully realising it is in fact a massive liability.

We arrive home, and as we enter the yard, I see my Dad's truck with Luke and his best mate Pete who run into the house. I detain my parents and drag them out into the middle of the garden after burying our slates in the sanitiser. My mother throws her arms around my father and sobs; I did not see that coming. He looks at me.

"It was bad, Dad, the whole outlook was raided, I know the only reason they did not pull the whole Allen house apart was that there were women and children there. Rachael, mum, and the older women kept their cool, knowing the Townies cannot cope with the smell of raw seafood." My mother regains control of her emotions and nods, smiling.

I look at them both. I feel stress and adrenaline pumping through my veins and my temple is throbbing. I say in a low voice, "We have to clean the house, and remove anything remotely religious or relating to your activities. You will have to help me, I have no idea what I'm looking for."

My anger is bubbling. My voice expresses sheer terror and rage as I swear and rant aloud for a moment, it's a first for me, and my parents are shocked.

"Esther! Watch your mouth!" my Dad says firmly.

"*No*, I am stuck in this terrifying world, I am sick of being raided and being stopped by the law. I need Simon, I miss him so bad and he is not here." I kick over a bucket with tools in it, scattering the contents across the yard. I continue kicking it across the yard. Hard.

"Oh, great Dad! You're not even *trying* to stay safe," I say as I quickly gather up items covered in ink. This must end today.

My parents agree and look remorseful.

"Esther, we are so sorry. We got comfortable; we have not been searched or raided like you have experienced. We know the dangers. We have not stayed vigilant."

"I have a plan, are you willing to listen?" They are shocked that I am being so assertive, and nod.

"Right, Mum, get rid of the rice paper packs, keep only what we need for meals, and get Luke and Pete to take the rest to Farmer and Fisher families."

She immediately retrieves them and heads inside to instruct Luke and Pete. They happily leave with bags of rice paper packs and points to buy lunch.

I look at my parents again. "Dad, remove anything remotely suspect out of the shed and has ink on it. We are going to wash, destroy, or hide it away from here. The house number that's on the gate, sand it back and repaint, I *know* it is a religious symbol." He looks at me, I look him in the eye saying slowly, "*E-v-e-r-y-t-h-i-n-g*." He just nods.

I tell Mum, "We will search the whole house, room by room and you tell me what has to go."

"I knew something wasn't right. The law is in some kind of frenzy, not even thinking logically," she says, pulling me into her arms in a vice grip.

"Esther, Simon's not here, you are, you underestimate how strong you are, you are not alone."

I finally submit to the terrifying day and cry for a moment. I brush away my angry tears as I look with my mother through each room for anything remotely suspicious, including items we inherited from our grandparents.

Fortunately, like most Farmers and Fishers, we have very little as we are minimalists with no need for decorative items, but we do love family heirlooms and hold onto them. I look at the small array of items we have from family or treasures of my parents. I ask about each item.

We move into Luke's room and pull it apart, searching every conceivable crevice. He has very little in his room; reminiscent of Simon and Andrew's rooms, he is just a grotty teen.

Sports gear is discarded, reeking in piles on the floor with several basket balls and, of course, a few plates and cups. His room stinks and we carefully reconstruct the filth as we found it. Regretfully.

We enter my room and my mother hesitates. "Mum, what's the matter?" She looks at me.

"You are a grown woman; it doesn't feel right to search your room."

"Mum, seriously, I have clothes and a whole lot of childish crap, but I don't know if any of it could be a risk." She nods and carefully looks at my collection of items, picking up the jar of coloured glass pieces.

She tells me, "These pieces belonged to a building called a church where people met regularly to worship God openly and spend time together. The stained-glass windows were beautiful I believe, depicting scenes from the Bible."

She puts it on the shelf again. "I think that will be okay. But this could have us locked up." She throws bunny at me, "He's trouble - always has been."

My mother opens the drawers so carefully you would think they were rigged to blow. I am exasperated at this behaviour. "Mum, what's going on?" I ask, then realising, my face heating up and colouring.

"Did you think I had protection in the drawer?"

She nods, looking embarrassed.

"Mum, it is okay. There's nothing in there that will make us feel awkward. Do you think Simon and I are ... *intimate*?"

She shrugs, "I don't know, I just wanted to respect your privacy, that's all. I see how Simon looks at you; he only has eyes for you. He looks like your father did before he married me."

"Oh, that's so sweet," I say - such a romantic anecdote.

"*No*, I mean he looked like a thirsty dingo in the desert." That floors me.

"Oh *Mum*, that's funny and cringy." She laughs. "Maybe, but it's true."

"We are not intimate Mum." She pats me on the arm as she makes her way out.

"Maybe you should go shopping. Just a thought."

We finish the search and wander out to the yard to discover a cleaning monster. Dad has pulled everything out of the shed and is sorting it.

My mother looks at him, "Mark, you had one job, now you've created a mess."

"How are we going?" he asks. Mum gives him the thumbs up.

Dad stands in the yard looking totally overwhelmed. "I know this is a mess but man I've got a pile of junk I can get rid of at the recycle yard and I got rid of all my frustration with the law." He hands me a small crate.

"Can you take this crate to Peter?"

"Sure, I will order a private transport."

"Can you afford it Esther?"

"Yes, I think it's the best option." He agrees.

"Thanks, Esther. You have been incredibly brave today."

I carry the crate inside and observe my parents laughing and smiling looking at each other like there is no one watching and realise that is what real intimacy is. It is knowing and trusting someone so well you can be yourself and know you are loved.

I feel an ache in my heart, reminding me that Simon is not here.

CHAPTER 29

Graduation day arrives for my friends. I catch the bus with Luke knowing that the harassment will be less now I am no longer at school. Despite the early hour it is crammed, stifling and loud.

On arrival I observe the Elite and Town families stepping out of private transports, Some have their own self-driven transports with private drivers and security detail escorting them through the check point like they are celebrities. I muse, especially when I see the private security following at a discreet distance, some are dressed in Town attire to blend, others are obviously security, their black suits and build scream security.

Heading through the security check point I walk towards the school auditorium for the graduation ceremony. The enormous automatic glass door opens on my approach.

Entering the foyer, I continue into the auditorium, and I sit at the back scrolling through my slate, laughing at my friends' sassy and humorous comments on our class page. They also share some awesome photos too; I am included in some of them.

The students remain outside. Parents and friends file into the auditorium greeting each other, and the Elite and Town parents find seats near the front, inclining their heads and speaking very softly. Farmer Fisher parents and friends sit together towards the back, chatting animatedly.

Rachael, Andrew, and Matt arrive with Jonah in tow. They greet me warmly and we all find seats together to endure the barely shielded contempt the Elite and Town families direct towards us.

Krystal and Peter sit with us; Krystal inclines her head and whispers hello. There is no eye contact or warmth in the greeting. She is clearly furious with Peter, wanting to be up the front with the Elite. Peter is oblivious, talking to everyone.

The principal welcomes us, inviting us to stand to honour our class as they walk in two precise lines, which separate at the stage and walk up the stairs on either end. They are seated on the expansive stage, in a single curved row. It is impressive to see them all in uniform, boots shone to perfection.

The assembly proceeds as they all do, lots of welcoming and kissing up to the local officials and the school board showcasing how great the school is performing and the numerous achievements this year.

The musical groups perform some boring classical pieces with the occasional squeak escaping from an instrument. Then we are entertained by kindergarten and final year photos displayed side by side in a slide show, which is hilarious.

Academic awards are given out. Ruby receives one for ancient and modern history as well as legal studies, which makes Peter proud, his smile says it all. Krystal's face does not move. Nobody claps as it is impolite until all the students have received their awards.

Andrew receives a technology award, which is incredible and Sarah, for science, she genuinely looks shocked. They join the other students at the front, and everyone claps politely. The students return to their seats, and we are informed they have received gift vouchers sent to their slates.

The next category is students nominated for scholarships or have been given early admission to university prior to exam results. There is an air of anticipation as this is highly sought after.

M O'Neill approaches the lectern and announces the recipients.

Immediate entry into Sydney City Precinct University

Pre Law –Ruby

Mathematics - Jason

The room buzzes with approval, Elite and Town parents nodding to each other and turning and acknowledging Peter and Krystal who look so proud.

Jason's parents act like it was expected. They are truly Elite, the way they dress and their whole demeanour screams there should be private schools for *our* children to separate them from us, not one equal education system.

Nominations for scholarships. The principal informs the auditorium that this now includes students who left earlier in the year now contributing to the work force but continued study via correspondence. They have been included in this year's selection process for equal access to further education, which he informs the crowd, was government mandated. This is a game changer; the crowd moves restlessly in their seats, and they are clearly unhappy. The principal steps forward smoothing his suit, adjusts his slate then announces the scholarship nominees.

Science-Sarah

Engineering -Andrew

Mathematics -Jonah

Law-Esther

History ……

The principal completes the list and is about to introduce the next part of the ceremony and looks up from his slate to a silent room of angry eyes glaring at him. A room of well-dressed ravenous wolves who are ready to devour him.

The atmosphere is heavy, the silence cringy, the school and government's mandate for equality throughout our society and education system has proven to be a complete sham. The Elite and Town citizens clearly want to be separated from the rest of society. Always have, always will.

A true professional the principal powers on and introduces the keynote speaker, Peter, to talk about history ….

Peter extracts himself from his seat up the back of the hall and confidently strides down the centre aisle to the front, bounds up the stairs in his very Elite suit, and places his slate on the lectern. He looks out at the crowd smiling. They thaw a little seeing their kind up front, and Peter proceeds to address the crowd, warmly congratulating them on raising our future.

He turns towards the students and claps. His talk brings civility back as he engages his audience with jokes about himself being an old dinosaur, which helps him understand history and shares interesting facts and images of historical artefacts. He has even slipped in a picture of Ruby's favourite childhood toy, Ellie the elephant, feigning surprise, wondering how it got there. Ruby seems to be enjoying being put on the spot.

Throughout Peter's speech, Jonah sits next to me looking at me and raising his eyebrows as if to say WOW we have a real chance here. He even reaches across and squeezes my hand for a moment, understanding that our parents were not here to be a part of the good news, and everyone hates us.

At the conclusion of Peter's talk, he casually walks back to his place and sits with Krystal who looks very proud of her husband. The ceremony closes with the students again filing out into the foyer and their guests follow, naturally from the front to the back in an orderly movement.

The stares and whispered vile comments our rows receive as the Elite and Town guests pass us are truly detestable, they do not hide their feelings.

Our rows eventually disperse and we arrive in the foyer to seek out children and friends who have wisely found a quiet corner and loaded several plates with food to share so we do not have to mix with the Elite and Town people.

Our group celebrates the end of school - proud of our friends surviving and their achievements. We are excited about the fact that we may see each other at Uni, which is comforting. It finally feels like it could be a reality.

I observe Andrew looking withdrawn and quiet while standing amongst our group. I ask him if he is okay and gently guide him away to another quiet corner.

"Okay, out with it." I hear myself demand just like my mother does. He looks at me then remembers he can talk to me and lets out his breath slowly.

"Esther, I cannot believe I can do something besides fishing. I feel so guilty too. If I leave to study, my parents will not have the help they need, only in the holidays. My Dad told me and Matt today he wants us to follow our heart in whatever occupation we want to pursue. He has assured me the business will be okay. I really miss Simon sharing today."

I nod listening, feeling his pain too. They are such a close family. I put my arms out and he happily lets me embrace him; I feel him holding back tears but submits to his disappointment in my arms. I release him.

"Remember we were friends first, soon to be family, you can talk to me about *anything.*" He nods and smiles a little. I move away to give his parents space to chat to him.

Andrew's parents approach and embrace him so proudly, Matt hangs around in the background looking the same as Andrew. As I pass, I squeeze his arm and whisper, "You, okay?" He just nods. No words.

I observe a murmur of voices that is not conciliatory. The school board has been bailed up by the Elite and Town parents against the hall entry glass windows, demanding explanations why *their* children did not receive scholarships and awards. Their rage is escalating.

Private security step in and whisk their delicate clients away before the whole foyer erupts into an ugly scene of a verbal and physical battleground.

Peter discreetly directs the security officers towards the angry mob who shepherd the board away to a safe building. The angry group disperses quickly when they sight Law Enforcers standing outside monitoring the disturbance. After they leave, their vile hurtful words still hang in the air.

The foyer is almost empty except for the Farmers, Fishers, and some regular town families. Peter remains but had encouraged Krystal to go home earlier away from all the drama.

He chats to everyone and is completely at ease, even teasing Jonah about how much food he has piled high on his plate, which reveals his sheer gluttony. We all laugh at his open love of food.

Ruby looks mortified and amused at the same time.

Ruby, Sarah, and I hug in a little circle like we do, savouring the last time we will be together in the school and before possibly separating for further study. Another precious memory. Bittersweet!

I observe Andrew embrace his best mate Thomas, and they sit and talk quietly. I am glad Andrew has a close friend to talk to, even if he cannot share all his worries; he seems to have perked up a bit.

Matt, his brother, looks pale and distant. Rachael and Andrew have put on a very brave face parking their distress by celebrating their youngest son's success today. Good for them.

We all head out the front door, stepping into the fresh air, and the principal farewells us at the doors, assuring us he is okay after our gentle inquiries. Smiling, he says, "You have to have a thick skin in this job."

He congratulates us all on enduring such blatant persecution throughout our school career. He tells us he has tried to eradicate it but to no avail.

He smiles at Jonah. "Some of us became great mates along the way, didn't we Jonah."

The principal looks at each one of us and says, "The awards you achieved were because you earnt them, and your grades were undeniably the highest; you did the work. Sometimes you need to be little hungrier than others to succeed." He waves goodbye, wishing us all well.

I am invited to join my friends at the local pizzeria to celebrate but decline wanting to go home and study. I realise I am only hungry to succeed and I miss Simon terribly, wanting to indulgently wallow in my misery a little today.

The next two weeks will be tough, especially without Simon to encourage me, and my future does not look as certain anymore.

Shaking off that selfish moment, I do not have time to worry. Like Andrew, we have a real opportunity to change the course of our lives, but we will need to dig in and work hard.

CHAPTER 30

I wait to be dismissed after the last exam. Jonah gives me a thumbs up from the neighbouring desk.

I collect my satchel and finding a seat near a huge glass window, I browse my social pages, sipping water before heading home.

Most of the chatter is about today's exams; we sit most of the same courses with a few exceptions. There are few choices. I just completed my hardest exam today, history.

Sarah and Ruby have several exams to go and will meet up with me on party day, which means I am officially free. To do what?

I sit for a moment thinking and taking stock, I do not need to study for a while, just work and read and ....

"Hey, what's with the frowny face?" My heart skips. Simon, he is back! I look up and see his tall frame leaning over me and smiling.

I hesitate, then throw myself at him, never wanting to let go. He is handsome, unshaven and his blonde curly hair looking unruly.

"You're back!"

Simon just nods. "How did your last exam go?" I shrug, trying to read the situation.

Simon senses that too, suggesting we sit in the park across the road and talk. We find a park bench under an ancient willow; Simon takes our slates, putting them at a distance, and we sit looking at each other in silence. He breaks it by asking can he share what has been going on in the last ten days.

"Of course, Simon," I whisper. He allows me to hold his hand.

Simon pauses. "I had planned what to say, but now it's disappeared." I gently squeeze his hand to encourage him as he launches into that terrible afternoon after the markets…

He tells me his family was so happy after the markets, they talked about how we had worked together like we were married, then something inside him snapped.

"No offense to you, Esther, but I felt like I had to escape the family's wedding excitement, the too much caring made me feel like I was suffocating. I felt rotten thinking those thoughts, I was sweaty, hyperventilating and feeling like I was going to pass out and throw up all at the same time.

"My parents thought it was heatstroke. My Dad got me to breathe and funnelled water down my throat, but I still felt sick."

He dragged me across the road to the pine forest reserve. It felt cool and peaceful, leaning our backs against the trees, facing each other, not talking. I started to feel a little better; all you could hear was the wind in the trees.

"My Dad sat for a long time looking at me and finally said, What is going on in your head son? You look sick and I know it is not heat stroke. If you want to talk, talk, I'm here.'

I sat for a long time in the silence looking at my feet, then I tell him how I am feeling. Can I share this with you?" I nod.

"I tell my Dad I am okay but lately I feel like my heart is racing, I'm dizzy and sick in my stomach, and sometimes I get bad headaches. I even wake up in a sweat, with my heart racing. I have felt like this for ages and thought it would pass. Esther, I am always happy with you. I just got stuck feeling that way.

"I got pulled out of school like you, but I was younger. I never begrudged helping my family but it was never *my* choice. I kept showing up, working. It is exhausting, hard work, Esther, as you know, and you have not even seen half of it."

"The long trips out in the middle of the ocean away from home and working in storms is terrifying. The waves come right over the boat, and I would think there must be something better than this."

"I felt hopeful about the future when I asked you out. You opened my eyes to having fun, being with you did not completely stop those sick feelings and pains in my gut. I just tried to ignore them, they never went away."

"I confessed all this to Dad. Peter got really close to discovering my issues when he pushed me to talk about and confront my feelings during a pre baptism chat."

"That's on me; the opportunity was there, and I didn't take it. I didn't see it and now it's built up. When I saw you in the park dressed like a Fishers' wife, I could not have been more in love with you or anxious. Suddenly I felt like everything was too much responsibility, so I broke.

"My Dad listened, he told me he appreciated my courage in sharing my feelings and suggested I take a break from fishing and rest, spend time with you, have fun, go on dates.

He asked for forgiveness, for being part of my stress. I told him I accept and respect our way of life.

"He looked me in the eye and said, *"No* son, not anymore, it stops today. You, Matt, and Andrew choose. You are grown men. I release you from any obligation to work on our trawler, your mother and I will work it out. Go live your life, spend time alone with God and find out what your real purpose is. We do not want to lose you. We love you, mate."

Squeezing his hand too tight, I see Simon's struggle.

"After the reserve talk I informed Dad that I cannot stay. I love Esther, but until I feel better it's not fair to her to be here. I told my family I'm leaving that day.

"Matt pleaded for me to stay, to talk it out with a counsellor. He told me he is here for me; my whole family did.

"My parents called some friends, and I headed further up the North Coast. The ride was long, but it felt good knowing I could get away.

"I stayed and worked with a young couple on their charter boats, taking tourists out on day trips around the bays and taking rich people out on deep sea fishing day trips.

"It was easy and even kind of fun. I learnt how to cook and prepare food quickly. I rented Zeik and Sarah's granny flat. Zeik showed me where the beach was down the road.

"Still rising early from habit, I would run on the beach, then sit and feel the breeze, watch the waves and the sun rise. Every day I prayed, waiting for some clue from God what to do with my life. I have made that my daily routine since.

"Zeik talked with me every evening in the backyard with the kids running around us while Sarah his wife made dinner. He did not pry into why I was there, he simply said stay with us until you are ready to face the world again. We are here if you need to talk. Commit time to reading God's word, then he gave me a booklet from the Bible like we have at home.

"The booklet was Philippians and written very neatly. He told me each scribe only works on one book from the Bible and distributes them, like your parents. He also gave me the contact details of a councillor Tim, who gets our kind of people. I got the sense he had seen Tim himself. I decided I could not feel any worse, it took courage to admit I needed help and to go.

"Speaking with James, he agreed I should try it at least once. The councillor guy Tim was so chilled and easy to talk to, like a mate. I was sorry I had not done it earlier. He explained to me that the minute a young guy admits he needs help he makes time to see them immediately.

"Tim explained if you cannot see the small leaks in the boat how will you know you are sinking, let alone weather any storms that come along?

"Tim listened a lot and got me to look at myself and accept it happens, people get overwhelmed with life, the lucky ones are rescued, like me.

"I saw Tim for five days; he was so generous, Esther. He moved appointments to accommodate me so we could do some intense work and to help manage my stress.

"He even got me a doctor's appointment for a full medical. They gave me some medication that I think has started to help a little. It's early days.

"I had the occasional check ins with him online for the rest of the time. I have never felt so exposed and raw. It was physically draining to talk about my feelings. I am so thankful to God and Zeik, who directed me to Tim.

"Yesterday I woke up refreshed, like I was seventeen again and I knew I was on my way back to you and my family. I went for my run and sat on the quiet beach, finally I was still enough to hear the Holy Spirit who said, "Fix your eyes on me, I will never leave you." I thanked Zeik and his family and headed home. You would love them, Esther. They showed me how to go with the flow in family life, do not overthink everything, just be in the moment and enjoy it. I looked up your exam timetable to find you. My beautiful, patient Esther."

Simon kneels in front of me, holding my hands, telling me he loves me so much, and has missed me, especially on the beautiful beach. He confesses he hurt me badly running away, not talking to me. He asks for my forgiveness and asks if I still want to be with him.

I look at him and throw my arms around his neck saying quietly, "Yes, I was hurt, angry and devastated but I was also terrified I was going to lose you forever. The fact that you were willing to go to a councillor and share with me your struggle says you are totally committed to working on yourself and for us. I see a peace and light in your eyes that I've never seen before. You were always forgiven, your struggle is my struggle, I love you. Let's agree to take each day as it comes."

He looks into my eyes, strong and determined. "Esther, I love you so much, but I really have nothing to give you. Will you live each day with me and marry me on the cliff top on New Years Eve? I am broken but with you and God's help I know I can get better if you will have me."

I just nod and throw my arms around his neck again and sob uncontrollably on his shoulder, relieved he is safe and still loves me.

My stresses of the last few weeks rush out. He kisses my cheeks, wipes my tears away with his t-shirt and holds me for a long time in such a strong reassuring embrace.

I am assured of his deep love, his heart beating slowly and steadily against mine. He has shown me he is the strong mature dependable man my heart has always desired and longed for but never acknowledged. I realised I needed this confirmation from him.

We separate and he pulls me to my feet.

"Have you spoken to your parents yet?" Simon assures me he has and his brothers too.

"They all cried, Matt too. They are so happy I'm coming home. My Dad told me the whole family prayed for me to come home when I was ready, and for God's protection. I'm humbled by their love and faithfulness, Esther."

Simon has arranged with his Dad that he will work two days a week with him and maybe one day a week with Zach, only for short trips. The rest of the time he will spend focusing on his quiet time with God, doing Tim's homework. He really wants to spend time with me, going on dates and meeting up with Zach and Hannah.

"I want to be here for you, Esther, I do not want to be the Fisher husband who is never home. I have saved a lot of points so I can afford to take time off."

"Simon, I have an idea, why don't we start renting the granny flat now, you have paid the deposit, you could move in immediately. You know I can afford to help with the rent.

"You could still go home for dinner if you want or cook for yourself, whatever you want. Just take your bedroom furniture and set it up in the spare room. You already told me you had plans for Zeb's bed in the lounge room; he could come with you or travel between houses."

"It is perfect. Thank you, Esther."

He pulls us further under the willows as a drone passes overhead. He gently kisses me, and his hands rest on my waist. I have craved his touch. We separate, looking at each other and smiling. I run through the long willow tree branches, Simon catches me. He pulls me to him, kissing me gently again.

This time, he pulls away from me and leans against the tree, breathing hard and smiling at me. "This is fun, I know it's not long until we marry but I can't stop wanting to be with you, Esther." I wrap my arms around him looking up.

"We are enjoying this part of our engagement, getting to know each other. We can wait, that is what we have always wanted. It is our private dance."

We retrieve our slates.

"Esther, can I take you on a date to recommit to you?"

I nod with a smile dancing on my lips, "I know this romantic place. It is a little Italian restaurant but you will need to book to secure the best table in the house."

He smiles, his blue eyes sparkle. "I think I know the one."

He leaves me saying he has some important jobs to do and book dinner reservations. Simon insists he picks me up like in those old romantic movies.

Heading home, I am glad no one will be there as I need to process everything.

We both will need to continue with counselling, together or separately, whatever is going to work, maintaining what progress Simon has made with his mental health.

Arriving home I fill the bathtub with bubbles and a few drops of essential oil I save as a treat as its smells so good and leaves my skin super soft. I light a candle and put on some soothing music.

I feel the tension of the last few weeks melt away into the silky suds. Dragging myself out, I dry myself, wrapping myself in my pink cotton dressing gown.

I lay down for a moment, a long moment and am awakened when I get an alert from Simon of our reservation time, one hour from now. I rush to dry and straighten my hair and pick out the perfect outfit that I can wear on the transport. I am suddenly nervous and excited, acknowledging this is a good sign we are going to be okay.

Messaging my parents, I update them what is happening, and they are overcome with happiness. They remain the same dependable parents. I love them for it.

Simon arrives with flowers filling his arms. He kisses me, telling me I look beautiful and gifts me with antique roses that are fragrant.

He has an arrangement of cottage style flowers for my mother; she will be touched. A bottle of scotch for my Dad, who will insist Simon shares it.

I look at him and see change. Simon has had another short haircut. You can almost see his scalp, blonde curls gone, clean shaven, a black linen shirt with sleeves rolled up exposing those strong tanned arms, black jeans and stylish new black boots peeking out. Casual but so, so classy.

"You get more handsome every day," I tell him, which he instantly deflects while blushing.

Simon helps me onto the transport and jumps on in front. I wrap my arms tightly around him; his cologne is just detectable and familiar. We ride silently into the early evening, weaving through the town, lights just starting to come on as the pinks and oranges of dusk fade. We're looking forward to an intimate night in our own private garden oasis and renewing our commitment to each other that has grown and matured into a deeper enduring love.

CHAPTER 31

I stretch out in my comfy bed. It is my eighteenth birthday; time to have fun!

I scroll through my messages and see many fun and thoughtful birthday wishes, the first from Sarah my birthday buddy, one minute after midnight. I send best wishes with a montage of goofy, fun, and beautiful photos capturing a lifetime of Sarah and me.

Rising to shower, I do not hear any activity in the house, it is so quiet; especially when it is market day and my birthday. Where is everyone?

A message appears from my parents, 'Happy birthday to our beautiful Esther. We are already at the markets to get our sales over with quickly. Have a relaxing morning, we will see you at lunch time to reveal plans for your birthday. The only hint is you will be a queen for a day!'

I am left pondering this hint and have a long shower. I take care with my hair, enjoying the hot water. I pamper my skin with lotion that brings it to life again after neglecting it for so long.

Making peppermint tea I curl up on a comfy chair on the veranda, with the Bellbirds tinkling in the distance. I scroll more birthday messages.

Simon's message is private, declaring his love for me with a beautiful candid picture of us, I have never seen, from the party in the city. We appear to be laughing and smiling, looking at each other as if we are the only ones on the planet. It is so simple yet says so much. I smile to myself remembering our great time touring the city together and the taste of our freedom to come.

Simon wishes his Queen Esther a happy birthday and that I need to be ready by 6pm as my carriage will arrive to take me to the party.

My excitement builds and I message Sarah, who is in knots trying to work out what is going on. She tells me that our Mums have made dresses for the occasion so no need to choose an outfit. She is so glad we can share this important moment together. I agree, acknowledging we are going to be truly spoilt today.

"I know, I can't wait, see you soon. The surprise is killing me though."

Sarah was never good at waiting for *anything*.

Lunch time arrives and my family arrives home, immediately moving into party prep mode. My mother flies in the door says a brief hello, then is busy in the kitchen. My father and Luke wish me a happy birthday with usual jokes about looking old then they disappear in the truck that fully laden with items covered by a tarp.

I wander back into the kitchen and make a simple lunch for myself amongst the food laid out everywhere on benches. I wonder where my busy mother finds the time and I see my favourite foods in small serving sizes packed in containers. She asks me to put lids on them.

My mother stops and comes over and hugs me for a long time, "Happy birthday, baby girl, I'm so sorry, I got caught up. It is time to get you ready."

Looking at the time I notice there are several hours to go before the party. I hear Ruby's voice with others on the veranda and rush to see what is going on. Ruby, Sarah, and the stylists from her favourite salon arrive in tow.

My mother and Ruby busy themselves organising the dining table and chairs like a salon. The stylists roll out hair and makeup kits across it, throwing capes around our shoulders. Sarah and I hold each other's hands, look at each other smiling and cannot stop shaking with excitement. We are informed to sit still and no peeking until they are done, as our hair is transformed over the next hour.

Sarah's mother arrives with two dress bags and takes them to my mother's room for hanging. Miriam, Sarah's mother, is an excellent sewer, so I can only imagine something beautiful awaits.

She reappears and kisses me on the cheek. "Happy Birthday Esther, you are so grown up now."

Miriam helps my mother with final preparations while observing what is happening with the stylists. Our mothers cannot stop smiling.

Our hair is finally completed, and I see Sarah's hair intricately braided and styled like royalty from the Renaissance. I gently touch mine and feel similar intricate braids twisted and pinned.

Our makeup is next and I feel layers of make up on my skin, wondering what I must look like, feeling like a stranger in my own body.

Sarah and I are ushered into my mother's bedroom, and our mothers tell us to close our eyes to carefully remove our clothes and lift our arms up. I feel a silky fabric slide over my body almost to the floor.

I look down at the layers of sheer organza fabric floating over the deep purple satin resting on my skin, flowing from a hand beaded bodice with spaghetti straps, and there is purple and gold detail sewn onto the organza layers. I am breathless and in shock at the sheer beauty and decadence of the dress. Sarah's dress is the same but pink and silver.

We are finally permitted to look in the huge mirror in my mother's room and gasp. The combination of the ornate hair, dresses and skilfully applied makeup has transformed us from girls to elegant women of an imagined renaissance fairytale.

The team is trying to stop Sarah from crying to protect their creation. I just stand quietly looking at my transformation, realising that in this very moment, I have emerged from the chrysalis of very ordinary and plain to the butterfly everyone else sees.

It feels so vain to think these thoughts but maybe I needed to see it in a dramatic way to believe it. I still look like me, just improved, with my best features highlighted - my eyes.

We are asked to pose for photos in the garden with our mothers and for the stylists for their portfolios. Sarah and I thank our mothers for all their surprises. They just smile saying we are so precious to them that they could not help it once they got started.

Our mothers excuse themselves, carrying the mountain of food out the door and saying our ride to the party will be here soon. Ruby helps them to the car and is in charge of driving them to the secret destination while we wait for our ride. Sarah and I stand alone in the quiet house wondering what is next on this magical day, looking at each other's dresses and hair.

I hear my Dad's truck toot and we walk outside to see our fathers have arrived in the truck, which has been decorated. Two chairs are positioned on the back like something for a parade, draped in fabric and flowers, the truck looks incredibly beautiful. Transformed. Luke appears to take photos of us and our fathers who then help us up onto the chairs.

Our fathers' smiles are incredible; they are so proud and excited. Sarah keeps asking where we are going, Matt tells her to be patient.

Luke carefully locks up the house and jogs behind the truck as it rolls out the gate and he locks that too, then jumping in the cab. He is grinning thoroughly enjoying the mystery.

We roll through town, and everyone stares. Sarah and I start to wave like we are on a parade float. The truck leaves the centre of town and heads slowly up the hill to the lookout. Sarah and I grab each other's hands knowing it must be in the Pine Forest reserve.

We arrive to see two handsome men dressed in linen shirts and satin vests that match our dresses waiting at the entrance to the reserve.

Our kings for a day smile as they see the truck approach and then stop momentarily when they see Sarah and me. They rush forward to help us down from the truck, handling us like we might break and damage our dresses.

Simon just holds my hands and stares at me and tells me he has never seen anyone look as beautiful in his whole life. He bows and puts out his arm for me to take, and Josh does the same.

They both look at each other and nod and push a hand-held button. Our dresses illuminate with hundreds of tiny lights sewn into the layers of organza. We stand for a moment looking at the beautiful creations Miriam has made.

Simon and Josh lead us carefully through the dark quiet reserve to the centre, where it has been transformed into a fairytale scene of chairs, cushions, and blankets that are scattered around in a circle. Food is laden on tables and two chairs have been decorated for us as if we are royalty and the party guests are our subjects.

Our friends and their families clap and cheer as we appear and sit as honoured guests. We are speechless. This is so spectacular we cannot believe it is real. Even the guests have made attempts to dress up for the occasion.

Ruby takes photos to capture the moment; she looks stunning in a red flowing satin gown. She keeps encouraging us to smile more if that is even possible.

Each of our parents share beautiful and funny memories with those present about us, which everyone loves and nods having known us so long. Finally it's Josh's turn, he talks about how he and Sarah's friendship grew to become love and shares everything he adores about her.

Naturally she cries happy tears and throws her arms around him, and everyone sighs at how romantic this scene is. He places a crown, which is lit with little fairy lights on her head. Her look is complete. Radiant. Even her happy tears twinkle.

Simon quietly approaches and kneels on one knee in front of me looking into my eyes. My heart is pounding. "Esther, all I can say is you know how I feel about you; you look so beautiful tonight. Will you be my queen forever?"

He arises and places an illuminated crown on my head like Sarah's. I feel like a queen and he is my handsome, humble king. No fancy words would have adequately expressed his feelings for me. He has expressed his love in so many ways over the time we have been together.

He stands, and I rise and stand on my toes to reach up and kiss him gently and wrap my arms around him, enjoying the precious moment of the fairytale come to life. Knowing our fairytale will not end tonight as this is only the beginning, to marry and live happily ever after like in children's stories.

Everyone cheers and someone yells, "Party time!" We all graze the endless supply of delicious finger food and enjoy the birthday song sung to us in front of a tower of frosted decorated cupcakes.

The adults and small children help clean up, say goodbye, and leave the young adults to dance the night away, I look up and see fairy lights in the trees circling our party. We dance and sing loudly as we are not disturbing anyone in such an isolated place. This party is far better than any end of school dance - no bullying just fun and complete acceptance.

After dancing and singing badly with my friends and a few slow magical dances with Simon in the middle of the pine forest, I sit on a blanket leaning on a pile of cushions. I admire the lights in the trees and enjoy a moment to take in all the wonderful events of the evening.

I hear the music turned down, just playing in the background, now carried on a gently breeze through the trees. Simon sits next to me, in silence, just looking at me and reaches for my hand. We sit for a while.

"Are you happy?" he asks.

"Yes, more than I thought possible," I reply, looking at him. He gently pulls me to my feet holding both my hands.

"I have a surprise for you." He leads me by my left hand towards the clearing overlooking the ocean. The breeze is gentle and my dress floats around me. I see small lanterns illuminating a blanket set up with cushions.

We stop and Simon holds my hands. He tells me how much he loves me and wants to enjoy this night for as long as possible. He then melts my heart completely saying how many days, hours, and minutes until we meet again, here in this very place sharing our vows and are married. He wishes we could be married right now in this moment.

The sun has almost set, and he brings out of his vest pocket a gold necklace with a small star and a sparkling diamond in the centre.

"Esther, the diamond is to remind you, you are the precious jewel in the centre of my life. Your name means, Star, as well as being named after a courageous woman who became a queen in the Bible. She reminds me a little of you. God was always with her guiding and protecting, despite the challenges she had to overcome." I am speechless, this is such a beautiful heartfelt gift and his words penetrate my heart and stay there. I just nod and throw arms around him and sob tears of happiness.

"I hope I can be half the woman you believe I am or could be one day, I will treasure this gift. Can you help me put this on?" Simon gently places the necklace around my neck and kisses me.

"You are perfect the way you are." We sit on the blanket and I remove my crown, rest my head on his chest with his strong arm around me. I am content to listen to the ocean, with his heart beating steadily and we look out and watch the sun slip below the horizon enjoying the quiet moment before our lives are transported into final wedding preparations, work and waiting for exam results.

CHAPTER 32

My slate rouses me from sleep after a late and beautiful dinner with Simon. Reaching for my slate, I lay in bed scrolling through the laws and see Ruby has invited a few of us to see some bands tonight, at a club in Sydney City. We can stay at her parents' apartment in the city, within walking distance to the venue.

I call Simon, "Hey baby, missing me already?" I ignore the comment and plough on telling him, "Just listen, I will talk since you're half asleep." I read Ruby's plan.

Simon nods, gives me the thumbs up, and then sits up suddenly fully awake and looks at me through the screen.

"Esther, let's plan a couple of dates while we are there. Thoughts?" He sits waiting for an answer. I realise I have been staring at his uncovered chest.

"*Esther*! Seriously, are you checking me out?" I finally blink.

"What? Oh, I was *totally checking you out*, Simon. You are so, so *shirtless*."

He puts his slate down for a moment then returns clothed.

"Esther, focus, what do you think about my plan?"

"Yes, cannot wait, I'll tell Ruby and the guys we're in. See you soon." I blow him a kiss.

Replying to the group chat I see that everyone is going. We will be small group, but it will be fun. I message work and I inform my mother what is happening. She is delighted we are finally all doing something fun and adds I am glad the boys are going too.

Showering quickly, I dress in my stretchy jeans, a cute new pink t-shirt that hugs my body and my soft soled joggers for walking.

Siting with Mum while she eats breakfast she says, "Esther, I'm so glad you are going out. There is so much ahead of you next year with study and running a home. This is such an important time for you and Simon to really build on your friendship. I'm going to miss my girl at our table."

"Oh, Mum I'll be home from time to time."

She shakes her head. "No Esther, I know you will want to be with Simon, or you will be in the city studying and working. That is okay. Just message me when you can." Kissing her on the cheek I leave her reading a novel on her slate and sipping tea in the peaceful house.

I jump on the bus, seeing that Sarah has minded me a seat. She is sweet. I sit listening to a detailed one-sided conversation. We step off at the station seeing Ruby chatting with Simon and Josh. No, Jonah, I leave that to come up in conversation organically.

When the bullet train arrives, we manage find an empty carriage, as it is the weekend. I listen to my friend's chatter. Sarah just blurts out, "Where's Jonah, Ruby? Is he busy today?"

Ruby sits up and looks us in the eye, "He acted like a huge disrespectful *jerk* and I dumped him. I don't have time for that kind of crap," she says bluntly.

We sit, unsure how to respond. Simon stretches out his long legs. "Fair enough, good for you Ruby," and leaves it at that. Josh fidgets uncomfortably.

Sarah and I look at Ruby both asking, "Are you okay?"

"Yep, it was cut and dried. I'm totally at peace with it." I just nod and give her a smile; she knows we can talk.

"Now we've got that awkward moment out of the way, what do we want to do, guys?" Ruby asks.

We spend the short trip planning a few activities for today then plan to work out the rest later.

We arrive at Sydney City Terminal and step onto the metro. We stand up, as it is a short trip, only a few streets, it is fun. I never tire of riding it, the sights, sounds and smells of the gourmet food of the city make me smile.

Simon leans over my shoulder and kisses me on the cheek. "Happy?" he asks seeing my smile.

"Happy," I reply.

We step off the metro and Ruby leads us to a huge apartment block in the residential Precinct. Entering the beautiful foyer, she is greeted by a concierge who take our bags. Then we find ourselves entering the two-bedroom apartment with stunning city views.

The two spacious bedrooms are beautifully decorated. Josh and Simon are given one with two single beds and the girls will share the master bedroom. I see two single beds have been made up for us. We insist Ruby take the king bed since she is providing the venue. We unpack and then all check out the stunning apartment and the city from the balcony.

Simon and I look out over the city. We take in the views of the Harbour Bridge and observe the Performing Arts Centre with its huge gleaming white sails on this stunning summer day.

Wandering back in, Simon heads to the bedroom to grab his slate to take photos. I head to the kitchen.

I see Simon push the bedroom door wide open and then propel Josh out the front door. He says to Ruby over his shoulder, "We will grab some lunch for everyone."

I look through the door to see Sarah dressing quickly. Simon stepped up as an adult. Not a comfortable moment.

Ruby and I scuttle to the balcony with juice.

I quickly message Simon, "I've transferred points for the shopping." He sends me a thumbs up and says they will be back in half an hour.

Sarah appears on the balcony looking happy.

"All good?" I ask casually.

"I was until *Simon* barged in."

I give Sarah a hard look. "Simon was not the problem here."

"What do you mean?" She is miffed.

"Sarah, wake up! You are not a kid anymore, be considerate of everyone. What you and Josh do in your own time away from here is your business."

"We weren't really doing anything, just mucking around."

I look at her, "*Really?* Sarah, it looked a lot more than that. Be careful is all I'm going to say, as your friend." She acknowledges what I am saying.

She smiles. "You're right, Esther. Being finally free, went to my head and Josh's too. He just started kissing me then …I will talk to him about respecting the space."

I give her a hug. "We love you guys; we are all adjusting to adult life. I suspect Simon and Josh are not just shopping for lunch."

We all laugh, knowing Simon is a man of few words and the look on his face as he left said it all. Treat the girls right or else.

Returning from our room I give her two condoms. She looks shocked. "Put these in your slate bag, and do not discuss it. Just leave them there, be prepared."

Ruby nods. "You're right Esther."

Ruby announces, "Time to have some fun." She loads her slate with music playlists and we start dancing around the apartment, singing the few words we can remember badly, and eating chocolate, much to the guy's amusement, as they re-enter. They are all smiles and loaded up with fresh produce.

Simon unpacks while leaving items out for lunch. He reaches for my hand and dances with me pulling me close, "Hello beautiful. We had a brotherly chat, all good."

I just nod, enjoying the beginning of a fun day ahead, smiling to myself thinking I have seen Simon and Matt interact. I'm thankful for the wisdom of an older guy.

Simon breaks the dance, asking everyone, "Okay if I prep lunch, I need to keep practising my cooking skills. I cannot be outdone by Esther."

Everyone cheers. We all sit around the huge kitchen counter and chat while Simon quickly preps a variety of salads and grills some chicken.

We all agree to hit the biggest Parkour Park in Sydney City first then go from there. Simon shyly brings up the fact he wants to take me on a date while we are here.

"Where are you going to take Esther?"

"It's a surprise," he tells us. "We might grab an early dinner and meet back here by eight to go out."

Ruby says that works, as she has some city friends she wants to catch up with. We all look at Josh and Sarah who smile.

"We both want to go to the zoo, so we will head there."

Simon announces that lunch is ready. He has managed a feast in record time: three salads and shredded chicken to put on wraps with leftovers for tomorrow. We all sit on the balcony enjoying the view.

Ruby says sadly, "I'm going to miss having lunch with you guys."

I nudge her with my elbow. "Ruby, we will be at the same Uni if I get the results I need and can meet up with you," she nods.

Sarah asks Ruby, "When do you start your pre-law and where are you going to live?"

Ruby brightens up saying, "I start in two weeks and I am going to live on campus. My parents have secured me a single dorm room thank goodness. Esther, message me any pre-Union events. I'll be there and most importantly; I don't want to miss the most gorgeous couple's union. Not long now guys."

I nod, slowly looking across at my handsome fiancé who is smiling back and think I am so lucky to have him in my life. He really wants to marry me, no casual decisions, he is all in.

Sarah turns to me and grabs my arm. "Esther, have you got a dress for the wedding? You have been so busy studying. Don't leave it too late."

I look across the table again, smiling at Simon. "I have already bought one right here in the city. It is being altered; I just haven't told anyone."

Simon looks at me, holding his gaze and inclining his head subtly to me, to say he is happy for me.

Ruby and Sarah go crazy yelling excitedly, "What! When? We need pictures, anything." I tell them I can message the store and see if I can try it on while in the city.

Ruby looks at me and the store name as I message. She knows it is the best wedding and evening wear store in the city.

The reply comes back, "We are open seven days. We need thirty minutes notice you are coming."

"Can we go now?" Sarah asks.

I look at everyone. "Is that okay?" They all agree.

I message them back and my fitting appointment is confirmed in thirty minutes. We all rush to clear up lunch and pull on our active wear for PK afterwards. Simon and I remerge first, Simon suggests we all come back, shower and change after the PK, which is a great plan.

While everyone is getting organised, I say quietly to Simon, "Tell me if it is too much, too soon, this wedding stuff. I was trying to keep everything low key until you were more settled from being away. Please tell me honestly if it is not okay."

He pulls me into his arms. "Thank you. It is nice to be asked. At the table I realised this incredible woman across from me is going to be my bride and I felt happy. Realising I need to get onboard with the fun and excitement, your friends reminded me this is very much a big deal. We did agree on more fun, let's go for it." I agree, then he starts tickling me until I cannot stand it any longer, yelling "Anchor."

We head down in the elevator. Simon holds my hand, which is sweet and does not let go all the way down to the store entrance.. Ruby shoos the two guys away like blow flies. "Come back in thirty minutes. Look, there is a sports bar, go hang out there."

We enter through very elaborate doors and are escorted immediately to the huge fitting room with a platform to stand on.

The two attendants I have met previously gush, "Esther, it's lovely to see you again." They usher me into the change room and are disappointed I am in my active wear. They help me into the dress, which is a strapless bodice covered in hand sewn crystals and beads with a full-length straight silk skirt that falls in silk pools at my feet.

I am escorted to the platform where Sarah and Ruby have been seated in front with sparkling water and high tea. They are speechless, especially as the attendants have pinned my braid up into a bun, which highlights my neck and shoulders and have added a small tiara.

They stand back so my friends and I can look in the mirror. The dress is simple but so elegant and the lights bounce off the crystals.

Sarah and Ruby just sigh and say, "Esther you are gorgeous." The attendants can be heard fussing behind me.

Ruby jumps up, Elite style, demanding to know what the problem is. They confess the dress is not fitting as well as it should. They whisper she has lost so much weight.

Ruby says, "*No, she hasn't*, she has gained lean muscle, look at her she so fit and toned, fix it." They immediately start pinning and pulling the dress to where they believe it should sit.

Ruby looks at me, "Esther are you truly happy with the fit now?" I nod.

She says, "Okay then, otherwise I'll make them keep going."

She tells them to go away and leave us for a moment. They scurry away to some far corner of the shop. They're now terrified realising Ruby is an Elite not a tame Farmer girl like me.

Ruby says to Sarah and me, "Let's be completely girly."

We all hold hands and just shriek at the top our lungs. "It's so amazing this dress I can't believe how well they have adjusted it."

We calm down and call the staff back. Ruby says in her Elite voice, "My friend Esther is happy to proceed with the final alteration." They nod and help me out of the dress again.

We remerge onto the street laughing. We have taken a picture to show my mother, who is never to know the girls were there.

We all walk towards the PK park just down the street. Simon grabs my arm, so we hang back a little.

"How did it go?" he asks curiously.

I look at him almost crying and say, "Simon it's so perfect for our special day."

"Happy?" he asks.

"Very happy," I reply, then cheekily say, "When I beat you at the PK park."

"We'll see," he says, grabbing my hand as we run to catch up, weaving around the city citizens who are not impressed.

We arrive at Hyde Park and locate the PK park within it. It is huge with simulated buildings, broken walls, rails, and ledges.

We stow our slates in nearby lockers and try to work out where to begin. A kind citizen shows us the colour coordinated zones to indicate beginner intermediate and experienced.

We all move to beginner and start there and let the guys start so we have the luxury of seeing how they go. They are slow working out their moves, we start and begin to gain on them. Josh is very quick and lean. He obviously has not spent too much time on trawlers yet.

Simon is a little slower, but his upper body strength gives him the upper edge on Josh and overtakes him to land on his feet at the finish.

The girls manage quite well. Ruby is not as strong but has great flexibility and agility to leap onto ledges and over walls. Sarah and I are close, but I overtake her as I have a lot more strength from yard work and I practise more often not being at school.

We all stand panting and sipping our water, refilling at the free water fountain. Our muscles and hands burn from the exertion.

"Who wants to tackle intermediate after a break?" Simon asks. We all are keen.

Josh has already removed his singlet top and thrown it in a nearby locker with his satchel. I look around and realise most of the guys do not wear a shirt, they must get too hot in summer. I do not blame them; I am not used to seeing citizens partly undressed. Back home the guys cover up a lot.

Disgusting rivers of sweat run down my back relentlessly. I wring out my long braid. Urgh! Simon sits next to me on the grass in the shade nudging me. "Looking good baby."

I shove him back. "Shut up."

Simon gets up and pulls his singlet top off and I see him for the first time, and I steal a long sideways glimpse. He is fit.

He grins at me. "See you at the other end, loser."

With that challenge and the chance to get near him, I throw down my drink bottle and rip off my active t-shirt to reveal my sports singlet top and run to catch up, realising my body is cooling a lot quicker without two layers on. We blend with the crowd now. I work every muscle to catch up and use my petite size and flexibility to get past Simon.

Simon catches a glimpse of me in the active wear and freezes momentarily, then curses under his breath, knowing he has been had.

His fiancé has played him big time. I leap off the last wall onto the cushioned rubber base that is marked 'finish' and wander casually over to my drink bottle and sip more water, waiting for him to finish and meet up with me.

Pouring water over my neck and face, I let it run over my back too and rehydrate. Everyone is doing the same. We are all done, and ready to rest.

I look for a seat to stretch my legs on. I discover one in the shade and slowly stretch all my muscles. It feels better already, a slight breeze cools me down and it dries me quickly. I see Simon approach and I avert my eyes. Nobody wants to be ogled like a piece of meat.

He grabs my hand and slowly leads me to a group of shady trees away from the others who are sitting on the grass. He looks at me, he is sweaty like me and has also poured water on himself to cool down.

He holds my hands and says softly, "Esther, you can look at me, it's okay." I nod and slowly look at him, staring into those bright blue eyes. Then I slowly look at his mouth, chin, strong shoulders and then his chest and torso.

I understand he is trying to remove any awkwardness between us, to be more comfortable with each other in a respectful way.

I tell him, "You can look at me if you want."

He laughs. "Already have, many times."

We smile at each other. Simon holds my face in his hands and says almost in a whisper, "You are so beautiful and strong I am even more attracted to you right now."

Reaching up I rest my hands on his chest and feel his heart beating strongly maybe a little faster at my touch and I stand on my toes and gently kiss him. He responds with the same gentleness and says, "I love you."

I respond, "I love you too with all my heart."

Simon holds my hands and we stand enjoying the moment of gentle intimacy. Now more comfortable with each other. We break apart and walk back pulling on our active t-shirts, modest again. The others are waiting patiently on the grass for us chatting.

Sarah says, "I can't wait to go and have a shower."

We all agree to decide to take the metro back to the apartment, much to the disgust of our fellow travellers. We arrive and tag team the showers, emerging clean and refreshed, and dressed for an afternoon of fun in the city.

Sarah asks Simon and me, "Where did you guys go at the park?"

Simon stretches out on the lounge like a satisfied cat, arms behind his head and looks at me smirking. "Just checking out the stunning view."

Sarah hurries Josh up, and he yells back, "The animals aren't going anywhere." They are amusing together.

Ruby appears, stunning in full Elite couture. She is wearing her hair down, which is a new look for her after years of school braids. Her raven hair is like a sheet of silk.

Simon says almost to himself, "I don't know what Jonah did, but he's a moron for letting you go Ruby."

"Thanks Simon, I needed that boost," she says smiling, flicking her long hair as she clatters out the front door in her ridiculously high heels, which she adores.

Sarah and Josh head out, informing us they will be back by seven pm. I grab a comb and start trying to detangle my long-wet hair.

"Sit," Simon insists and asks for the comb. I sit on the floor in front of him and he patiently combes out my long hair until its smooth. We talk about the PK course and which level we liked best for variety and challenge; we are determined to be fit enough to tackle the hardest one. Simon tells me all the knots are gone; I am touched by his thoughtfulness and thank him.

"Where are we going? Is this okay for the date?" I twirl in a simple full length cotton dress in navy blue, a nice change to work scrubs or jeans.

He nods, saying, "You're perfect, just wear comfy shoes."

I quickly blow dry my hair so its smooth and shiny, opting to leave it down and slip on some white soft soled flat shoes.

CHAPTER 33

We step out into the city, feeling the summer heat hitting us instantly. Simon waves down a private transport, giving the driver directions. We are driven to the older part of the city, Darlinghurst.

The daylight disappears quickly with the old buildings blocking any remaining sun as it drops a little lower in the afternoon.

The driver lets us out in Crown Street, near a row of older unmaintained shops, reminiscent of the much earlier days before shopping centres. I see boutique clothing and vintage stores.

Our bodies are buffeted by strong wind. I shiver, as the wind tunnels converge onto this street. Simon directs me quickly into a shop with an old grimy glass door, tarnished ornate handle and a scruffy sign that is hard to read.

It could easily be a scene out of my favourite zombie slayer stories. We are greeted by a friendly elderly gentleman whose warm brown eyes twinkle. I look around and see it is a cosy boutique vintage jewellery store with custom pieces displayed.

I look at Simon who just squeezes my hand and smiles, giving no clue to why we are here.

Simon asks the man, "Are you John?" He nods. "My father sent me to see you especially, Andrew Allen."

"Ah yes, welcome Simon and Esther," he says. Simon reveals his tattoo, which the gentleman acknowledges and shows a tattoo of symbols under his watch. Simon nods.

"Follow me," John says. He holds out his hands for our slates and puts them into a safe and locks it with a huge brass ancient key.

I try not to be alarmed as he leads us into his back workshop. He turns a circular handle and opens an enormous ornate safe door and walks through it.

John pokes his head out smiling and beckons us. We look at each other as if we have entered another world and follow him into a secret room and the false back panel is quietly closed behind us.

We look around and take in this softly lit windowless room and are relieved to see more jewellery displays and elegantly upholstered chairs.

The gentleman formally introduces himself as John. He settles us in two antique chairs arranged in front of a small antique desk covered with black velvet and sits on the opposite side.

He looks at Simon. "So, Simon the Fisherman, what brings you to John's shop?"

"I have brought my fiancé Esther with me today so we can choose our wedding bands together."

I see Simon smiling at me as he reaches for my hand.

"I hope that's okay Esther, I wanted to surprise you." I am speechless, I had accepted I would keep wearing my commitment ring like so many of us do. This is an extremely costly exercise we are undertaking.

John nods slowly, surveying Simon.

"Now Simon, look at me. Why do you want a wedding band? Why do you want to give *Esther* a wedding band? I can see she has lovely commitment ring already."

I am puzzled by this questioning, then sense this is a significant exchange between the two men. I sit ready to watch what unfolds, trying not to hold my breath.

Simon fidgets for a moment in his chair then sits up straight and looks John in the eye.

"I want to present my bride Esther, with an outward sign of my commitment to our marriage covenant I will promise to her. If she is willing, she will gift me a wedding band, an outward sign of her commitment to me and our marriage covenant she promises to me."

I am floored by his confident eloquent speech that transports me back into last century.

John nods, seeming satisfied. He indicates we put out our left hands on the velvet cloth.

"Simon, what does the ring mean to you besides a reminder of the covenant of marriage and your promises?"

Simon looks at me smiling and says, "The ring symbolises to me that our love has no end. It also reminds us that God is at the centre of our marriage and that his love for us is eternal. That he is the alpha and omega, and his kingdom has no end."

John places his hands on ours, "Heavenly Father, bless this young couple who have shown that you truly are the centre of their relationship and have a deep understanding of what a marriage covenant is. Watch over them, bless them, and keep them in your care. On their wedding day they will honour you and praise your name. Amen."

We say Amen, totally overwhelmed by this sacred moment. Simon, still looking at me, leans over and kisses me gently just for a moment. John averts his eyes respectfully.

John pats our hands and removes his, smiling. He looks at me and says, "You are going to marry a wise and Godly man Esther. You are blessed. He has shown he studies and understands the scriptures. Esther, are you willing to trust Simon as the leader in your home and acknowledge that God is the centre of your marriage, that everything you do should honour him?"

I nod, "I'm willing with God and Simon's help."

I had not really thought about this before until now. I think of the times Simon has shielded me and guided me and am thankful he is willing to put himself out there for me, despite having my own strength and independence.

John looks at Simon. "You are truly blessed to be engaged to Esther. I can see she is wise and humble and will be a faithful partner."

Simon looks at me for a long time and touches my cheek gently.

"I know. Thank you for taking us through this preparation John. It has been incredibly inciteful and really helped me, us, to be personally challenged to acknowledge how sacred marriage is. I had no idea what to expect when my dad sent me here. He just said see John; he will help you with wedding rings." I nod in agreement.

John rubs his hands together. "I never know where God will lead me when I meet a new couple. Okay kids, you have done the hard work, let's have some fun choosing rings." His demeanour has flipped from serious elder to fun uncle.

John brings a tray of ladies' rings and places them in front of me. He explains in detail the specifics of each, including the intricate engraving and their meaning. He does the same for Simon and then discreetly leaves us to decide together.

The minute he has gone I throw my arms around Simon. "This is too much, such a surprise. Such beautiful words, I have never heard anything like it."

He wraps his arms around me, pulling me onto his lap and stroking my long hair saying, "No, it's what's right." He looks at me with a serious face.

"This is important Esther, even if we are poor and have absolutely nothing, we will have our rings to remind us of our love, our wedding day and God's goodness and faithfulness. I love you so much Esther I am so grateful to have you in my life," Simon whispers.

"I love you too, Simon." We kiss with such gentleness and love for one another in this private moment holding each other.

I see the importance of a conversation like this. It is the foundation strengthening our bond and reminding us of what marriage really is, it is not frivolous wedding celebrations and dresses. It is a partnership even through the tough times and not bailing out when it is too hard.

We sit in silence, sitting in the ornate chairs, again looking at the rings in front of us.

I look at Simon, somewhat embarrassed, "Simon, there are no prices on these. I cannot just choose one not knowing." He nudges me with his shoulder. "All of these are in the right price range for us."

I look at him. "Really? They are all so beautiful."

I look again carefully and choose a simple but intricately engraved one and slip off my commitment ring and place it on my left hand and just sit looking at it. I look across at Simon who has chosen the exact same design and has placed it on his finger. I laugh lightly. He looks at me saying, "What is so funny?" I hold up my hand and he laughs too.

"John will think we are hopeless romantics. Oh well, I think that seals the deal, we are both officially on the same page."

John appears and discreetly looks in. "Everything going, okay?"

We nod and hold out our hands like proud children. He looks from one to the other and laughs out loudly, "You two have got the love bug bad." He slips them off and sizes us properly. "Do you want an inscription inside?"

Simon nods and says, "Esther?"

I tell John, "I would like the same as my commitment ring." Simon agrees, "Perfect I'll have the same."

John says, "What am I going to do with you two, hey?"

We happily follow him through the mysterious entrance out to the shop where our slates are waiting for us. Simon opens his slate ready to transfer the points. John waves his hand and says, “No charge, Andrew and Rachael have said this is their wedding gift to you both.”

Simon and I stand there stunned, unsure what to do. It is a very generous gift and such a powerful way to express their love for us both.

Simon suddenly has silent tears running down his face. I do not know what to do. He is my tall strong Simon, now silently dissolving into a puddle. I wrap my arms around him tightly, holding him. He is shaking. He finally manages to calm himself to tell John and me, “I am overwhelmed. I know this is such a huge sacrifice for them. They have done so much for me already; I do not feel worthy of it.”

John pulls Simon onto a chair in the middle of the shop. He sits and faces Simon looking him in the eye. “Simon, your parents told me they couldn’t be prouder of how you have carried yourself as a faithful son and grown into the man you are today.” He touches Simon’s wrist. “And as Esther’s future husband. They love you both so much they could not find a better way to express it. The fact that you had saved and was prepared to pay for the rings is a test of your character. They bought their rings from my father and see the value of this process and wanted you and Esther to experience it too.”

Simon just sits and is calm and he dries his tears on his sleeve. He stands up and hugs John who happily returns the hug. They separate. Simon is back to his old self again, so I leave John and Simon to manage the final details.

Standing, unsure what to do with myself, I look out the glass front doors and see some small restaurants dotted along the street and decide this is a great place to have a cosy dinner on a perfect day. I look around the shop and see rows of antique and vintage watches, cufflinks, pendants, necklaces, and lockets rarely seen in my community unless passed down from family. They are quite beautiful, exquisite, and understated. Each design is unique. My understanding is the Elite purchase them as rare collectables.

I thank John as we leave for his time, wisdom, kindness, and that we appreciated his help. He waves us off with a big smile and says, "Go have fun, young people."

We step back out onto the breezy street. Looking up at Simon I ask, "Are you truly okay? You seemed so broken a moment ago."

He assures me he is fine. Just the last few weeks had been such a huge roller-coaster of emotions and experiences it hit him hard with his parents' generosity, an unexpected moment; it moved him.

Satisfied Simon is okay I suggest, "Let's have an early dinner here before we go out for the night, after Parkour today, I'm so hungry. I would love to sit together and enjoy this moment alone."

We walk, looking at the different cosy cafes and restaurants. The air is filled with alluring scents of international cuisine and the sounds of people enjoying themselves. We decide on Lebanese. The restaurant is very small and intimate and appears to be run by a family.

We settle into a cute booth and order an array of dishes to sample and discuss our day. We each share how we felt about our experience with John.

Simon shakes his head smiling, "Dad really dropped me in it with John. No warning, boom, just to face the big questions unplanned and unrehearsed, in front of my fiancé, so awkward."

I squeeze his arm. "Simon, I had no idea you could speak so .... wisely."

He looks at me, kissing me on the cheek. "It just came out from the heart not my head for a change."

I hold his face in my hands very close to mine, "I loved your words so much, they touched my heart; I really feel they should be our vows. What do you think?"

Simon leans forward, his forehead resting on mine and whispers, "It's perfect."

Our food arrives and covers the small table and breaks our sweet moment. We shift into casual mode and discuss the Parkour park; a highlight and we are keen to tackle another time. Simon insists next time we are taking towels and a change of clothes as we were drenched.

"I almost lost my grip several times my hands were aching and so sweaty."

I smile asking, "Is that the only reason you lost your grip?" He nods, grinning and kisses my cheek, "Absolutely *not!*"

CHAPTER 34

Our group reluctantly leaves the lively club at two am. Our bodies accepting defeat after a long day. The cool air is a soothing balm; the heat of so many dancing bodies in one space was claustrophobic.

We walk slowly back to the apartment chatting about the bands we saw and the club scene that is so new to us. Ruby has given up on her heels and is carrying them. Sarah and Josh only drank water, being so broke and wanting to dance all night.

Simon and I enjoyed the freedom away from home. We danced, sat, and enjoyed the music and met people we knew from the party at our friend's flat. It was great to catch up. We enjoyed a few drinks and Simon is very relaxed, chatty, and not shy anymore. We walk hand in hand behind the others so we can have some space to talk and be alone. He looks at me the whole time telling me everything he loves about me, which is adorable, right down to the time he saw me at the party dressed as a beautiful queen.

I nod, enjoying the moment on the quiet street except for the loud friends ahead.

Simon unexpectantly pulls me into an alcove of a shop front and kisses me with such unrestrained heat, and confidence it takes my breath away. His hands sliding down my shoulders to my waist wrapping himself tightly around me, I respond to the spontaneous moment my own desire barely restrained, not wanting to put the brakes on and caught up in the moment. Then the cool air hits me suddenly, clearing my head.

Realising that I only had a few drinks, but it clouded my judgement, eliminating my inhibitions, the same as Simon. Now, with a clear head, I stop for the moment, breaking us apart and leading Simon by the hand down the street, letting the cool air from the wind tunnels cool his feelings. He becomes alert quickly and focused as we walk approaching the entry of the apartments.

He stops, reaching for my hands, apologising, "Esther, I'm so sorry, I realise I was not in full control of myself, my feelings for you, and my behaviour, it came over me fast." Simon looks remorseful.

"I was the same, but my head cleared. Simon, we want what we want, which is good but not in the street, not a month before our Union and not when we are under the influence of alcohol. I had a really good time tonight dancing and hanging out with you."

"Me too, you look incredible, Esther." He leads me through the foyer and nods to the concierge. We enter the elevator and he pulls me into a loving embrace. I enjoy the few peaceful moments we share before entering the apartment, exhausted.

We are awakened by Ruby's alarm, annoying but a great plan. We lay talking quietly about last night and Sarah asks, "Where did you guys go? You disappeared, and I was worried."

I simply say, "We were enjoying being on a date and didn't want to rush back."

Ruby looks at Sarah. "*Seriously!* They're almost in a union, give them some space."

Ruby really gets it; she's such a loyal friend. I suggest we come up with something to do that does not involve too much walking as the lactic acid in my body is terrible this morning.

They agree. Ruby says, "Right, showers, first then decide."

We are restored by the warm water and lay on the couches eating fruit Simon and Josh have kindly prepared for an easy breakfast. Sarah asks excitedly, "What do we want to do today?" Ruby suggests the aquarium, which we all agree on and then back here for lunch.

"No walking, I will pay for the private transport door to door, I can barely move," Ruby insists. We do not object, pull on comfy shoes and head down in the elevator.

A large transport drops us at the entrance to the aquarium. We climb out and look around at the beautiful Sydney City morning. The summer's heat is rising, and the harbour looks incredible with the luxury boats docked on the nearby wharf. Simon and Josh are already wandering towards them; Sarah and I steer them back to the aquarium.

"No boats, just sea creatures," I say firmly to Simon.

Ruby manages to get us discounted entry, which really brightens our day, and we enter exploring the huge exhibits. Josh and Simon drive us mad by pointing at the various sea life playing a game 'grill or kill.'

We all wander off in different directions to look at exhibits. I see Ruby happy to be alone, and we leave her be. She obviously is hurting from the breakup with Jonah but has buried it for the moment. She sits looking at a huge exhibit, looking but not seeing.

Simon leads me to the ocean tunnel exhibit where you walk through a glass tunnel with larger and smaller sea creatures swimming overhead. We sit on the seat and enjoy the sharks and rays gliding past.

Simon holds my hand and names as many sharks as he can and other sea life he knows, which is incredible and he brings these creatures to life for me. I lean my head on his shoulder, enjoying the moment of peace. I feel his slow steady breathing and realise he needed a moment of peace too.

Simon stands and guides us to other exhibits. My favourites are the sea horses and the jellyfish, which are incredible the way they move. Simon kills the mood by saying, "Until you get stung by one." Fisherman!

We accept we need to leave and want to come back again one day.

Our friends browse the gift shop while Simon and I stand and wait. He leads me outside in the sunshine and turns me to face a huge, beautiful hotel with shimmering glass across the road from the aquarium.

"See that hotel, that's where we are staying for our honeymoon. I finally looked up the address. I would love to take you on a date to the underwater restaurant they have here one night on our honeymoon."

I look at him excitedly and ask, "That's the hotel? It is beautiful and close to everything. An underwater restaurant? It sounds incredible."

Simon looks very excited about the plan too. "It's really only a month and we'll be back here exploring the city together," he pauses and whispers, "and each other."

Simon leads me around a corner away from the front entrance of the aquarium. He wraps me in his arms, looking down at me in the way he does when he really, really desires me, and kisses me gently.

The others have extracted themselves from the gift shop, finally, and wandered out the front entrance to discover us. They now quickly back up awkwardly trying to pretend they did not see our public display, which they have never, ever witnessed.

We are always so discreet. My girlfriend's reaction is, "Aww how romantic."

We break apart and Simon grabs my hand and says, smiling, walking past them, "What do you think we get up to when you're not around?" They follow us out to the waiting transport.

We have lunch together on the balcony again. The view is stunning.

My slate beeps, and my mother informs me the girls' party before the wedding is planned for next Saturday and can I invite Sarah and Ruby. She says she will message them later with all the details.

I relay this to them and they get excited; I tell them it is a bunch of women hanging around eating cake and giving marriage advice. They look at each other smiling, and say, "Not if we have anything to do with it." I look at them and inwardly groan but I am also intrigued to see what they come up with.

Josh kicks Simon under the table. "What?" Simon says. "That means the guys are going out on the town," Josh says, "my first bucks' night, if I'm invited."

"I am sure you will be. Zach is in charge, apparently. It could go two ways, cringy marriage talk, oh no. Check, already done thank goodness. No it's a straight-out pub crawl."

The guys high five each other across the table. Simon points a finger at him, saying, "Don't drink too much, you're not used to it."

I laugh out loud.

"Simon, you only had a couple last night and you were acting stupid."

He looks at me smiling. "I promise, my beautiful bride, to behave *terribly.*"

As I head inside I wack him saying, "You better behave."

We pack up the apartment and jump on the metro, enjoying the sights, then head back to Sydney City Terminal. We step off and head up to the entrance to see lines of fellow travellers being stopped, questioned, and searched. As we get closer, I see the physical searches are intense and detailed.

There are rows of Law Enforcers sitting at tables processing numerous lines of travellers and their belongings. The scene is overwhelming, and confronting, but the crying and pleading is the worst. You can see and feel the terror. Citizens' personal effects are bagged and tossed into tubs marked *Property of Historians* like worthless trinkets.

Feeling utter disgust for this process I observe the Law Enforcers taking liberties and inflicting fear and unnecessarily touching citizens, which you could only describe as depraved. Now I'm acutely aware of why Simon spoke up for me back at the unit when we came to the city previously.

I am fearful and absolutely terrified for our safety. My heart is pounding and sweat is already trickling down my back. My ring is a direct violation, if they see the words inside or even catch a glimpse of the fish.

I look at Simon and know his tattoo could give him away big time, or at least need a lot of explaining.

"Ruby, give me your concealer, *now.*" I ask as a directive. She hands it over, not questioning it.

I tell Simon, "Put out your wrist." He looks at me and the concealer and follows my lead.

I pull back his leather strap and coat his tattoo in concealer, blending it with his skin and fanning to dry it quickly. It's working. I am grateful the tattoo is small enough to hide, but it is very dark.

Fortunately, Ruby wears expensive concealer to cover a small birthmark so I know it blocks out everything. I gratefully pass the concealer back to her. She raises an eyebrow as if to say a tattoo?

Simon pulls Josh to his side, and I am sure he is checking if Josh has any Christian markings or items. I see him shaking his head. Simon, Josh, and I know our two friends are completely ignorant about our faith, so they are safe.

The lines move slowly as rows of citizens line every available wall inside the enormous historic sandstone building. They are being very roughly searched and released. Word travels up and down the lines that they are looking for anything illegal - religious signs' markings, jewellery, possessions, or weapons, and where we are going and why.

Simon tells everyone to be calm. He asks Ruby to transfer each of us our copies of the band tickets to validate our reason for being in the city.

The line starts moving quickly as some are excused. Naturally, they are Town and Elite and only receive light searches.

Putting my ring down the centre of my bra, I know that it would not be appropriate to check in that much detail without good reason.

Simon squeezes my hand tightly; he knows we are so close to being caught. He wraps his arms around me tightly, kisses me and whispers, "I love you; we'll be okay no matter what. We have to suffer these trails for the harvest." I nod step, and turn, ready. I am next.

The girl in front of me is being roughly searched, and the Enforcers show her no mercy. They extract some items from her pocket and she is restrained by two Enforcers.

She starts screaming hysterically and thrashing about, declaring her right to believe in whatever she wants. Refusing to be cavity searched. Her screams mixed with everyone else's yelling and crying is chilling, a living nightmare. She is removed forcibly to an awaiting van.

I step forward handing my slate over to the Enforcer. They tell me to step aside. They spend a lot of time scrolling my extensive travel logs and then ask my reason for being in the city today and then why I travel to and from the city so often.

I tell them I went to see some bands last night and I work between several Medical Precincts and am now heading home. I indicate my friends who are now lined up, that I was with them. The Law Enforcers look at all our slates comparing them to see if my story holds up.

They verify it but are not satisfied. We're directed to a vacated wall and we put our arms out for a full body search and cavity search if they think that is required.

I have a female Law Enforcer who is respectful and carefully runs her hands over me without missing any chance of finding anything. She steps back and tells me to turn around and looks me in the eye saying, "You are a bit of a queen aren't you, *Esther?*"

I shrug and reply, "I guess!"

The Enforcer moves on to Simon who now endures a humiliating thorough search too. She touches the wrist band as if checking it then steps back and looks at him in the eye, then at his slate.

"Simon the *fisherman,* you and your queen are free to go." We nod and thank her.

"Follow the laws guys." She moves onto another group.

Our friends, already released, are waiting on the other side of the barrier. We tap our slates and run as fast as we can to catch the next bullet train out and throw ourselves in the carriage doors as they are closing. We want to escape this terrifying place.

We try to catch our breath gasping; I retrieve my ring out of my bra and slip it on my finger again. Simon holds me tightly whispering, "Are you okay baby?" I nod. He looks at me; our faces are so close; we are still catching our breath.

"We just experienced incredible grace from that woman," he says smiling. I nod slowly looking back at him smiling too and whisper, "If God is for us who can be against us?" Simon holds my face in his hands and kisses me firmly.

"Exactly, you remembered Romans 8 verse 31."

I grin, "Oh wow, I did. Now, what is this about me being a queen?"

Simon smiles. "I think it's time you heard about your namesake, you're more than ready."

We find seats where we can store our luggage and sit digesting the interrogation. Simon and I check everyone is okay before finally settling. Simon looks at his slate scrolling messages as I power nap on his shoulder. He whispers, "Is dinner tomorrow night with Zach and Hannah, okay?" I just nod and fall asleep.

We arrive at our home station and there are Enforcers, with only their eyes visible. Once they know we came from the Sydney City Terminal they wave us through, knowing we have been checked.

This experience leaves me feeling unsettled.

Sarah and I order a private transport to travel home. Ruby will walk home. Simon and Josh will jump on a bus.

"See you tomorrow, Simon. Thank you for an incredible date; I'll never forget it."

He smiles looking down at me. "That's the whole idea. I will never forget it either, it was such a private moment, I can't quite describe how I feel."

"It was a sacred declaration of our love and commitment," I tell him.

Simon kisses my cheek and gives me a brief hug. We separate, looking at each other, smiling and say goodbye, reluctant to go home.

I arrive home feeling elated and tired. I say hello to my parents and share with them about our city trip, including that Simon took me to buy our wedding rings and how it was a special moment.

I do not expand on what happened. This is a private matter between Simon and me.

My parents are quite moved by Simon's decision to arrange such a personal and important symbol of our marriage and are overjoyed for us.

Sitting on my bed I take a deep breath, sending a message that has taken all my courage, and knowing it is essential after my experience today in the city.

I fully grasp the desperate fight of my parents, community, and Peter. Fighting for freedom, freedom of religion and religious expression of all people. Knowing in my heart that each person deserves to be treated with respect, acknowledging that their body, mind, and spiritual life are intricately interwoven, not separate and are one.

Simon's words in that private moment in the secret room, were so eloquently demonstrated, that his response was both physical, emotional, and spiritual.

Seeing so clearly now that eliminating a citizen's right to express their faith, which is inherently part of them, is like removing a vital organ. It leaves them to struggle day to day to function incompletely.

My stomach aches, truly, deeply grieved for our Christian community and citizens living under the weight of the oppressive laws. I feel deep regret for not immediately accepting Peter's call to serve our community covertly with others working to free them from the current laws, charges and return what is rightfully theirs to live peacefully.

I reflect on the fact that I am still in my spiritual infancy, learning the ancient writings, and observing how Christians live in our community. I am beginning to understand how it all comes together, but in my heart, I am still seeking that incredible personal relationship with God that others have, like Simon and James.

I am unsure of my role in helping people, using the few skills I have, but I trust Peter can use me and he has assured me Simon will help. It is a terrifying and dangerous challenge that lays ahead. I type and hit send.

Hi Peter,

I have been thinking about your kind offer to use your home gym. Are you able to show me how to use the equipment? I am available before my union to pop over at your convenience.

Many thanks, Esther

Peter responds, "So glad you decided to take up the offer, see you soon, Pete."

Sitting on the floor I unpack my bag. My hand rests on my blue dress reminding me of one of the sweetest moments I have ever spent with my future husband.

Simon, in that moment, revealed what is in his heart, a very private, mature relationship with God, which is intimately entwined in every aspect of his life and love for me. I am humbled, observing his life so completely and confidently surrendered to God.

CHAPTER 35

Today I head to the gastroenterology floor. Lots of mess to clean up. Great!

Logging onto the work slate I see an endless list of tasks to clean rooms, not just linen changes, it's body spills too. I am so grateful I wear an apron over my clothes, or I would have to change my scrubs regularly.

Lunch time finally! I put my work slate on charge at the nurse's station, remove my coverall, and head out back to my locker to retrieve my lunch and slate.

I opt to eat in the fresh air after my morning. Having discovered a sanctuary outback in the open ambulance bay, the staff set up for themselves and anyone else, I am grateful knowing Town and Elite will not be there.

Opening my licence handbook, I read through the road rules skimming them. They are very simple, but the road signs will take some practise as there are so many. I reach for a snack and see CEO Ward standing in front of me.

"Hello Esther, I see you're studying for your licence already, excellent! I'll wait for you to notify me when you've passed, then we can arrange lessons." His voice is formal.

I can only nod, and he pauses asking, "Is everything okay?"

"It's just I've never seen you out here before, CEO Ward." He smiles for a moment, and it's gone.

"There's a lot about me you don't know." He strides off inside. I realise the boss is everywhere.

Attempting my first trial test on the transport licence I am delighted to receive a good result, feeling hopeful I can get my licence quickly.

Packing away my satchel I check my slate and see a delivery alert. Hooray, I am released from my present tasks. I know that my shift manager would be informed that I was sent elsewhere in the hospital.

I leave my satchel in the locker and slip across to the other and covertly grab out the delivery satchel. I will be delivering several towns away, thankfully. I will be back home ready for dinner tonight with Hannah and Zach.

Passing through the station I am stopped by Law Enforcers again. I inform them I have been sent to work at another Medical Precinct. They look at my scrubs and wave me through.

This scrutiny is getting oppressive, one of many that occur every week. My delivery is successful and happily pass through the stations without further interrogation - no Law Enforcers, they must have quit for the day. I realise the merit of wearing scrubs helps evade searches.

I message CEO Ward to arrange a meeting, terrifying as it is. This is not something you send a message about. He responds quickly and directs me to come to his office when I am back. On my return, I change into my full length running active wear and then head to the business offices. The CEO's assistant barely acknowledges me, except when the office door automatically opens.

Quietly walking in I stand awkwardly in the centre of the sparsely furnished room and see a wall of multiple images constantly changing and realise it is the hospital security system. The CEO observes how his hospital runs all day.

CEO Ward's hands work quickly on another wall illuminated like a huge slate with numbers and documents all over it. He turns suddenly, realising I am there, and touches the wall slates, and they shut off.

He apologies profusely for not acknowledging my arrival. I assure him it is okay. He indicates we sit and then looks at me briefly with those dark unreadable eyes and expression.

"How can I help?" he asks.

I indicate with a finger on my lips. He nods and leads me into the inner office, which must block signals.

He looks expectantly, and I relay the increasing inspections at the stations and the level of scrutiny and how wearing my scrubs seemed to make my passage easier. He nods and briefly looks at me.

"Can you pass the licence quickly?" I nod. "Good, I am going to book you into an intensive single transport programme. I will send dates and details once I have a copy of your licence to get you on the road quickly to reduce the chance of our deliveries being detected and you being searched."

I shrug, "I'm okay, I'm used to it."

CEO Ward really looks at me and says firmly, "No, it's *not okay* to routinely subject citizens to searches." He averts his eyes again.

As I am about to leave the outer room he asks, "Off to the gym?"

"No, I jog home most days after work or do PK."

"Oh, good for you." He farewells me then turns on his walls of screens again.

I jog home, shower, and dress for dinner to allow time to study the manual for my licence. I am grateful when Simon messages he can pick me up. More time to read.

Skimming the manual quickly, I subject myself in the next few hours to as many sample tests as possible to see where I am weak and quickly realise it is not the signs I am struggling with it is the rules pertaining to alcohol. I really hone in on that section of the test.

The process to sit the online exam is easy. I just transfer a lot of points and then sit the test with my camera on so they can see me completing it. I am grateful I do not have to travel for it.

I look at the clock on my slate. I have one hour before Simon picks me up. I decide to go for it. Loading the exam, I turn on my camera and sit my slate in a stand so I can be observed and take a deep breath and start the one hundred multiple choice questions. You can get two wrong to pass.

Working my way through at a steady rate, I reach the end and review my answers and feel I have done my best and then hit END. The screen shows its processing the exam and I sit staring around the room, then get some veggies out for Hannah and Zach, trying not to be impatient.

Simon arrives. “Is everything okay?” I must look distracted.

“I just sat my licence and I’m waiting for the result.”

He is by my side, instantly staring at the screen too. He reaches for my hand saying, “You’ve got this Esther, I know it.”

We wait in silence, then there it is just a number on the screen.

“What’s that?” He looks at me proudly, “Look again, that is your licence number.” I stand frozen; I cannot believe it.

Simon puts his arms out and I accept his hug, whispering, “I can’t believe it is happening.”

He whispers, “I know.” I remind him nobody is to know. “I must message my CEO so he can book me into the transport course. He does not want me travelling on the trains after he heard about the stop and searches.”

Simon nods, “For such a scary boss he is a decent bloke. I have been scared for your safety too Esther.”

After saving the details of my licence I am ready for fun.

Simon leads me by the hand, “I’m going to show you how to start the transport. You want to look smart at your course don’t you?”

He makes me sit on the seat and talks me through the steps to start the engine, which is easy. He kicks up the centre stand and I suddenly feel the full weight of the transport and am balancing on my toes, fortunately he is holding it steady and places the stand back down. I move back and he jumps in front. “Lesson one done, let’s go.”

Simon accelerates as we head up the steep hill to the lookout, the view of the water never disappoints, especially at dusk. He stops outside our little place, soon to be called home and takes his helmet off. I do the same.

Simon informs me, "I have moved my stuff in today into the second bedroom and taken a few cooking items to get by. It is very empty, but it felt good to just have my own space to think. Did you want to come in?" he asks.

"No, I think its best we keep our personal space until we are in a union."

Simon starts the transport again and we glide down a few houses to Zach and Hannah's cute house and Simon parks out front. It is a tiny house, not a granny flat with a veranda and I see the garage open, bursting with fishing gear. A glimpse into my future life.

I have brought veggies and Simon has banana bread. I am surprised.

"It's Mum's doing, she said. "Simon, you don't take fish to a fisherman's house." I make a mental note. We knock on the door and Zach greets us, all smiles, he waves us in.

The guys hug briefly, and they follow me. I see a warm inviting family room with the kitchen attached. The table is set for four, Hannah has even lit a candle.

Hannah comes immediately to me and gives me a warm hug and saying, "It's been ages since we have spoken."

"Exams are over; I'm just working until our union day." She places the slates outside.

"Now, where were we?" Hannah hugs Simon too. He submits to it, Zach grins. "It's easier to go with it." She laughs. "Like you've got any complaints." He shrugs. "You got me."

We all sit down and they tell us there is no lecture on marriage, just hanging out together and chatting about day-to-day stuff in married life.

Simon and I look at each other across the table, relieved. Simon breaks the ice. "Good, I cannot be subjected to Zach's men's mentoring group again. That was brutal."

Zach almost spits his drink out laughing, "Oh man, your face was priceless that day, the guys talking about their feelings and marriage."

Hannah and I exchange amused looks as if to say we do not want to know.

"Anyway…" Hannah gratefully intervenes, "we have a gift for you." She hands us carefully tied bundles of paper and a pencil each. She quickly explains, "These are for you to write your vows."

Zach jumps in saying, "And to write a list of dates you would like to go on and then exchange lists so you can surprise each other. You have a few weeks before the wedding."

I thank Hannah and Zach; it is such a heartfelt gesture.

"Hannah, is this the paper off surgical supplies?" I ask her.

"Yes, I had to save it, it's such good quality sitting in the recycle bin."

"I've never held a pencil before," I tell her.

"It's like a stylus on your slate you just push firmer, and you don't have an eraser." I nod, vowing to practise.

Simon thanks them and says, "This is cool."

Zach cheekily says, "Wait until you're married, then you get to write your suggestions for date nights, it's different to being engaged."

Hannah shoots him a look. "*Zach!*"

He and Simon give each other high fives, much to our dismay.

Hannah brings bowls of hot steaming chicken curry to the table and then suddenly waves at Zach to get the rice as she disappears and reappears moments later.

Hannah sits down and Zach reaches for her hand telling us, "We are expecting our first baby. We are thirteen weeks and keeping it a big secret, but we wanted you guys to know as you are such close friends. Hannah gets a bit queasy at times."

We express our happiness.

Simon says, "Zach had to grow up eventually."

I throw my arms around Hannah and whisper, "I'm so happy for you, this is huge news." She nods a little emotionally.

We share a meal together and the conversation flows easily as Zach and Hannah candidly share their day-to-day life with us and how they juggle work, study, managing a home and Zach running his own business.

Hannah tells us that Zach helps with the cooking, which was a huge help during her study and she just graduated.

She is now a doctor officially and has even landed a job at our Medical Precinct as an inhouse doctor and her role will be treating mostly the Farmer and Fishers, as well as the community.

Hannah turns to Simon, "Can you cook?"

He says, "Yes, I can, nothing fancy but it's edible."

She stands up and says, "Outside you two," looking at Zach and Simon.

"Go and talk about something besides fishing while we clean up."

"Sure," Zach says, diving into the fridge and grabs two beers. "Come on Simon, outside and I'll show you the BBQ I'm building."

Simon laughs, "This will be interesting."

They disappear, and Hannah sits down saying she feels very tired. I offer to clean up and place the leftovers in the fridge for her.

"Tea, Hannah?"

"Yes please, ginger to settle my tummy."

I find a jar on the bench with fresh ginger for tea making and steep it in a mug for her. We sit in the lounge room where she curls up, sipping her tea.

She looks at me. "How's Simon going? Zach told me what happened." I tell her he is working hard on de-stressing and doing the homework the councillor gave him. I am checking in with him regularly.

"That is good. Are you praying and studying God's ancient writing together?" I shake my head, and tell her, "I would like to now he's back."

She tells me that it will strengthen our marriage, and it is important during our engagement to pray together to share more deeply with one another our feelings and concerns. This builds another level of intimacy and trust.

"Esther, do not worry about being intimate, you guys will work it out together. Too much emphasis is put on sex when it's everything else leading up to that point that makes it good. Being loved, feeling safe, trusting your partner completely, as well as being able to talk about everything, even the hard stuff.

"I get the impression from Zach that you guys have always communicated well but on an even deeper level when Simon came home after being away. You guys are probably doing better than couples who hurry to be intimate first and then work out the communication later. Even Farmers and Fishers are guilty of that."

I sit for a moment thinking about what she is saying.

"Thanks Hannah, I needed to hear that. We are in a good place. Even talking about the hard stuff, especially keeping each other accountable about abstinence, and telling each other if we are struggling. As for intimacy, we have arrived at the same place, we are both looking forward to freely expressing our love for each other."

Hannah nods, saying, "I am so happy for you guys. I see how you look at each other without speaking, that's intimacy right there."

Laughingly I reply, "Sometimes I don't want to read what he's thinking at this stage of our relationship."

Hannah laughs out loud and says, "Wait until you are married, they look at you with one look and do not hide their meaning. I'm totally okay with that. I can't help it as I am totally in love with Zach."

We sit quietly, lost in our own thoughts, enjoying the private moment between friends. Hannah has confirmed to me that I have arrived at a good place to move forward with my life with Simon, but we need to keep doing the work together.

The guys come in talking loudly and see us sitting quietly talking.

"Here they are." Zach sits next to Hannah who immediately snuggles into his arms.

Simon leans over the lounge and says, "Are you ready to go?" I nod.

Hannah asks, "Same time next week?" We happily accept and thank them for their hospitality insisting they do not have to see us out.

It is still early and there is enough light to enjoy the evening. Simon holds my hand leading me to the transport. "Do you need to be home yet?" I shake my head.

"Good." He opens the storage on the transport and places our gifts there, places our slates inside and retrieves a small booklet. It says Esther, "you got a copy for me to read."

He nods and kisses me. "It is yours to keep eventually."

I am overwhelmed and fascinated by this little handwritten booklet, and it has so much work in it.

Simon leads me by the hand with a blanket tucked under his other arm. We walk to our new home, down the long driveway past the main house to ours, which has a tiny veranda on it.

Simon lays out the blanket on the veranda and says to sit smiling. He sits next to me, our feet dangling almost touching the ground. He reaches under the low veranda and brings out a candle and lights it, Citronella. I sit and look at him smiling, "You had this planned."

"Esther, I know you well enough to respect you are a woman of integrity and knew you would not enter this house until we were married. So here I am sitting on the veranda with the love of my life knowing mosquitos will eat her alive if I do not light a citronella candle while reading to her a compelling story of a courageous woman, Esther." Simon never fails to surprise me with his deep thoughtfulness and attention to detail.

I am excited to read this book of Esther. I hold his hand asking, "Can we talk about tonight? I really enjoyed spending time with you, Zach, and Hannah. I understand why you are so close to them."

Simon explains, "They're the best and they are honest. Man, Zach is blunt and excruciatingly honest."

I smile a little to myself, and he nudges me. "What are you thinking about?"

I tell him, "I hope you are still in love with me as much as they are after many years. I swear, Hannah acts like she is still on her honeymoon." Simon grins.

"Yep, I got that loud and clear from Zach. He is still crazy for her too. Oh, and he gave one piece of advice for the wedding night."

"Really? What is it?"

"You'll have to wait, nah, all he said was that you guys will work it out." I laugh. "That is what Hannah said but the follow up was full of wisdom."

Simon puts his arm out and I tuck up my feet and lean my head on his chest as he starts with a prayer.

"Heavenly Father thank you for tonight, for sending us good friends who are wise and perfect examples of what a God centred marriage should be. Bless them and their baby. We ask you to help us learn more about you through studying your ancient writings together and show us your purpose for our lives. Amen."

I say, "Amen," quietly realising that I sincerely agreed with Simon's prayer. I look up at him.

"Whatever you went through recently, however painful, was worth it. It has transformed you into the incredible man that I am impatient to marry. I love you."

He is very quiet for a long time, just holding me in his arms and looking out into the night. He kisses me on the cheek and says very quietly, "Thank you, I have been impatient to marry you from the moment I picked you up in your family kitchen and knew I had a chance."

He switches on a torch and proceeds to read the first chapter of Esther....

CHAPTER 36

Simon finishes reading the first chapter of Esther, and I ask him, "So when does Esther show up?"

He smiles, stepping down onto the grass.

"Soon, it's not a fairy story, Esther. You'll be shocked what happens."

"Simon, are you still having your quiet time? I am worried you are not getting the time you need to rest or meeting up with your councillor."

"I am, every morning, I promise. It always starts with prayer, what I am thankful for. I realised I am feeling a little better; my thankful list is longer than my requests. I look at Tim's questions he sends to reflect on and sit and think about us, a lot, and this house, wondering what you are doing and wanting to be a part of it."

I wrap my arms around him, my head on his chest. His arms are wrapped around me too. We look at each other in the candlelight. "I'm so happy Simon. So how do you think our life will look?" Simon looks embarrassed.

"What did I say?"

He leads me by the hand and grabs the torch, turning it on.

"This is how I imagine it will be. Promise you won't laugh." He leads me back down the driveway. I assure him I won't. We walk back down the driveway and up the two steps to the front door.

"I arrive home after fishing and I take my boots off at the door and drop my gear just inside. I tell you I'm home and you come and meet me with…" I jump in, and say, 'A kiss.'" He nods looking really embarrassed.

"Keep going," I encourage him.

"Then I shower and come into the kitchen where you have started dinner, and we finish cooking together while you tell me about your work and studies. and I bore you to death with fishing stories. We eat dinner then…."

I nod smiling, "I'm sure we can mix it up." He wraps his arms around me holding me tight stirred by the thought of our cosy dreams of domestic life, and I feel myself melting into his arms.

Simon suddenly looks worried.

"Esther, we haven't talked about birth control, I want to share the responsibility. We haven't talked about how many kids …*man* that cooled me down." He laughs and sits on the steps looking down. I sit next to him.

"Simon, I have an apology to make. I did not talk to you or involve you in any discussion about birth control. I went weeks ago and got an implant put in my arm, it lasts five years and you can take it out if you want to have kids earlier than that. It is a yes to kids, let us just work that out later, much later."

He reaches for my hand. "It's okay Esther, more than okay, I am thankful you're organised. I went shopping ages ago, just in case we got carried away, to be prepared, but this is good. More reliable. Thank you, I want us to have time together before more responsibility." He squeezes my hand gently nudging me. "I love that you want what I want too," Simon says shyly.

"Birth control?"

"*No.*" He smiles and kisses me slowly while saying, "You *want* what I *want* …."

I redirect Simon's attention. "I'm ordering a transport and you can walk me back to the transport. I need to collect my paper bundle, so I can write down some fun date ideas."

We walk back to Hannah and Zach's.

"Simon what are you up to tomorrow?"

"I have not been given any work by Dad so a quiet time, and I'll write down my date ideas, maybe my vows too."

I browse my schedule, "I'm free, how about we meet up for a couple's quiet time together at the river. You tell me when."

"Sounds good. How about lunch time so I get in my run and quiet time, and I have an online follow up with Tim too. So, what is the plan, Esther?"

"Well, I need you to show me how to pray, so we can pray together for citizens we know and maybe us too. Then you could read me more of Esther, swim and have a picnic. How about I meet you at the bush fire trail near my place about twelve pm?" Simon happily agrees.

My transport arrives driven by Joel, a friend of ours.

Simon says goodbye and helps me in, which is very sweet. As we pull away Joel asks, "Hey Esther, how's it going? Not long until your union day."

"I know I can't wait."

As we drive the short distance home, I message my licence details to the CEO who replies immediately with a celebration picture, this guy never takes a night off. Did he show he is human by sending a fun picture back?

I arrive home. My parents are chatting in the lounge room.

"How were Zach and Hannah?" my mother asks.

"Cute as usual, they were so kind to share some helpful tips." I hold up the paper bundle and the pencil and say without giving away what is in my hand to AI, "I will need help with my homework." They both laugh. "Simon set up a blanket on our veranda. He and I spent time just talking about the day-to-day stuff that couples must deal with."

They listen, then I take our slates and dump them in the sanitiser.

"Simon prayed and read to me a chapter of Esther, it was incredible. He is really taking being a wise husband seriously. He even brought a citronella candle, so I didn't get bitten by mozzies."

Mum smiles, seeing our relationship deepen. Dad says, "Well, sounds like he's gone soft in the head, blankets and candles, then again only the best for my girl."

He puts his arms out, allowing me to be small again, wrapped in my fathers' arms. I put my head on his shoulder and I tell my parents more about the city trip and Simon's date choosing rings. They smile at each other sharing a silent moment and then with me. I wonder if they had a similar experience? My father releases me and pats me on the hand.

"It sounds like all you need is a dress and a fiancé." I run off and get my slate to my parents' amusement and reveal the picture of me in the wedding dress.

They are speechless. Dad has tears in his eyes and my mother hugs me sayings that it is perfect.

* * *

Awakening just before dawn, the house is silent except twittering and a repetitive mix of bird calls outside. No kookaburras, so this means a perfect day for a picnic.

Reaching for my slate I look up the weather map. Sunshine and a hot December day; not long until my wedding day. I browse the laws for the day. Still depressing.

Scrolling through my social pages I see my friends, Josh and Sarah at the beach. Sarah is trying to surf and she's out and about when Josh isn't working on the trawler until exam results come in.

I sit up. It's today. Nine am. I am fully awake with butterflies.

I scroll messages of upcoming events and see one from the CEO who has sent a message.

'Esther: Intensive transport training booked next week in the city Friday to Monday. Accommodation at Sydney City Medical in staff quarters. All costs covered.

Travel to training via metro each day.

Do not break anything.

CEO WARD'

I will be learning to ride and living in the city for part of a week, so I will need to postpone my women's party. My mother will be disappointed but will understand. My reason will be I have work and undertake essential training.

Getting out of bed, I see my white silk wedding shoes in a box tied with a ribbon. I gently tug at the ribbon opening it and just look at them. I have chosen shoes like slippers, as I will need to walk through the forest. They are so beautiful. I carefully retie the bow.

I sort my clothes and make a pile for Sarah to look at. I stack Sarah's pile in the bottom of the wardrobe and have a small quality assortment of clothes to take to my new life.

I shower, ready for another incredible day. It is already hot! I pull on a loose cotton dress with spaghetti straps and make a fruit smoothy and sip it on the veranda. I enjoy the sounds of our house waking up, my parents getting ready for work, and calling Luke to get out of bed, repeatedly.

I muse I will be sitting on my own veranda soon - a sweet moment of contemplation.

My parents rush past saying message us your results or at least a hint.

Getting up I look for Luke who is moving slowly. I make his lunch and fill the water bottle. Luke emerges eventually with his basketball and satchel. I pass him his lunch and drink bottle. He just nods and is gone.

Tidying the house, watering the garden for Dad, I enjoy the finches and the little blue wrens hanging about watching me work. The time drags on until almost nine am. I cannot believe my HSC results are minutes away, sitting in the lounge room alone with my slate in my trembling hands.

Several incoming messages appear. I am curious to see if I will be a lawyer, paralegal, Law Enforcer, or stuck at the Medical Precinct.

I open the results and the other messages and just sit - my future laid out in front of me, and tears running down my face. I hear a noise and see the most beautiful sight, Simon coming through the door with flowers.

He rushes to my side calling, "Baby, are you okay? I wanted to be here for you when you opened the results, I am so sorry I was late." He puts his arms out and I let him hold me tight.

He says nothing, just waits. not caring if his shoulder is covered with tears. Pulling myself together, I grab a tissue and sit on the lounge again. Simon remains silent taking everything in, unsure what is going on, holding my hand, and looking at me.

I turn, smiling through tears still silently trickling down my face.

"Simon, you are the love of my life. I'm so glad you are here to hear my news first. I have been informed I have received everything I have worked for." Simon looks happy but still confused.

"I just got a really good exam result, a scholarship to the Sydney City University and three offers for internships as a trainee in law, acting as a paralegal at businesses in the city."

We sit and look at each other, realising we are set. I will be busy, but our future is certain if I can get my degree. I will also be earning a wage working part time while studying.

Simon's face radiates pride. He hugs me tightly repeating, "I knew you could do it."

"Simon, it's going to be hard for the next few years."

"I can help, I will be here for you, cooking, cleaning, and fishing. I want you to succeed and not worry."

"Thank you for supporting my selfish crazy dreams, Simon."

He holds my face in his hands, his look intense.

"Esther, it is so much more. I feel hope, you can be the change, Ruby also, to bring justice and change to this toxic place. Peter and so many citizens are working on change." I realise what he is saying, I need to succeed and he is my partner in this.

Placing our slates in the sanitiser I return to Simon, the connection between us is electric. I slowly run my hands down his neck and shoulders wanting to feel connected and wrapping my arms tightly around his neck. Simon submits to my touch with restraint; his kisses are strong and determined, encouraged by my responses.

He whispers how beautiful I am, that he loves me, brushing my hair from my face and looking intently at me. I stand up holding his hand, indicating I want to lead him to my bedroom, not breaking his gaze.

"*Okay?*"

"Esther, are you sure?"

"I'm very sure."

We sit on my bed still gazing at each other and holding hands for a long, long time, Simon leans down and kisses me so gently. I hear his heart beating, his breaths increasing and he whispers, "Okay?"

"Okay," I can barely reply.

Simon kisses me gently, sliding my dress strap off my right shoulder. His hand and kiss pause for a long moment, then he slides the strap back up slowly laying his hand firmly on my shoulder and stands up looking at me steadily.

"Esther, I am sorry, my heart and mind said stop, wait. My fire for you suddenly extinguished. Like a bucket of sea water chucked on me. I still love you; I still *desire you.*"

Standing I reach for his hands.

"It is okay, thank you. My feelings suddenly shifted too; I love you, Simon. I acknowledge now I really want to wait until we are married. My feelings were so intense, then they suddenly vaporised, weird. Do you think God has intervened?" Simon shrugs, blushing deep red.

"Maybe, Esther, I felt an overwhelming wave of deep respect and love for you. I heard words repeated in my head and heart that were so loud, 'She is a bride waiting for her bridegroom, she is a bride waiting for her bridegroom.'

"My body was screaming to keep going, and my feelings were so intense. Yet suddenly I am totally cooled down, and it's okay to wait, which shocks me because in that moment I did not want to stop being intimate with you."

I lead us back to the lounge room and sit on the lounge and I ask for his forgiveness.

"Simon, I am so sorry I started this intimate moment. It was not fair on you as a committed Christian guy, let alone emotionally and physically."

He smiles, looking at me shyly, explaining, "It's okay Esther, I really wanted to show my love for you. At least you understand that I am a guy with guy stuff to deal with. We got great news; you look so pretty… your beautiful eyes looking at me and we are alone..."

I leave him while I get water and brownies. On my return, we sit calmly talking through our next few weeks, realising we need to keep our wits about us.

I inform Simon about the intense transport training course in the city; it is a secret. I will tell my family tonight that it is for some intensive work training. I will be gone from Friday to Monday evening and will bring my wedding dress back with me.

"Let's spend the day as we planned, have lunch together here, you can read Esther to me, and we can finalise anything we need to do before I head off for a few days. How is our little home going?"

Simon smiles and nudges me with his shoulder. "Esther, it is the best decision we made. I feel peaceful, no pressure, and when I am not with you, I have meals with my family. They are adjusting, even Zeb finds his way and camps out with me most nights. We just chill on the veranda under the frangipani tree you and I love so much. I have cooked for myself several times, which is good."

He leans over and grabs my hands. "Esther, I have good news too, if you agree to it. Zach and Hannah have made me an offer to work with them in a new business venture. Zach got excited about my experience up the North Coast with the shorter day trips and private deep sea fishing trips with tourists. He thought it could work here in our town and with the baby coming, that he could be around more to help Hannah. We can share the trawler work and day runs between us, managing hand selected crews. We would trial it and if it does not work out, we go back to commercial fishing full time."

I feel so happy seeing him excited about his passion working on the water again but scaled back. Less long trips, closer to home working with a friend and having a say in the day-to-day operations. Hannah and I will need our husband's home to help us, not be absent like their fathers were, out at sea, a lot.

Simon adds, "Zach and I agreed that you and I should decide together."

"If you think you guys can make a go of it, do it. I trust whatever decision you make, being around for your families is an amazing plan. Simon, I never asked were you okay with me being at Uni and working in the city. The trains are fast, but I'll be leaving early and coming home late depending on my schedules."

"Esther, you have always been upfront about your plans, I never want to get in the way of that, it's a huge opportunity."

I hug him. "Let us go for it, I transferred points to the real-estate agent the other day to cover the next six month's rent, so we do not have to worry about that. I don't spend points on much and I had heaps. It makes sense, then we only need to feed ourselves and pay any utility and travel costs."

"I think we have been showered with so many of God's blessings, everything is in place for the wedding and our plans for the year ahead," He pauses, smiling and says, "Your face says, that I need to pass this transport course and get back to Simon next week without any broken bones."

"Thank you for reminding me God has blessed us with so much, yes, I am terrified."

Retrieving our slates we look at our schedules.

"So, love of my life, the night after my return we have dinner with Zach and Hannah scheduled then the next day I will be working but the day after I am totally free."

Simon nods. "I will be fishing but it will be a shorter run. Could you meet me at the wharf with a picnic dinner? I have an idea for a date, which involves a picnic, a sunset, and my gorgeous bride to be. I can shower at the wharf, so I do not reek. Can I message you when I'm closer to home?" I nod, loving the plan.

CHAPTER 37

Exiting the Sydney City Terminal, I take the metro to the Medical Precinct. Walking through the automatic doors I ask for directions to the staff accommodation and am directed to a far corner of the precinct.

Finding the tiny reception area to the dorm rooms I see a shared bathroom and kitchenette. I am greeted by the housekeeper who inclines her head and shows me to my room. The beginning of many new things to come.

Sitting on the single bed, looking around the tiny room, I am unsure what to do. My slate flashes with incoming messages, one from Simon, so sweet.

The next from CEO Ward confirming I have arrived and the address for tomorrow's course. He informs me he has arranged an interview for me, in one hour in the business suites with CEO Copeland, for an intern position. I thank the CEO.

I dress quickly and restyle my hair up into a town style bun and apply light makeup with tinted lip gloss. My black linen pants and white silk top look smart with my heeled boots.

Locating the business floor almost at the top, I step out of the elevator into a huge open office space tastefully decorated with work hubs dotted around the centre of the room with executive suites located to optimise the views.

Reception welcomes me, depositing me outside the CEO's office. His assistant Todd introduces himself, with no eye contact and inclines his head while discreetly scanning me like a drone.

Todd is easily the best dressed in an understated Elite tailored suit and crisp white shirt. His hair is Elite styled, never to move, with stunning stud diamond earrings. Todd's cologne expensive, and overpowering.

Scanning complete, Todd sends me through saying a little sassily, "Good luck honey, you will need it," under his breath.

Entering an enormous office, I see two wall screens reminiscent of CEO Ward's office but double the size. This office has stunning views of the city.

CEO Copeland, a middle-aged man, well-dressed without Todd's flair for fashion, immediately welcomes me, directing me to a chair facing his desk and informing me he has reviewed my profile.

"Your grades are excellent M Williams; you work hard. How do you feel about doing junior work, learning medico and legal processes, getting coffee, drycleaning etc?"

"I am happy with that opportunity. How many days are you offering?"

He waves his hands dismissively. "A few days a week to fit around your Uni degree. Naturally you will be paid for each of your *skills* you provide to this precinct."

"I have hundreds of applicants, but you have a unique skill set that works for me handling *correspondence*." I get his meaning.

"CEO Ward insisted I meet you. I understand you are attending the transport course for a few days. That will be an asset getting my *correspondence* across town. We have several smaller transports for that purpose. What are your thoughts?"

I thank him for seeing me and inform him I want to learn every aspect of law while I am studying.

The CEO coughs uncomfortably. "There is the private matter of your upcoming union. I trust your life partner understands the privilege extended to you and is supportive of this and the commitment required as an intern."

I assure him that Simon is supportive and not privy to the *correspondence*. The CEO looks impressed. "Not an easy decision but I am determined to protect him and others from knowing."

He looks me up and down, trying to work out what I am in this cookie cutter society and like Todd, is at a loss to pigeonhole me. I am enjoying messing with their heads.

"The internship is yours if you are willing to do all the dirty work nobody wants to do around here."

"Yes, yes, I really want it. It can't be any worse than the hospital cleaning I have done."

"Okay, see you the first week of the new year, I will forward the details. I have secured one of CEO Ward's prized couriers. I must thank him for referring you. He was very accurate in what he told me about you. You may see Ward in the city working alongside me from time to time, he is a whiz at numbers that baffle me." He waves his hand over the door, and it slides open.

Walking out, Todd pretends to be engrossed in his work. I know he was desperately trying to hear through the frosted glass. Todd looks at me intently. All I say is, "See you next year, Todd." I swoop into a waiting elevator seeing Todd's shocked expression.

Back in my room I message Simon about my internship. I send a short message of gratitude to CEO Ward.

I chat to Ruby and Sarah, filling them in. They insist we reschedule a girl's night out on my return.

Searching for dinner, I settle on a café close by and head back upstairs to review my transport manual before falling asleep on the crisp sheets.

The following morning, I pull on jeans, t-shirt, and joggers and make a coffee in the kitchenette and purchase a muffin from the vending machine.

Sitting on a tiny lounge, I scroll the laws sipping excellent coffee and pausing at a new law. I take a deep breath. From New Year's Day every citizen must be implanted with a chip. No exceptions. Even children. I will need to read all the petty new laws if I want to stay ahead of trouble.

Following my navigator, I jump on the slow-moving metro, enjoying the freedom and early morning activity around me. Many citizens are exercising, walking, or having breakfast in cafes. Stepping off, I arrive in the older part of Sydney City.

The transport training office is a repurposed warehouse. I am welcomed, checked in. Citizens sit quietly and incline their heads acknowledging me. No eye contact, of course!

I still struggle to be acknowledged in public. Back home, I am made to feel invisible. Inclining my head, I mirror the custom. A female sits next to me. She nudges me. “I’m Anna.”

“I’m Esther.”

Our lesson starts on the transport mechanics; I listen intrigued. The lesson moves quickly and at break we try on protective clothing. The assistant asks me what kind of riding I will be doing and I inform her. She directs me to look at fashionable tailored pants and jeans that offer the protection of leathers, they’re easier to move in.

The assistant looks up at me. “You have an allocation from your employer, two pairs of corporate style pants, two jackets and one pair of boots. All paid for, you just need to be fitted.”

I am thankful and try on the clothing, selecting black stylish ankle boots that will look okay in the office too. We are then directed for the rest of the afternoon to work on realistic VR simulators until the instructors are satisfied. We can ride safely tomorrow.

Anna and I sit side by side enjoying the healthy competition, and ourselves. The simulator is incredible, I feel my body naturally shift with the corners and my hands relax on the handlebars. I am determined to master inner-city riding; the challenge is not to speed and to park legally.

The lesson ends with us all synced to race each other to the Art Gallery, without too many errors. It is a simulation of the city streets, and we can take any route we like. Unfortunately, I do not know Sydney City, but I arrive in reasonable time.

We are released for the evening. Grabbing my clothing I see Anna hanging around waiting for me. She asks, "What are you doing tonight?"

I inform her I am heading back into town to my accommodation then calling my fiancé. She nods. "Okay, see you tomorrow."

My brain is at capacity. I enjoy the metro trip back to the Medical Precinct. Law Enforcers jump on; I will never get used to just seeing eyes. They are talking and laughing with each other, but I see them scanning everyone at the same time.

One of the citizens fidgets in their seat and the Enforcers sense something amiss and immediately pulls the citizen to their feet, who declares their innocence. The Enforcer hits the stop button, and they alight at the next stop.

I see the citizen's belongings upended on the street and the citizen is lying on the ground face down with an Enforcer's boot resting on their back! I shiver - trouble is everywhere.

Grabbing a simple takeaway of aromatic chicken curry, I set myself up at the tiny table in the common area and call Simon. He answers, he's still on the trawler close enough to home to receive my call.

He holds up his hand as if to say, wait' and carries his slate to the back where it is more private. I see him reattach his safety harness to a new safety point. He sits chatting to me about his day while I eat.

He looks at me with those blue eyes, "How was your day baby?" *No injuries*?"

I laugh saying that we only did VR training, only imaginary pedestrians got cleaned up. He is impressed with the fast-track training.

Simon spends fifteen minutes expertly teaching me the finer points of riding the single transport in the city. I appreciate his tips.

Simon whispers, "I think about how beautiful you are all the time, and that I am going to be with you every day soon. I love your long silky hair, your green eyes that are so mysterious, your perfect lips that are so soft…"

I put my hand up saying, "Simon. Love of my life, have you had a few beers on the way back?" He nods slowly. "How do you know!"

"I know *everything,* also you are super sweet and uninhibited after a few drinks but promise me you won't have anymore." He nods, continuing his list of my attributes, which I am enjoying.

I smile at him, unshaven in his bright orange safety gear. He looks strong and handsome.

We sit and just look at each other for a long moment and hear the trawler engines slow and see it being steered towards the wharf. The crew yell, "*Goodbye Esther.*"

I whisper, "Goodbye, I love you, see you soon." He nods and waves looking a little sad, then grins telling them to shut up as he hangs up. He really loves hanging out with me and I with him.

Entering my room, I kick off my joggers and put my clothes out for tomorrow. I shower and lay on my bed, reviewing my day, and trying to remember everything I learnt, but my mind drifts back to the handsome guy on the screen out on the water. I feel lonely away from him. I set my alarm and drift off to sleep quickly tonight.

Waking early, I dress and head downstairs to a cafe and order a full cooked breakfast, knowing it is going to be a busy day. I revise my notes from yesterday as I plough through the mountain of food nearly choking me, when I see CEO Ward at the counter ordering a smoothy, looking literally like a hot mess.

He is in gym shorts and t-shirt; his face is red and he is sweaty like he has just finished a run. I am in shock, as he is always so polished, professional, and in a suit. He chats easily to the server, while they make his very green smoothie. The Elite usually only talk to their own kind. He reminds me a little of Peter.

Sitting very still I hope not to be detected. Fortunately, he grabs his smoothie and walks past talking business. I am relieved, resuming my breakfast and revision.

Heading out, I throw my satchel across my body jump on the slow metro, tap my slate and opt to stand near the open door, enjoying the breeze and glimpses of sun starting to reflect off the huge expanses of glass. The city has its own kind of beauty, which I am enjoying.

I see Anna ahead and run to catch up. "Hey, how was your night?" she asks.

"Pretty tame, a takeaway and revision. You?"

She smiles and says, "I didn't do any revision, but I studied Rob over there, all night long." She indicates one of our class mates.

"Oh, okay," I manage, inwardly cringing.

Two people are assigned a transport taking turns around the course. I happily let my partner, Anna go first and watch her carefully, balancing, initially on her toes then wabble a little as she starts moving forward then disappears around the extensive course, which consist of back streets blocked off for us to practise.

Anna returns looking quite happy. I pull on my helmet realising it is so different when you are not the passenger.

I balance, starting the engine as I have been shown, kick up the stand then gently start rolling, I am away, the VR training really helped. I feel the natural shift in my movements as I travel around corners and practise what Simon taught me about gentle transitions between speeds and stopping. I cannot deny the first run was exhilarating. We continue and complete five circuits of the course, becoming more experienced.

Feedback is given by our instructor after each run.

We gather at the end of the day and are informed we can be examined tomorrow as we have achieved good results in our VR training and practical. Tomorrow we will ride out to a quiet part of the city with the instructor following, giving directions behind through a helmet comm. If we pass, we get to go home, if not we do the test again.

I look across at Anna, looking morose next to me, a complete change from half an hour ago. She has been so excited and energised, now she's miserable.

"Is everything okay, Anna?"

"Rob doesn't want to hang out with me tonight. He's going out with someone else."

Realising I have no real response, I just listen. I see the pitfalls of casual dating.

I suggest we have dinner together. She declines politely saying she will work something out. We are all excused and told to review our personal footage running the course, which will be uploaded, so we can critique our own riding. Leaving the warehouse, I feel very tired and have sore muscles. I'm not used to riding a single transport.

Another wonderful metro trip tonight at dusk observing citizens out for dinner or heading home from work. I glimpse signs for the underwater restaurant at the aquarium and feel excited about our date night soon at the restaurant. I pick up takeaway and enjoy a hot shower, trying to loosen my sore muscles, especially in my lower back.

On my return from the communal bathroom, the housekeeper appears with a small box and informs me it arrived this afternoon. I thank her and carry it into my room. I see a pair of super soft riding gloves with a fine grip, some liniment and chocolate with a card from CEO Ward, wishing me good luck. It is unexpected and thoughtful.

I grab my slate and reheat my dinner and send Simon my footage to look at with me to get some constructive criticism. This will certainly test our communication and relationship.

He calls back half an hour later looking very relaxed in a t-shirt in our little house sitting on a very nice lounge chair I have never seen before.

"Hi, nice lounge."

"Hi Esther, just got it today. Ruby had it dropped off. Her parents are redecorating so she offered it to us, hope that is okay."

"It's more than okay, it looks comfy." Simon pans the slate to reveal Zeb tucked up next to him. Simon helplessly says, "I couldn't say no to him."

"Simon, we are going to be hopeless parents if Zeb is our trial child."

Simon laughs giving Zeb's ears a scratch and leans in and says, "Esther, seriously, how are you going? I have been thinking of you all day, out there riding and hoping you do not hurt yourself and end up in a cast for the union. I have been looking at your footage, this is a cool course with awesome technology, so much better than the crappy course James and I did where if you didn't die you passed." He grins.

I am so happy to see a familiar smiling face.

"I'm doing okay, just tired and have very sore muscles. What did you really think of my course runs? Be kind but honest Simon, I need to pass."

He sits back looking at me for so long. I think there is buffering then he leans forward and says, "You are truly amazing, I'm so proud of you baby."

"Really? I'm surprised it is not hopeless. I'm in with a chance of passing?"

"Esther, you are going to pass easily. You just need to relax so your body moves more freely and not grip the handlebars so hard then your body may not be so sore. Otherwise, revise the road rules, that's where you'll get caught, on petty rules."

I mention we must get an implant. He shrugs, "I'm surprised we have got away without having it this long. We will navigate this like anything else, *together.*"

"I have missed you, so glad I can see you tomorrow at Hannah and Zach's. Don't forget to bring something, Simon," I remind him.

"All sorted, I picked up something to bring. Good luck beautiful."

"Thanks, I need to go study, love you." He waves smiling as he shuts off the slate.

I sit for a moment contemplating tomorrow, rubbing liniment all over my body. It soothes my aching body. Feeling a little better I look at rules and footage before falling asleep, vowing to wake early to revise as I am so tired. I set my alarm and drift off.

My alarm wakes me, and my muscles burn. Crawling out of bed I grab my clothes and have a very hot shower, which helps, and slather on more liniment especially on my lower back. I suspect the gift from CEO Ward was reminiscent of him learning to ride.

Feeling better, I dress into my riding gear, pack my bag, and make a huge coffee, and sit on the lounge to revise.

My slate alerts me that study time is up. I roll along with my bag thinking this will be my workplace next year, feeling like my life is heading in the right direction. I'm glad the internship has been finalised.

I will pick up my wedding dress on my way home today. The staff at the store have assured me they will wait if I am held up at my course, which is sweet and they have packed it to travel.

Arriving at the warehouse I pull on the gloves the CEO gifted me, they feel skintight and barely noticeable. I am willing to give them a go; my hands are raw.

Our young examiner appears looking happy. He runs us through the morning agenda. It is more practise and when ready, we can go for our test. I am determined to get on a transport as quickly as possible so I can go home to my Simon.

I manage to secure a transport first with Anna and several others, and I nod to them and wish them luck. They all look terrified.

Quickly completing five circuits and feeling good I go for the test. The examiner checks my clothing and my helmet is on tight. He asks me if I know the city, I shake my head. He assures me he will give plenty of notice when to turn and stop.

He looks at me, "Why are you so nervous?"

"I'm terrified of letting everyone down if I fail." He laughs out loud.

"Esther, I have seen your footage and stats, this is merely a formality unless you really stuff it up. You are a natural rider. Let's go and have some fun."

I am relieved this guy is kind. He syncs our helmet comms. and tells me to head off, directing us out towards the harbour We cruise around the beautiful city, stop occasionally at traffic lights or park somewhere, which I am careful to observe where I park. He tells me it is time to head back.

On arrival, I stand waiting. The examiner shows me his slate, PASS. He smiles at me, "I told you that you were a natural. Where will you be riding?"

I tell him the city mostly, he nods and says looking me straight in the eye, "Let me know when you are in town next and we can meet up. I like you; you are hot."

I blush, feeling awkward. I politely decline and say I appreciate the compliment. He is disappointed. I grab my bag heading back uptown to collect my wedding dress and head home.

I message Simon that I passed and forward my licence details thanking the CEO for the opportunity, clothes, and thoughtful gift. He quickly replies with his congratulations.

I gratefully step on a bullet train with my beautiful dress heading home to my incredible life up the North Coast.

CHAPTER 38

Simon and I arrived at Hannah and Zach's home at the same time.

Simon congratulates me on passing my course. He looks at me with admiration then kisses me with such sweetness and gentleness. I look at him and say, "I missed you too."

I hold a basket of fresh produce. Simon has a six pack of beer. I look at him raising an eyebrow.

"Seriously?"

"Yes, *seriously,*" he replies.

We enter finding Hannah chopping vegetables, she welcomes us warmly and tells us Zach will be home soon. Simon nods, and tells us their trawler was a little ahead of Zach's.

While she is finalising her prep, we sit at the counter. Hannah asks us how we are going with our work and any updates on the wedding plans. We report in, she nods.

"How is the communication going between you since we last spoke and the list of questions, I sent?"

Simon reaches for my hand, looking at me, "Going well. We talked through all the questions, it was good, stuff we had not really thought about. Tim, my councillor even sent us a stack of questions too. Man, they are brutal, still working through them, still love each other."

Hannah smiles looking up, "It helps especially if Esther's going to be studying in the city, it is all about communication and sharing the load. That's what we did. Zach is great at reheating leftovers; he even talks about *feelings.*"

Hannah suddenly stops her food prep. She is very pale and holds onto the kitchen bench, she puts her head down saying, "No, no, no, *no.*"

Simon and I look at each other, not sure what is happening. She looks at me holding her stomach. "I think I'm miscarrying, Esther please help me to the bathroom." She is so pale and stricken.

I help her, looking at Simon, who is frozen on the spot. I tell him to wait outside for Zach and then immediately call their parents who live up the street. He reanimates, quickly moving out the front door, unsure what to do.

Helping Hannah to the bathroom I offer to order an ambulance. She says, "No."

"If it's going to happen, I know what to expect, I just never wanted it to happen to me. Esther, please stay with me until Zach comes home." She then asks me to stand outside the bathroom. I hear her crying. Then silence.

I knock on the door.

"Hannah, are you okay, can I come in?" she says I can weakly. I open the door slowly and see her wrapped in a towel on the edge of the bath.

"Did you lose the baby Hannah?" She robotically tells me it happened quickly, which she says means she can go to the hospital tomorrow.

"Are you sure?"

She nods sobbing, "Zach will be devastated."

I wrap my arms around her and cry with her. I feel helpless.

Running a tepid shower, I assist Hannah. She leans limply against the shower as the water washes over her, then I dry and dress her into soft pyjamas following her instructions how to help. Hannah is so gracious to let me.

Simon knocks on the bathroom door.

"I messaged Zach, checking his ETA, he's almost home."

I open the bathroom door and indicate Hannah with my head to Simon who carefully scoops her up very gently in his strong arms. She puts her head on his shoulder and cries silently; he looks at me as if to say, "Did she lose the baby?" I nod. He looks at her with such compassion.

We tuck her into bed and Simon runs immediately out the front, now desperate for Zach to get home.

I switch on Hannah's beside lamp brush her hair and sit, holding her hand. Hannah looks so small and pale. She asks me to make her some tea and squeezes my hand.

"Thank you, Esther, I'm so glad you're here, praise God for sending you guys."

While the water is boiling, I quickly clean the house, leaving everything tidy. As I am carrying tea down the hallway, I see a scene unfolding in the front yard, which is gut wrenching.

Simon runs to Zach's truck as it pulls up, Zach climbs out and I see Simon telling him what happened. Zach looks like he wants to run inside immediately, trying to push past him. Simon blocks him, slows him down, hands on his shoulders looking at him, talking quietly, then pulls him into his arms and holds him tight.

Zach submits to the heartbreaking news and looks like the wind has been knocked out of him.

I see them separate, talking quietly again. I scoot down the hall and prop Hannah up with extra pillows, she sips the peppermint tea slowly and a little colour returns to her face and she stares at nothing. I tell her Zach's home, and she looks relieved.

Zach runs down the hall in his socks and work gear. I leave the room quietly pulling the door behind me, observing profound grief shared as they wrap their arms around each other and cry.

Walking outside I find Simon in the front yard pacing, agitated. I run to him.

"Stop. What is going on in your head? Talk to me." I wrap my arms around his chest tightly, he starts crying and shouting at the same time, saying repeatedly, "I didn't know what to do, I could not help them. Hannah and Zach are heartbroken."

I nod, saying, "I know."

He sobs saying, "The worst part was having to tell my best mate his wife just miscarried and see his face. It was like I punched him in the guts. The poor guy is devastated."

"I was so touched with how gentle you were with Hannah and strong for Zach. All I could think the whole time is this incredible guy is going to be my husband and I feel safe. I can trust him and that everything is going to be okay."

Simon kisses me gently on the cheek. "Thank you, I had no idea what to do, my body just started moving and I am sure God was directing my words to console Zach."

We sit on the edge of the little veranda holding hands silently, swinging our feet. There are no words. The birds and cicadas have stopped their song.

We see Hannah and Zach's parents running towards us. They greet us looking concerned, asking what happened. They embrace Simon and me, expressing their gratitude that Hannah and Zach were not completely alone in this. They stand outside the front door with heads bowed in silent prayer, then enter the house quietly.

Simon and I follow discreetly, retrieving our slates and observe the women gathered around Hannah speaking softly. Zach and the fathers are in the lounge room sitting quietly.

Zach gets up and hugs us both. Simon promises to call tomorrow. We slip out the front door and close it. Simon takes my hand quietly saying, "Let's get out of here." We ride to our favourite beach.

Parking, we leave our slates behind and kick our shoes off. We walk down onto the sand and sit, looking out at the ocean, and the sun is setting. The weight of what we just experienced together lifting a little, soothed by this beautiful place.

Simon wraps his arms around me and leans his head against mine. I take his hand. "They will be okay. I saw Zach and Hannah in that moment, I cannot explain it, but their bond was so strong. They did not need to talk."

Simon holds my face in his hands, looking at me so gently.

"That is what marriage is, a covenant made by two people, stronger than just words on a document, it is a commitment. That is what I want for us, that God binds us together like that strong rope on the trawler for mooring that can withstand whatever storm we face."

I nod saying, "That's what I want too. That's beautiful Simon, we could use that for our vows."

Simon smiles. "It reminds me of a song my parents sing, apparently they had it at their wedding. My mother sings it when we are alone out on the boat, and my Dad just smiles and hums along."

"Sing it to me. I have never heard you sing except with a bunch of guys after few beers. Do you know the words?" Simon looks like he wants the beach to engulf him. He says slowly, "I won't sing but I'll tell you the words then my mother can sing it to you one day, deal?"

"Deal."

"Let's walk along the sand." Simon proceeds to tell me the words of the song that he can recall holding my hand. It is beautiful.

Simon pauses and sighs and holds both my hands.

"The moment Zach went inside, I realised everything I have been thinking about lately was so shallow and utterly selfish. I really thought I was a grown up, but I am not. Far from it. Tonight, I was shown what marriage is, what happens when you step up as a husband. It's us, you, and me. Esther, you know I have feared responsibility. It got real tonight. I kind of freaked out a little thinking this could have been you."

I squeeze his hands, "You're right, it's you and me, stronger together, when I'm weak, you're strong, when you're struggling, I'm strong," I remind Simon.

"Are you hungry? I am starving, it has been a long day. Let's buy dinner at the food truck and have a picnic on the beach," Simon says.

We carry our food to the beach and sit on a blanket. We sit in long comfortable silences eating our seafood and looking at the ocean as the incoming tide laps gently at the shore, each of us lost in our own thoughts.

We call our parents, telling them what happened tonight, realising we need them. They are saddened by the news, but grateful we are willing to share our struggles with them.

I overhear Simon's father tell him he is proud of him being there for his mate.

My mother asks, "Are you okay Esther? That was a lot to handle."

"Yes, Hannah and Zach were so strong. Simon was here with me. We managed together." She tells me Simon and I were very mature handling something so unexpected and remaining calm.

After we finish our calls, I tell Simon, "I think we should give Zach and Hannah space for a while."

He agrees. "I think our pre-wedding training is almost complete. We can work on more of Tim's questions together for the moment. We just got front row seats of how to face a major challenge in a marriage and still be strong."

I admit I do not know much about pregnancy stuff.

"Esther, who really does? Doesn't everyone work it out as they go? That's what my parents did and I turned out great."

I laugh for far too long to his dismay. "*Did you*?"

"Yep, they made all their mistakes with Matthew. Andrew and I turned out great," he replies smiling cheekily.

"*Really*?"

"Really."

We walk back to the transport, dust the sand off our feet, and pull our shoes on again. Simon takes me home, lingering outside. I think that he needs some space. He holds me for a long time then looks down at me.

"Will you promise to meet me at the beach every week to hang out? I really enjoyed how peaceful it was. I think I need that."

I remind him of the date he is organising for tomorrow.

He nods smiling and saying, "All sorted, you just bring food. I want to share with you a secret spot I discovered." He kisses me for a long time seeming not to want to break our connection. Gently and lovingly, wrapping his arms tightly around me, it is comforting after a challenging evening.

I just nod wrapped in his arms thinking of those beautiful words of the song Simon's parents had at their wedding.

Waving goodbye, I watch Simon's light fade into the distance. I wander into the quiet house and say hello briefly to my parents on my way through to my room. I need space too.

I climb into bed and lie there looking at my beautiful wedding dress hanging from the top of my door - it gives me peace after tonight. I realise I am exhausted from my busy week and happily drift off.

CHAPTER 39

Arriving on the tiny beach inlet near the wharf, I drop my picnic basket, stretch my legs, enjoying the peace after so many busy weeks. I lay on my blanket and see Zeb! He has wandered off again.

Zeb trots up awaiting his customary scratches then lays his full weight across my lap, his furry body resting on me. I run my hand down his fur; there is no response but his breathing. Alarmed I look into his eyes, he looks miserable.

"Are you ill Zeb?" His ears flicker. I move him to the picnic blanket and get a bowl of water. He sniffs then turns his head away.

I wonder if he has been foraging from the bins near the co-op. I sit and stroke his back and head like a sick child as I stare at the first signs of dusk. The trawler will be back soon, and Simon will know what to do. Maybe take Zeb to the vet. I lay down next to Zeb still stoking his back.

Awakening I feel cool. It is getting dark, my heart races, I have lost track of time, so I quickly message Simon; he may be in range to check on his ETA. No answer, he's obviously too far out. I pull on my light jacket and joggers, encouraging Zeb to follow. He reluctantly comes, with his tail down; he really is poorly.

Walking towards the wharf, I encounter a sickening scene unfolding. Women and fishermen are gathered on the wharf. There is no sign of the trawler Shalom that my Simon is on.

I drop my basket, running and stumbling along the old wharf to Rachael. She turns and everybody follows her gaze, she looks terrified, shaken, and pale. She says nothing to allay my fears.

In my head I'm screaming. "No, no, no, *no*!" Not Simon, it cannot be!

"Rachael, what's happening?" She says slowly, "Andrew radioed in, Simon was washed overboard from an unexpected swell and a freak storm. His harness broke from the fastening and they have been looking for him, *for hours* ..."

I cannot move, feeling hot tears. I shout, "No, no, *no,* he said he would meet me here." I stand looking out to sea hopefully, looking for the trawler. Instead, I see the fishing community move with experienced urgency. Most of the trawlers have left and the coast guard is co-ordinating the search along the coast line, but they leave too.

The wharf is silent, and women and local people stand in the semi darkness illuminated by the small wharf lights. The reality covers us like a suffocating blanket.

They are all staring at me.

"They are going to find him. He is an excellent swimmer, he is strong, he is my husband in my heart, I am not giving up on him," I tell them fiercely.

I throw my arms around Rachael. We sob together sharing our pain and shock of the unknown and walking together towards the carpark gratefully accepting a ride, Zeb has not left my side. I realise with sickening reality he already knew something was amiss.

Someone shouts that Shalom is back, and we run to the wharf seeing a very dejected crew of Fishers. I see Skipper Andrew, Andrew, Matt, James and Jonah on deck, their devastation is heartbreaking to see.

As the trawler is being secured, the men run to Rachael. James and Jonah run to me and wrap their arms around me tightly and telling me that they were all on deck. There was a calm patch of water so they were prepping the catch and as Simon was throwing scraps overboard a sudden swell arose and a huge storm hit the boat, which started to roll. Simon's harness fastening broke and he was thrown overboard from the force of it. They did everything right and couldn't find him. The sea was wild then became calm. They searched for hours, and other trawlers in the area came to help.

I look up, and these two young men cry ugly tears of loss and exhaustion. They witnessed their friend's terrifying ordeal and unable to verbalise the terrible truth that Simon could be one of the many Fishers lost at sea.

Simon's family gather in the lounge room of their home, the house is a noisy, bustling workplace, a steady flow of women and children packing food into keep containers. The Fishers are studying maps and tides on their slates tracking possible directions Simon may have drifted to.

The Fishers all wear life jackets but the harsh elements of the sea make it hard to survive. He has strength and youth on his side.

I see my parents, Luke, and the community of Farmers flood the room. I am so grateful for them. My parents hold me, tears in their eyes, and my mother reaches out to comfort Rachael and my Dad joins Skipper Andrew as they pour over the maps together.

Luke hugs young Andrew who finally breaks down having witnessed his brother thrown overboard. They head outside.

One of the men quietly outlines the plan. Groups of our community will be given areas of the coastline to monitor. He reminds the adults that we need to reach out to the ultimate lifesaver as we search, leaning on him for his help and support.

Everyone nods, knowing his message is clear: pray without ceasing and place your trust in God.

Those who can search leave with directions and food, children are taken home to bed. Only adults remain in the house; it is going to be a long night.

I have been operating on autopilot; I feel numb, but there are no tears anymore. I enter Simon's empty room, searching in the wardrobe for anything. I notice he has left winter clothes behind when he moved.

I find a warm jumper that covers me; it smells like him. I wander back into the lounge room to find a circle of people praying silently. I sit and observe this faith in action, still desperately seeking an understanding what it is all about.

All I know is what I am observing can only be the power of the Holy Spirit. It is undeniable as these citizens' faith seem stronger in this adversity, sharing what little they have. They are reaching out for help - the room has an incredible peace and it rests on me too. It gives me comfort.

Curling up on a lounge, I think about Simon's ordeal out in the ocean, fighting for his life and I am terrified for him. I ache for his suffering and his family searching and waiting.

Zeb squeezes himself onto the couch next to me, we sit in companiable distress, his large sighs heartbreaking. We eventually sleep.

I awaken at dawn, grab food and Zeb. Everyone has gone to sleep in a bed, couch or gone home. We walk quickly across the road and along the familiar path through the pine forest to the clearing looking out to the ocean. I stand and start looking for orange clothing on the water below and out far.

Zeb paces along the edge, sniffing the air looking out, sensing this is our mission. It feels better doing something, I have hope that Simon will be found, he is a strong swimmer, he may have managed to survive the night and be washed up on the coastline somewhere.

The heaviness in my stomach nauseates me.

The sun rises and the visibility is better; I see small boats in the distance searching. I check for updates on the coastguard's site - still no news but the whole town is looking. I see citizens in the distance searching the coastline, feeling hopeful Simon will be found with so many eyes on the water and coastline.

Zeb flops down on the grass looking morose. "Come on buddy, we have to keep looking for your mate." He does not move but sighs again, his head on his paws. I search for hours looking and pacing the full length of the forest cliff.

I try to feed Zeb but he refuses. The waves are playing tricks on me, I keep thinking I see him, but *no*, only waves.

I feel comforted being alone. My anguish can be real and raw. I have screamed into the wind, to God to bring him home and sobbed to the point there are no more tears. My mind flip flops from hope to loss in an instant, not willing to even think about a future without Simon. It is too soon, so many people are looking, he will be found.

The sun is sinking and visibility is difficult. I hear my slate alert me, and I see a message from Simon, my heart races and then stop momentarily. It is pictures of him and the crew sent early yesterday at sunrise, but it took a long time to come through to my slate; it looks like a perfect day. The sky is clear with a stunning pink backdrop, and the water is blue and calm. I stare at Simon's bright blue eyes staring straight back at me. I look at everyone in the crew then I notice Simon's hands down low making a sneaky heart where his mates cannot see. I feel a sob stuck in my throat.

I run through the pine trees, tears blurring my vision and see my parents walking towards me, they must have sensed where I might be. We stand together quietly.

"I know, he's gone, isn't he?"

They nod. My Dad informs me, "They have called off the official search, they found Simon's jacket with his name on it with his life jacket washed up near the shore. The search is scaled back. We are going to sit with Rachael and Andrew, and their family. Do you want to come?"

We enter the house, and Zeb immediately rests his head on Rachael's lap; he will be her companion now. We join Simon's family, the crushing loss is physically painful, they are broken. I sob in my parents' arms, knowing there is no relief from this pain.

* * *

A week passes and I return to work still grieving. We will farewell Simon at the end of the week in a simple memorial.

I work robotically in my day-to-day activities, only thinking moments ahead at a time, the future too painful to contemplate.

Everyone at work is kind but the pity in their eyes grates on my raw nerves. I move quickly through tasks. My slate alerts me that I need to go to the CEO's office.

CEO Ward greets me, ushers me in, and he immediately expresses his condolences in Simon's passing. He offers a chair and proceeds to update me on my tasks for next week - in the city delivering packages to smaller outer city Medical Precincts as a relief courier. He pauses and looks me in the eye in a rare moment asking, "If that is, okay?"

"Fine with me. Can I work in the city permanently? Are there any positions available?"

The CEO stops and stares at me saying, while carefully choosing each word, "Isn't it a bit *soon* to move away from your family and...community considering *everything?"*

My bottled-up emotions are generating pressure inside me and I cannot contain them. To my horror I explosively spill my every thought for the last week all over the CEO, someone who does not know me and is my *boss*.

The rant goes for five excruciating, heart wrenching minutes as I tell him, "I can't stand being here anymore, the pity looks from friends and co-workers, missing Simon, life plans ruined and I don't know what to do with myself. All I know is when I'm busy at work I don't have to think."

He sits perfectly still, respectfully looking at an imaginary object on the carpet and listens to this rant, witnessing floods of tears of frustration and pain flowing without ceasing.

He passes me tissues and sits quietly on the chair opposite me awkwardly until I gain composure. My moment passes and I feel lighter and clearer in my head than I have for days.

The CEO moves his chair closer, hands me a bin indicating if it is okay to touch my arms, I nod. He rests his hands gently on my arms looking into my puffy eyes and says, "I am so glad you felt comfortable to talk to me Esther. I was concerned you were back at work too soon and coping *too well* having experienced such profound loss, when in fact you were not.

"May I suggest, which you can consider. Use the gift I gave you and Simon to stay in the city; we move the dates and make it a week's accommodation.

"Next week, you go and rest, away from all this tragedy and clear your head, and work in the city, staying at the hotel. I will find you a permanent position. If you decide the city agrees with you and an agreeable position comes up, you can transition there until your internship starts."

He gently takes his hands away, "How did you go in your exams? Sorry, that is personal."

"I did really well in fact, I got offered a scholarship at Sydney Uni in law and I had three offers for internships starting next year. As you know, I have been offered and have accepted the internship in the City Medical Precinct, thanks to your kindness."

CEO Ward stands, moves his chair back to its perfect position, straightens himself as if the moment of vulnerability is never to be witnessed again.

"Thank you, this is exactly what I need."

I throw my arms around him pinning his arms to his side. I remove myself from his person, take a step back to establish boundaries again. He politely smooths his shirt and suit saying, in his modulated professional tone, "Okay, I will make the arrangements and update you."

He waves his hand over the sensor and the door slides open; he farewells me loudly, "Take care of yourself, I am sorry for your loss."

I finish work, happy to be home, and pack my bag to leave, no longer thinking of what to pack for my life with Simon. I am grateful for the numbness that is present as I methodically fold and pack my clothes to take to the city potentially for longer than a week's posting.

Sorting all my clothing, adding to Sarah's pile, I simplify my wardrobe to a few key pieces.

My few childish knick-knacks sit on a shelf, redundant, glimpses of my childhood, and precious treasures proudly displayed. I leave them, unsure how to move them on. Mum will help me with that at some stage when I am ready.

I open the wardrobe, fully confronted with my wedding dress hung carefully out of sight. I hang it on the wardrobe door and stare at it for a long time. No tears come, just a dull lump sits in my gut that does not move.

I feel very little looking at it - just a muted sense of loss of what could have been but no longer is. It seems so indulgent and vain. Putting it back in the empty wardrobe with my packed suitcase I close the door firmly. Mum will know what to do with it. She will consult me even though I do not care what happens to it.

Realising I am angry and bitter at everything, I am disgusted with myself for such selfish thoughts about my loss with no real thought for anyone else.

I didn't get thrown around in the ocean and drown, I didn't lose a child, I lost my fiancé and love of my life but I am also mourning the long awaited happiness I have been savouring in my heart, and projected romantic scenarios in my head, of building a life with Simon, Having fun setting up our home, being loved and cared for by an adoring husband until we grew old together. All these scenarios have been building up in my mind for so long.

GONE. Destroyed. Washed away…

Sitting on my bed I feel exhausted carrying these heavy emotions, hiding them from friends and family who secretly worry, watching over me. I lie down holding bunny, looking at his worn silky ears, and drift off to sleep.

I awaken to a warm blanket carefully draped over me and sounds in the distance of dinner preparations. I jump up, realising I was going to cook dinner. I rush to the kitchen and my mother says, "It's okay, it was good to see you rest."

She has been so constant in her care yet not dwelling on the events and talking about it or the future. She has the wisdom of her years to let things be and let time and the citizens involved work through it until they are ready. I am grateful for that, conscious of the personal grief my parents endure too, but remain selfless.

I know leaving will be okay. Mum and Dad will understand and wait patiently for me to return home when I am ready, I am grateful for that.

Snapping out of my reverie, I help set the table and sit watching the family moving around me in their comforting routine. We share the meal sitting in silence.

My father discusses the arrangements for Simon's memorial. Simple, honouring his life on the beach and a wreath taken out in the trawler by immediate family and close friends to be tossed into the sea as a final farewell.

My mind wanders elsewhere. I look out the window unfocused as he tells the family of the details of times and date.

It all seems too late and too little to remember such a vibrant person in the best years of his life, but it is what is done and expected, so we will participate and go.

We clear the table and I walk outside to breathe, and I am greeted by a bouncy Zeb who has appeared. I look up and see the familiar truck in our driveway and my heart skips for a fleeting moment.

Andrew has come to chat to Dad in the garden. Andrew opens his arms wide and I walk into them. No words needed. I realise I have missed Simon's loving family and Zeb.

I am released and leave the men to talk; Zeb follows me to the kitchen for leftovers. His sweet face makes me smile for a moment then we sit on the veranda and stare at the yard in companiable silence. Our relationship is simple; we just hang out together.

CHAPTER 40

The day arrives to farewell Simon. We gather on his favourite beach at sunrise. There are so many people from our communities, Fishers who knew Simon and his family working alongside them at the wharf, surfer buddies and those who searched for him.

The water is calm; the sun is shining and people talk quietly to one another in small groups. Everyone wears the ribbon of mourning, united in grief.

As this is a very public gathering the farewell will be generic and socially acceptable. Simon's family has been excused from the mandatory formal Town farewell considering the devastating circumstances.

Peter gently starts Simon's farewell on behalf of his family. His parents are visibly distraught, his brothers, standing still, and rigid. Mathew's girlfriend Elizabeth, has her arm round him and resting her head on his shoulder.

The familiar farewell is rhythmic and familiar, personalised where appropriate. It is surprisingly soothing to my ears, maybe it's detached just enough not to cause pain.

At the conclusion everyone is invited to take a frangipani flower from the many baskets lining the shore and cast one into the outgoing tide in memory of Simon. The scent of frangipanis is sweet and the sight of them gently floating out to sea is a gentle and a beautiful tribute to a tragic death.

I feel a tight choking in my throat and realise my detachment from Simon's passing is over and I am feeling the deep loss through my whole body. I walk towards the baskets and take a handful of flowers and pick up my long skirt. I tie it in a knot, kick off my sandals and wade deep into the water. The initial feeling of cold water jolts me awake from my mental slumber, the sand between my toes and the water lapping at my bare legs is real and brings me into sharp focus of what is happening.

I am farewelling my Simon and there is nothing I can do to bring him back.

Staring out into the distance I see the ocean and sky meet. Beautiful. I slowly place one flower at a time in the water, giving thanks for each of Simon's loving characteristics and moments bestowed on me and others.

Our time together was so precious. Only we knew the depth of our connection that made it unique. The moment is gone as I place the last sweet flower in the water. I turn and wade out, and my parents greet me with open arms and wrap them around me, warm and safe.

Luke joins us. We stand quietly together feeling each other's grief.

We walk to Dad's truck ready to farewell Simon on the trawler. I am not ready for this, but I must. The trawler is ready to leave when we arrive, the engines are warming up.

Matt is skippering for his father. A large group of Fishers and Farmers are assembled on the trawler, and we leave pulling away from the wharf slowly. Everyone visibly relaxes as they feel safe in the group and can talk freely. A special place has been chosen not too far from the shore, the exact coordinates of where Simon started as a Fisher.

Each of the older men speak about Simon's character as a man, his strong faith, and give thanks for his life entrusting him to his Heavenly Father, and Saviour.

They speak so confidently of the life to come, living in eternity with their Heavenly Father through the Grace of Jesus Christ.

Everyone nods and agrees with what they are saying. Others pray aloud, expressing the gut-wrenching grief then giving praise and thanks. I feel I am surrounded by a warm comforting breeze that swirls around us on the trawler. There are no longer tears, only a celebration of a wonderful life lived and the promise that we can have eternal life too.

A final prayer is said, and a simple wreath is tossed into the calm water by his heartbroken family and the group is silent, only the gentle lapping of the water against the trawler can be heard. Peter says, "Amen," to end the respectful moment.

Jonah, James, Andrew, and Matthew come up to me and we all hug. Then Jonah says, with his usual twinkle in his eye, "I know it's early, but we better open these and share one with our mate Simon."

He opens a discreetly hidden box of beer; grabs out one bottle, twists the cap, and pours it over the side as we travel back to the wharf.

He says simply, "We will miss you, mate, you were one of a kind." He hands out the beers.

"Let's toast our mate, Simon." We all tap bottles and take a sip. I taste the yeasty flavour and pull a face, swallow it but hand the bottle to James. They all laugh out loud; the sadness has lifted.

We arrive at the wharf and all head to Simon's family home for a shared meal. There will not be any singing or dancing as it is still raw grief for all, unlike Paul's passing, which was a life fully lived.

I stay for a while, politely chatting to different people who kindly check in on me.

I slowly walk away from the house towards what would have been our little home together, stepping onto the veranda and enter the passcode opening the cool interior.

Walking for the first time from room to room I see beautiful boxes of homewares, ready for the newlyweds to unpack together, given by our community. I finally enter our bedroom.

Simon's wedding suit hangs in the wardrobe ready. I run my hands over it and feel something in the pocket, and I retrieve a small silk bag containing our two rings and several folded pieces of paper. I carefully open it and gasp, it is his vows all ready for our special day.

I take the rings in the bag and place it on the kitchen bench. I remove my ring Simon gave me and place it on top, and I take the paper with me.

I message Matthew saying, "I have left my commitment ring for you to propose, a gift from Simon to me. Marry Elizabeth, do not waste a moment, the house is yours, the rent is already paid for six months, everything you need is here. A gift from Simon and me."

Retrieving my suitcase, I placed just inside the door yesterday, I close the front door and walk towards the outlook, not looking back.

I leave my bag at the entrance to the Pine Forest reserve and walk through to our special place. The cool interior is welcoming, and the sweet scent of pine soothing and familiar.

I take in the stunning ocean. There is a gentle, warm summer breeze, with the brilliant midday sun reflecting off the waves like jewels as I read aloud his vows, reminiscent of our precious time together choosing wedding bands.

'Esther, this ring symbolises to me, that our love has no end. It reminds us that God is at the centre of our marriage and that his love for us is eternal, that he is the alpha and omega, that his kingdom has no end. Jesus taught us how to love selflessly…' Simon's precious words about a God centred marriage, his love and adoration of me flow across the pages ending with faith, hope and love, which produce torrents of happy tears.

I clutch the pages tightly to my heart, feeling his words as they pour out. I have never seen his handwriting before.

Simply, a final love letter to me, his bride. I feel the depth of his love for me through every handwritten word and his unshakable faith.

I am a bride waiting for her bridegroom.

The wind becomes stronger, whipping up my hair and clothes. I cannot see, my hair is in my eyes, the wind swirls around me and rips the pages from my hands and I am standing helpless and devastated when I hear my name whispered repeatedly in the wind and in my head, in my heart.

I now know his voice; I am not afraid. I am ready to respond.

"Here I am Lord, your servant, Esther."

The wind stops and the voice says, "I am with you."

The wind stops; the voice leaves me.

I am at peace.

Walking slowly back to my bag at the reserve entrance, I smooth my hair and clothes and order a private transport to take me to the station, which arrives quickly. It is Joel our friend.

Joel helps me load my bag and politely makes small talk having just left Simon's farewell. He asks me, "So Esther, where are you going?"

I smile, "Wherever God leads me."

THE END

www.ingramcontent.com/pod-product-compliance
Lightning Source LLC
LaVergne TN
LVHW050921080826
845145LV00001B/155

* 9 7 8 1 7 6 4 3 8 2 0 8 3 *